THE MORROW
BOOK OF
QUOTATIONS
IN
AMERICAN HISTORY

THE MORROW
BOOK OF
QUOTATIONS
IN
AMERICAN
HISTORY

Joseph R. Conlin

WILLIAM MORROW AND COMPANY, INC.
New York

To E.J.C. and A.L.C.

Library of Congress Catalog Card Number: 84-60613
ISBN: 0-688-02068-2

Printed in the United States of America

BOOK DESIGN BY BERNARD SCHLEIFER

PREFACE

WHAT WAS THE FIRST "quotations book"? As a lifelong connoisseur of the genre, I have my nominee. But I will not name it here. "A reasonable probability is the only certainty," to quote Edgar Watson Howe from *Country Town Sayings,* and I am just that certain that if I mention a title and a date some reader somewhere will start like a night nurse and exclaim, "Aha! Got him there!" thence informing me in a long, all too persuasive letter that another collection of quotations was published earlier than my nominee. I am not particularly sensitive to being corrected. A few lines below I want to invite critical letters and suggestions for improving this book. But it is in the nature of quotations books that *every* reader of them is sooner or later disappointed to find that a personal favorite has been overlooked or deliberately omitted. I can wait to hear from the critics of the guts of this book.

If, however, I shall pass over the question of which was the first quotations book and, therefore, what it was like, I shall generalize boldly about the second quotations book. *It,* we may be sure, was put together by copying a goodly part of the first and adding personal favorites. Since the unknown pioneer, all compilers of quotations books have been pilferers. Except for the liars. Mindful of Numbers 32:23 ("Be sure thy sin will find thee out"), I hasten to align myself with the former venial sinners. The easiest part of preparing *Quotations in American History* was the initial phase, when I thumbed casually through the numerous general quotations books in existence and many of the very, very specialized quotation books, pocketing each pertinent item that was not fastened down by copyright or tainted by highly dubious authenticity.

Pleasant work. But not without its demands. There are a great many quotations books on the shelves. The *American Books in Print* for 1980–81 listed no fewer than 184 titles under the rubric, although many of them bore names of less than compelling appeal, things along the lines of "The Quotable Rock Guitarist."

I decided not even to look at the British catalogs for fear of find-

ing "Immortal Epigrams by the Womenfolk of Dorset" and worrying
if, just maybe, there was something in there I should be including
here. And a feeling of being anesthetized by a dentist descended
over me when I contemplated just how many nineteenth-century
collections of quotations I would discover if I visited certain libraries
where one's footsteps echo off frescoes on ceilings high above. The
nineteenth was a great century for quotations books, as for discur-
sive prefaces and miscellaneous other crotchets.

Why so many? Why have quotations books been so popular?

The answer, I think, is that the well-done book of quotations is
both useful and enjoyable, not a common combination. A book of
quotations serves its readers as a book of reference, a place to find
the exact wording or context of a half-remembered saying or the
name of its author. A book of quotations can also be a compendium
of capsule biographies of famous men and women, an impression as
from a cameo or snapshot of a person from his or her own words.
Then, a book of quotations is a textbook, an educational tool. Ralph
Waldo Emerson may have said, "I hate quotations. Tell me what
you know." But he was just being silly for his friends, as Emerson
often was. One cannot become learned on a steady diet of epigrams
and terse remarks, but wisdom is to be found in them.

A quotations book ought also to be a book that can be read, or
rather perused, for pleasure, an undemanding and not entirely "serious" kind of book that is picked up on a lazy day and leafed
through for the joys of little discoveries. Has there been a collector
or compiler of quotations books who did not get started in the business in just so idle a way?

In any case, these have been the purposes I have reminded myself of daily whilst assembling this book. I have made sure that the
well-known American *mots* are here—"Don't give up the ship," and
all that—accompanied by enough contextual information to guide
the earnest searcher farther along the way. But there are also a great
many obscure quotations here, the kind that will be familiar only to
experts on a particular person or historical topic. Meeting them for
the first time will, I hope, bring a little amusement, edification, or
enlightenment into the casual reader's lazy day.

The question will, no doubt, have occurred to many readers,
why, with so many quotations books in existence, prepare yet another? The answer is that there is none quite like this one. It is
general and comprehensive but, unlike *Bartlett's*, the *Penguin Book
of Quotations*, the *Oxford*, and others, it is historical rather than
literary or philosophical in focus. Its subject is American historical

development and not universal human wisdom, nor the intrinsic literary merit of its stuffing. But I can best explain the unique character of *Quotations in American History* by explaining the kinds of quotations I have included and the kinds I have not.

First, I started with the "familiar" sayings (in John Bartlett's happy use of the word), those quotations widely known but easily enough misquoted or misattributed. Then I looked for concise statements that were *signal* in American history, trip-hammers of historical development, or *representative* of the individual who said or wrote them.

It is in these categories that my choices are likely to disappoint some readers. For, once beyond refusing to give up the ship, holding fire until the whites of their eyes are clearly discernible and proclaiming a New Deal for the American people, I have fallen back on my own knowledge, personal taste in quips, and judgment as to what will be most valuable or entertaining to most people. Each and every reader, I daresay, will be chagrined to find that a favorite quotation is missing here, and I should be a greater fool than I am willing to allow if I insisted that every item I did include is indubitably a wiser choice than every one of the hundreds of quotations I hovered over, pen in hand or teeth, and, often with a murmur of lamentation, set aside. I hope to hear from readers. With luck there will be other editions, and I look forward to all suggestions and critiques, including those intemperately phrased. If nothing else, they wake you up in the morning.

A fourth category of quotations in this book consists of those that are *reflective*, statements that address the meaning of the United States and the character of Americans. I hesitate to call this a separate category. Self-definition has been and continues to be a preoccupation, even an obsession of Americans and those Europeans and other foreigners who have been fascinated by their cousins in the New World. As a consequence, their remarks might be said to be as much quotations *in* American history as the words of politicians or generals that moved or justified events. In this book, the remarks about the United States and Americans run the gamut from excerpts of the illustrious Alexis de Tocqueville, so familiar as to rank in familiarity with the boldest military charges, to observations by lesser-known people that have struck me as particularly perceptive. Once again my judgment is at the mercy of readers.

Not included in this book are quotations of the literary wit-and-wisdom variety. I will correct that. There are quotations from literary figures and many diabolically witty remarks, but only because they are also historically pertinent. Thus, Edgar Allen Poe, a conspicuous fellow in most quotations books, especially those that emphasize Americans, is represented here by only one acerbic remark (in prose) on the subject of American dollar-worship. Dorothy Parker, who richly merits the several pages she is allotted in collections of wit and wisdom for her reflections upon the modern human condition, makes an appearance below only with her response to the news that former president Calvin Coolidge had passed away. Recalling his habit of sleeping up to sixteen hours each day, a fact of some historical moment, Parker remarked, "How could they tell?" Historical pertinence is the theme of this book and its special characteristic.

A final word about the substance: The book is a dictionary of quotations in American history, not a book of American quotations. There are foreigners here, both those who have been and continue to be the shrewdest analysts of the American historical experience, and those who, like Winston Churchill with his observation that an iron curtain was descending across Europe, profoundly influenced the course of United States history. In the case of such persons I have identified their nationality. Where there is no such label, the person quoted was either American-born and bred or so intimately associated with the United States as to render foreign birth (or flight abroad) beside the point.

On the use of this book as a reference tool: The quotations are arranged alphabetically by author with, after the zees, a grab bag of Slogans and Catchphrases that includes anonymous quotations that, despite their shadowy origins, had an impact on American development, and manifestos, mottos, and *mots* that were group written.

I could go on and on as to why I opted for the alphabetical author format rather than, for example, a chronological or topical structure. However, on the assumption that readers who pick up a book of quotations do so in order to read quotations and not overlong prefaces, I shall restrain myself. Suffice it to say that the shortcomings of an author structure that the other structures transcend are replaced by at least as many equally grievous problems in chronologically or topically organized books. For all the sensational innovations of the computer people in organizing knowledge, there is still nothing like the alphabet for finding things in a book.

For those who are interested in quotations dealing with a specific subject, a subject index is included.

J.R.C.
April 1984

ACKNOWLEDGMENTS

I have obligations to more persons than those I have quoted. Barbara Corchero and Cynthia Davis helped me catalog my piles of cards at different stages of the project. Jean L. Harvey twice typed the copy into readable form. Ric Machuga and Marilyn Murphy helped me verify some quotations and located contextual data which, in several cases, I had concluded were irretrievable. Colleagues and cronies, William H. Hutchinson, Carl Peterson, and Thomas Wagstaff, read a preliminary draft and pointed out a number of omissions, some glaring, some just glimmering, but all significant. Their attentions improved the book. Finally, Elizabeth Terhune and Bruce Lee of William Morrow and Company supervised the transformation of an unwieldy pile of papers into a book I hope readers will find useful and enjoyable . . . or both.

THE MORROW
BOOK OF
QUOTATIONS
IN
AMERICAN HISTORY

A

E. C. "Teddy Blue" Abbott (1860–1939): *Texas cattleman*
Living that kind of life they were bound to be wild and brave. In fact there was only two things the old-time cowpuncher was afraid of, a decent woman and being set afoot.
(*We Pointed Them North*, 1939)

Bella Abzug (1920–   ): *Feminist congresswoman*
Congress is a middle-aged, middle-class, white male power structure. . . . No wonder it's been so totally unresponsive to the needs of this country.
(Speech in Washington, 10 July 1971)

Goodman Ace (1899–1966): *Writer*
Every time a gun goes off in a have-not country another Communist is born.
(*Saturday Review*, 12 June 1965)

Dean Acheson (1893–1971): *Secretary of state under President Truman*
I do not intend to turn my back on Alger Hiss.
(To a reporter on being asked for his reaction to the conviction of Alger Hiss for perjury, 1950)

I doubt very much if a man whose main literary interests were in works by Mr. Zane Grey, admirable as they may be, is particularly well-equipped to be chief executive of this country, particularly where Indian affairs are concerned.
(On the presidential candidacy of Dwight D. Eisenhower, June 1952)

I will undoubtedly have to seek what is happily known as gainful employment, which I am glad to say does not describe holding public office.

(On retiring as secretary of state, 22 December 1952)

Abigail Adams (1744–1818): *Wife of John Adams*

In the new code of laws which I suppose it will be necessary for you to make, I desire you would remember the ladies and be more generous and favorable to them than your ancestors. Do not put such unlimited power into the hands of husbands. Remember, all men would be tyrants if they could. If particular care and attention is not paid to the ladies, we are determined to foment a rebellion, and will not hold ourselves bound by any laws in which we have no voice or representation.

(Letter to her husband, 1777)

Brooks Adams (1848–1927): *Historian*

The West Indies drift toward us, the Republic of Mexico hardly longer has an independent life, and the city of Mexico is an American town. With the completion of the Panama Canal all Central America will become part of our system. We have expanded into Asia, we have attracted the fragments of the Spanish dominions, and reaching out into China we have checked the advance of Russia and Germany.

(*The New Empire*, 1902)

We are penetrating into Europe, and Great Britain especially is gradually assuming the position of a dependency. . . . The United States will outweigh any single empire, if not all empires combined. The whole world will pay her tribute. Commerce will flow to her from both east and west, and the order which has existed from the dawn of time will be reversed.

(Ibid.)

Charles Francis Adams (1807–1886): *Statesman and businessman*

It would be superfluous in me to point out to your Lordship that this is war.

(Note to Lord Russell on the construction of two ironclad Confederate rams at Liverpool, 5 September 1863)

Failure seems to be regarded as the one unpardonable crime, success as the all-redeeming virtue, the acquisition of wealth as the single worthy aim of life. The hair-raising revelations of a skullduggard and grand-scale thievery merely incite others to surpass by yet bolder outrages and more corrupt combinations.

(See Martin Duberman biography)

Henry Adams (1838–1918): *Historian*

That, two thousand years after Alexander the Great and Julius Caesar, a man like Grant should be called—and should actually and truly be—the highest product of the most advanced society, made evolution ludicrous. One must be as commonplace as Grant's own commonplaces to maintain such an absurdity. The progress of evolution from President Washington to President Grant, was alone evidence enough to upset Darwin.

(*The Education of Henry Adams*, 1906)

Boston had solved the universe.

(On the smugness of the Unitarians, ibid.)

Although the Senate is much given to admiring in its members a superiority less obvious or quite invisible to outsiders, one Senator seldom proclaims his own inferiority to another, and still more seldom likes to be told of it.

(Ibid.)

James Truslow Adams (1878–1949): *Historian*

God looks after drunks, children, and Americans.

(*Virginia Quarterly*, July 1934)

John Adams (1735–1826): *Revolutionary leader and second president, 1797–1801*

Facts are stubborn things; and whatever may be our wishes, our inclinations, or the dictates of our passions, they cannot alter the state of facts and evidence.

(Speech in defense of British soldiers on trial for the Boston Massacre, 1770)

As the happiness of the people is the sole end of government, so the consent of the people is the only foundation of it, in reason, morality, and the natural fitness of things.

(Proclamation, 1774)

I have passed the Rubicon; swim or sink, live or die, survive or perish with my country—that is my unalterable determination.

(Conversation with Jonathan Sewall, July 1774)

Every man in it is a great man, an orator, a critic, a statesman; and therefore every man upon every question must show his oratory, his criticism, and his political abilities.

(On the Continental Congress, 1776)

Public virtue cannot exist in a nation without private, and public virtue is the only foundation of republics.

(Letter to Mercy Warren, 16 April 1776)

All great changes are irksome to the human mind, especially those which are attended with great dangers and uncertain effects.

(Letter to James Warren, 22 April 1776)

Yesterday the greatest question was decided which ever was debated in America; and a greater perhaps never was, nor will be, decided among men. A resolution was passed without one dissenting colony, that these United Colonies are, and of right ought to be, free and independent States.

(Letter to Abigail Adams, 3 July 1776)

The second day of July, 1776, will be the most memorable epoch in the history of America. I am apt to believe that it will be celebrated by succeeding generations as the great anniversary festival. It ought to be commemorated as the day of deliverance, by solemn acts of devotion to God Almighty. It ought to be solemnized with pomp and parade, with shows, games, sports, guns, bells, bonfires, and illuminations, from one end of this continent to the other, from this time forward forevermore.

(Ibid.)

The happiness of society is the end of government.

(*Thoughts on Government*, 1776)

Fear is the foundation of most governments.
(Ibid.)

The divine science of government is the science of social happiness, and the blessings of society depend entirely on the constitutions of government.
(Ibid.)

There is a Feebleness and a Languor in my Nature. My Mind and Body both partake of this Weakness. By my Physical Constitution, I am but an ordinary Man. The Times alone have destined me to Fame—and even these have not been able to give me much. When I look in the Glass, my Eye, my Forehead, my Brow, my Cheeks, my Lips, all betray this Relaxation. Yet some great Events, some cutting Expressions, some mean Hypocrisies, have at Times, thrown this Assemblage of Sloth, Sleep, and littleness into Rage a little like a Lion.
(Diary, 26 April 1779)

A government of laws, and not of men.
(Original draft of Massachusetts constitution, 1779)

I must study politics and war, that my sons may have liberty to study mathematics and philosophy, geography, natural history and naval architecture, navigation, commerce, and agriculture, in order to give their children a right to study painting, poetry, music, architecture, statuary, tapestry, and porcelain.
(Letter to Abigail Adams, 1780)

The essence of a free government consists in an effectual control of rivalries.
(*Discourses on Davila*, 1789)

The history of our Revolution will be one continued lie from one end to the other. The essence of the whole will be that Dr. Franklin's electrical rod smote the earth and out sprang General Washington. That Franklin electrified him with his rod and thence forward these two conducted all the policy, negotiations, legislatures, and war.
(Letter to Benjamin Rush, 4 April 1790)

The Revolution was effected before the war commenced. The Revolution was in the minds and hearts of the people.

(Letter, 1818)

Thomas Jefferson still survives.

(Last words, 4 July 1826. Jefferson had, in fact, died several hours earlier.)

John Quincy Adams (1767–1848): *Sixth president, 1825–1829*

Think of your forefathers! Think of your posterity!

(Speech at Plymouth, Massachusetts, 22 December 1802)

I take it for granted that the present question is a mere preamble—a title-page to a great tragic volume.

(Diary, March 1820, concerning the first congressional debate on the morality of slavery)

It is now established as an irreversible precedent that the President of the United States has but to declare that War exists, with any Nation upon Earth, by the act of that Nation's government, and the War is essentially declared. It is not difficult to foresee what its ultimate issue will be to the people of Mexico, but what it will be to the People of the United States is beyond my foresight, and I turn my eyes away from it.

(Speech in Congress on President Polk's presidential declaration that war existed with Mexico, May 1846)

Samuel Adams (1722–1802): *Revolutionary agitator*

Let us contemplate our forefathers, and posterity, and resolve to maintain the rights bequeathed to us from the former, for the sake of the latter. The necessity of the times, more than ever, calls for our utmost circumspection, deliberation, fortitude and perseverance. Let us remember that "if we suffer tamely a lawless attack upon our liberty, we encourage it, and involve others in our doom." It is a very serious consideration . . . that millions yet unborn may be the miserable sharers of the event.

(Speech in Boston, 1771)

Among the natural rights of the colonists are these: first, a right to *life;* secondly, a right to liberty; thirdly to property; together with the right to support and defend them in the best manner they can.
(Resolution of the Boston town meeting, 20 November 1772)

What a glorious morning for America!
(Upon hearing the gunfire at Lexington, 19 April 1775)

We have no other alternative than independence, or the most ignominious and appalling servitude. The legions of our enemies thicken on our plains; desolation and death mark their bloody career; whilst the mangled corpses of our countrymen seem to cry out to us as a Voice from Heaven.
(Speech at Philadelphia, June 1776)

From the day on which an accommodation takes place between England and America, on any other terms than as independent States, I shall date the ruin of this country.
(Speech in Philadelphia, 1 August 1776)

Driven from every other corner of the earth, freedom of thought and the right of private judgment in matters of conscience direct their course to this happy country as their last asylum.
(Ibid.)

Our union is now complete; our constitution composed, established and approved. You are now the guardians of your own liberties.
(Speech in Boston, 1777)

Jane Addams (1860–1935): *Social worker*
The new demand of women for political enfranchisement comes at a time when unsatisfactory and degraded social conditions are held responsible for so much wretchedness and when the fate of all the unfortunate, the suffering and the criminal is daily forced upon woman's attention in painful and intimate ways.
(Speech, 1914)

Morris A. Adelman (1917–): *Economist*

Those fellows are not considerate and they're not malicious. They're just trying to do the best for themselves, squeezing the goose without killing it.

(On OPEC's increase in the price of petroleum, December 1978)

Spiro T. Agnew (1918–): *Vice-president under Nixon*

To some extent, if you've seen one city slum you've seen them all.

(Speech in Detroit, 18 October 1968)

Now anybody who knows me, or has taken the trouble to read what I have to say, knows that I respect the right of dissent.

(Speech in Washington, 3 December 1969)

The day when the network commentators and even gentlemen of the *New York Times* enjoyed a form of diplomatic immunity from comment and criticism of what they said—that day is past. . . . I do not seek to intimidate the press, the networks or anyone else from speaking out. But the time for blind acceptance of their opinions is past. And the time for naive belief in their neutrality is gone.

(Speech in Montgomery, 29 November 1969)

It is not an easy thing to wake up in the morning to learn that some prominent man or institution has implied that you are a bigot, a racist, or a fool.

(Ibid.)

We seem to be approaching the age of the gross.

(Speech in New Orleans, 19 October 1969)

The Republican Party has a place for every American who believes that flag waving is better than flag burning.

(Ibid.)

Bronson Alcott (1799–1888): *Transcendentalist philosopher*

I consider it the best part of an education to have been born and brought up in the country.

(Attributed)

Nelson W. Aldrich (1841–1914): *Senator from Rhode Island, financier*

A delusion and a sham, an empty menace to the great interests, made to answer the clamor of the ignorant and unreasoning.

(On the Interstate Commerce Act, 1887)

Nelson Algren (1909–   ): *Writer*

Never play cards with any man named "Doc." Never eat at any place called "Mom's." And never, ever, no matter what else you do in your whole life, never sleep with anyone whose troubles are worse than your own.

(In conversation with H. E. F. Donohue, c. 1950)

Muhammad Ali (1942–   ): *Heavyweight boxing champion*

Float like a butterfly, sting like a bee.

(Describing his boxing style to reporters, 1964)

I don't have nothing against them Vietcongs.

(To newspaper reporters, on his refusal to be inducted into the armed forces, January 1967)

I'm the greatest!

(On winning the Heavyweight Boxing Championship, 1964)

Saul Alinsky (1909–1972): *Agitator and organizer*

A racially integrated community is a chronological term timed from the entrance of the first black family to the exit of the last white family.

(*Reveille for Radicals*, 1946)

Change means movement, movement means friction, friction means heat, and heat means controversy. The only place where there is no friction is in outer space or a seminar on political action.

(*Rules for Radicals*, 1971)

True, there is government harassment, but there still is that relative freedom to fight. I can attack my government, try to organize to change it. That's more than I can do in Moscow, Peking, or Havana.

(Ibid.)

I'm very critical of the U.S., but get me outside the country and all of a sudden I can't bring myself to say one nasty thing about the U.S.

(Ibid.)

Ethan Allen (1737–1789): *Soldier and politician*

In the name of the Great Jehovah and the Continental Congress.

(Attributed reply when asked by the British garrison at Ticonderoga in whose name they were being asked to surrender, May 1775)

William "Foghorn" Allen (1803–1879): *Congressman from Ohio*

Fifty-four Forty or Fight.

(In reference to the disputed boundary between Oregon and British Columbia, speech in Congress, 1846. The boundary was compromised at 49 degrees north latitude.)

John P. Altgeld (1847–1902): *Governor of Illinois*

None of the defendants could be connected with the case. Wholesale bribery and intimidation of witnesses were resorted to. The defendants were not proved guilty of the crime.

(Pardon of the three surviving Haymarket anarchists, 26 June 1893)

No community can be said to possess local self-government if the executive can, at his pleasure, send military forces to patrol its streets under pretense of enforcing some law. The kind of local self-government that could exist under these circumstances can be found in any of the monarchies of Europe, and it is not in harmony with the spirit of our institutions.

(Letter to President Cleveland protesting the use of federal troops in the Chicago Pullman strike, 6 July 1894)

In writing *Progress and Poverty*, he dipped his pen into the tears of the human race, and with celestial clearness wrote down what he conceived to be eternal truths.

(Memorial Address on Henry George, 1897)

Fisher Ames (1758–1808): *Federalist politician*

A monarchy is like a merchantman. You get on board and ride the wind and tide in safety and elation but, by and by, you strike a reef and go down. But democracy is like a raft. You never sink, but, damn it, your feet are always in the water.

(Speech in the House of Representatives, 1795)

Oakes Ames (1804–1873): *Congressman from Massachusetts and lobbyist for the Union Pacific Railroad*

I have found there is no difficulty in inducing men to look after their own property.

(On his distribution of railroad company stock to congressmen voting on railroad subsidies, 1868)

Marian Anderson (1902–   ): *Opera singer*

Sometimes, it's like a hair across your cheek. You can't see it, you can't find it with your fingers, but you keep brushing at it because the feel of it is irritating.

(On racial prejudice, *Ladies' Home Journal*, September 1960)

Sherwood Anderson (1876–1941): *Writer*

The beaten, ignorant, Bible-ridden, white South.

(Attributed)

Susan B. Anthony (1820–1906): *Women's suffrage leader*

The true Republic: men, their rights and nothing more; women, their rights and nothing less.

(Motto of the feminist newspaper, *Revolution*, 1868)

The only question left to be settled now is: Are women persons?

(Common conceit in speeches)

Modern invention has banished the spinning-wheel, and the same law of progress makes the woman of today a different woman from her grandmother.

(Ibid.)

Mary Antin (1881–1949): *Immigrant writer*

So at last I was going to America! Really, really going, at last! The boundaries burst. The arch of heaven soared! A million suns shone out for every star. The winds rushed in from outer space, roaring in my ears, "America! America!"

(*The Promised Land*, 1912)

Thomas G. Appleton (1812–1884): *Writer and artist*

Good Americans, when they die, go to Paris.
> (Attributed)

Lewis Armistead (1817–1863): *Confederate general*

Give them the cold steel, boys!
> (Charge to his troops at the Battle of Gettysburg, 3 July 1863)

Philip D. Armour (1832–1901): *Industrialist*

I like to turn bristles, blood, and the inside and outside of pigs and bullocks into revenue.
> (Attributed)

Neil Armstrong (1930–   ): *Astronaut*

That's one small step for a man, one giant leap for mankind.
> (On setting foot on the moon, 20 July 1969)

Chester A. Arthur (1830–1886): *Twenty-first president, 1881–1885*

It cannot be. I have heard nothing. I hope, My God, I do hope it is a mistake.
> (To a reporter upon hearing of Garfield's death and his accession to the presidency, 19 September 1881)

We have to deal with the appalling fact that though thousands of lives have been sacrificed and hundreds of millions of dollars expended in the attempt to solve the Indian problem, it has until within the past few years seemed scarcely nearer a solution than it was half a century ago.
> (Message to Congress, November 1881)

John Jacob Astor III (1864–1912): *Multimillionaire*

A man who has a million dollars is as well off as if he were rich.
> (Attributed)

Brooks Atkinson (1894–1984): *Writer*

We cheerfully assume that in some mystic way love conquers all, that good outweighs evil in the just balances of the universe and that at the eleventh hour something gloriously triumphant will prevent the worst before it happens.

(Once Around the Sun, 1951)

There is a good deal of solemn cant about the common interests of capital and labor. As matters stand, their only common interest is that of cutting each other's throat.

(Ibid.)

W. H. Auden (1907–1973): *Poet*

It is a sad fact about our culture that a poet can earn much more money writing or talking about his art than he can by practicing it.

(The Dyer's Hand, 1962)

What the mass media offer is not popular art, but entertainment which is intended to be consumed like food, forgotten, and replaced by a new dish.

(Ibid.)

Jane Austen (1775–1817): *English novelist*

With regard to an American war . . . they consider it as certain, and as what is to ruin us. The [Americans] cannot be conquered, and we shall only be teaching them the skill in War which they now want. . . . I place my hope of better things on a claim to the protection of Heaven as a Religious Nation, a Nation in spite of much Evil improving in Religion, which I cannot believe the Americans to possess.

(Letter to Martha Lloyd, 2 September 1814)

Mary Hunter Austin (1868–1934): *Novelist*

It is the proper destiny of every considerable stream in the west to become an irrigation ditch.

(Land of Little Rain, 1903)

B

George Baer (1842–1914): *Industrialist*

The rights and interests of the laboring man will be protected and cared for, not by the labor agitators, but by the Christian men to whom God in His infinite wisdom has given control of the property interests of the country.

> (Letter to a journalist during a strike by anthracite miners, October 1902)

James Baldwin (1924–   ): *Writer*

The making of an American begins at that point where he himself rejects all other ties, any other history, and adopts the vesture of his adopted land.

> (*Notes of a Native Son,* 1955)

It is only in his music, which Americans are able to admire because a protective sentimentality limits their understanding of it, that the Negro in America has been able to tell his story.

> (Ibid.)

Aunt Jemima and Uncle Tom are dead, their places taken by a group of amazingly well-adjusted young men and women, almost as dark, but ferociously literate, well-dressed and scrubbed, who are never laughed at.

> (Ibid.)

Our dehumanization of the Negro then is indivisible from our dehumanization of ourselves; the loss of our own identity is the price we pay for our annulment of his.

> (Ibid.)

This world is white no longer, and it will never be white again.
(Ibid.)

Money, it turned out, was exactly like sex, you thought of nothing else if you didn't have it and thought of other things if you did.
(*Nobody Knows My Name*, 1961)

A ghetto can be improved in one way only: out of existence.
(Ibid.)

Europe has what we do not have yet, a sense of the mysterious and inexorable limits of life, a sense, in a word, of tragedy. And we have what they sorely need: a sense of life's possibilities.
(Ibid.)

It is a great shock at the age of five or six to find that in a world of Gary Coopers you are the Indian.
(Speech at the Cambridge Union, 17 February 1965)

Consider the history of labour in a country in which, spiritually speaking, there are no workers, only candidates for the hand of the boss's daughter.
(*The Fire Next Time*, 1963)

White people in this country will have quite enough to do in learning how to accept and love themselves and each other, and when they have achieved this—which will not be tomorrow and may very well be never—the Negro problem will no longer exist, for it will no longer be needed.
(Ibid.)

Arthur Barlowe (1550?–1620?): *English explorer*

We were entertained with all love, and kindness, and with as much bountie, after their manner, as they could possibly devise. We found the people most gentle, loving, and faithful, void of all guile, and treason, and such as lived after the manner of the golden age. The earth bringeth foorth all things in aboundance, as in the first creation, without toile or labour.
(On North America, *Discourse on the First Voyage*, 1584)

Frederick A. P. Barnard (1809–1899): *Educator*

We have in Herbert Spencer not only the profoundest thinker of our time but the most capacious and powerful intellect of all time. Aristotle and his master were no more beyond the pygmies who preceded them than he is beyond Aristotle. Kant, Hegel, Fichte, and Schilling are gropers in the dark by the side of him. In all the history of science, there is but one name which can be compared to his, and that is Newton's.

(Toast at a testimonial dinner for Herbert Spencer, New York, 1882)

Phineas T. Barnum (1810–1891): *Showman*

This is a trading world and men, women and children, who cannot live on gravity alone, need something to satisfy their gayer, lighter moods and hours, and he who ministers to this want is in a business established by the Author of our nature. If he worthily fulfills his mission and amuses without corrupting, he need not feel that he has lived in vain.

(*Struggles and Triumphs*, 1871)

I am not in the show business alone to make money. I feel it my mission, as long as I live, to provide clean, moral, and healthful recreation for the public to which I have so long catered.

(Ibid.)

There's a sucker born every minute.

(Attributed)

Money-getters are the benefactors of our race.

(Attributed)

How were the circus receipts at Madison Square Garden?

(Last words, 1891)

A. H. Barr, Jr. (1902–): *Historian*

Except the American woman, nothing interests the eye of American man more than the automobile, or seems so important to him as an object of esthetic appreciation.

(Commenting on sculptures incorporating automobile parts, 1963)

John Barrymore (1882–1942): *Actor*

America is the country where you buy a lifetime supply of aspirin for one dollar and use it up in two weeks.

(Attributed)

Frédéric Auguste Bartholdi (1834–1904): *French sculptor of Statue of Liberty*

Everyone is running to and fro, pressed by the stomach ache of business.

(Letter to his mother, 12 June 1871)

Bruce Barton (1886–1967): *Advertising man and writer*

He picked up twelve men from the bottom ranks of business and forged them into an organization that conquered the world. . . . Nowhere is there such a startling example of executive success as the way in which that organization was brought together.

(*The Man Nobody Knows: A Discovery of the Real Jesus*, 1924)

Bernard Baruch (1870–1965): *Financier and presidential adviser*

Let us not be deceived. We are today in the midst of a cold war.

(Speech at Columbia, South Carolina, 17 April 1947)

Take the profits out of war.

(*Time*, 25 February 1957)

You talk about capitalism and communism and all that sort of thing, but the important thing is the struggle everybody is engaged in to get better living conditions, and they are not interested too much in the form of government.

(At a press conference in New York City, 18 August 1964)

Luigi Barzini (1908–1984): *Italian journalist*

I still believe the world would have been a better place if some of the American ideals of my youth had prevailed everywhere and, first of all, in the United States itself.

(*O America*, 1977)

Katherine Lee Bates (1859–1929): *Educator and poet*

O beautiful for spacious skies,
For amber waves of grain,
For purple mountain majesties
Above the fruited plain!
America! America!
God shed his grace on thee,
And crown thy good with
brotherhood
From sea to shining sea!

("America the Beautiful," 1893)

Bear Rib (?–?): *Hunkpapa Sioux chieftan*

To whom does this land belong? I believe it belongs to me. If you asked me for a piece of it I would not give it. I cannot spare it, and I like it very much. . . . I hope you will listen to me.

(During treaty talks at Pierre, South Dakota, 1866)

Charles A. Beard (1874–1948): *Historian*

The movement for the Constitution of the United States was originated and carried through principally by four groups of personal interests which had been adversely affected under the Articles of Confederation: money, public securities, manufactures, and trade and shipping.

(*Economic Interpretation of the Constitution*, 1913)

Jeffersonian Democracy simply meant the possession of the federal government by the agrarian masses led by an aristocracy of slave-owning planters.

(*The Economic Origins of Jeffersonian Democracy*, 1915)

Simone de Beauvoir (1908–   ): *French writer*

America is one of the world's pivotal points: the future of man is at stake here. To like America, or not to like her: these words are meaningless. Here is a battlefield, and one can only be stirred by the struggle she carries on within herself, a struggle whose stakes are beyond measure.

(*America Day by Day*, 1953)

Carl Becker (1873–1945): *Historian*

Twice tricked by the British into a European war in order to pull their chestnuts out of the fire.

(*Progress and Power*, 1935)

No class of Americans, so far as I know, has ever objected . . . to any amount of governmental meddling if it appeared to benefit that particular class.

(Attributed)

Thomas Becket (?–?): *English actor*

> O, Columbia, the gem of the
> ocean,
> The home of the brave and
> the free,
> The shrine of each patriot's
> devotion,
> A world offers homage to thee.

(Song, written in Philadelphia, 1843)

Bernard E. Bee (1823–1861): *Confederate general*

Let us determine to die here, and we will conquer. There is Jackson standing like a stone wall. Rally behind the Virginians.

(Of General Thomas J. Jackson at the Battle of First Bull Run, 21 July 1861)

Henry Ward Beecher (1813–1887): *Prominent clergyman*

The Negro is superior to the white race. If the latter do not forget their pride of race and color, and amalgamate with the purer and richer blood of the blacks, they will die out and wither away in unprolific skinniness.

(Speech, New York City, 1866)

The trade union, which originated under the European system, destroys liberty. I do not say a dollar a day is enough to support a working man, but it is enough to support a man. Not enough to support a man and five children if a man insists on smoking and drinking beer.

(Sermon at Plymouth Church, New York, 29 July 1877)

Is the great working class oppressed? Yes, undoubtedly it is. God has intended the great to be great and the little to be little.
> (Ibid.)

The real democratic American idea is, not that every man shall be on a level with every other man, but that every man shall have liberty to be what God made him, without hindrance.
> (*Proverbs from Plymouth Pulpit*, 1887)

The commerce of the world is conducted by the strong, and usually it operates against the weak.
> (Ibid.)

The ignorant classes are the dangerous classes.
> (Ibid.)

When a nation's young men are conservative, its funeral bell is already rung.
> (Ibid.)

Alexander Graham Bell (1847–1922): *Inventor and entrepreneur*

Mr. Watson, come here; I want you.
> (First words spoken by telephone, Boston, 10 March 1876)

Daniel Bell (1919–   ): *Sociologist*

Although action is typical of the American style, thought and planning are not; it is considered heresy to state that some problems are not immediately or easily solvable.
> (*Daedalus*, Summer 1967)

Francis Bellamy (1856–1931): *Baptist minister*

I pledge allegiance to the flag of the United States of America and to the Republic for which it stands, one Nation, indivisible, with liberty and justice for all.
> ("The Pledge of Allegiance," 8 September 1892. The Pledge was officially amended by Congress in 1954 to include the words "one nation under God, indivisible . . .")

Melvin Belli (1907–   ): *Trial lawyer*

My idea of the ideal jury is twelve Irish unionists deciding the case of my client, Patrick O'Brien, a union bricklayer, who was run over by Chauncy Marlborough's Rolls-Royce while Marlborough was on his way to deposit $50,000 in the bank.

(Attributed)

Saul Bellow (1915–   ): *Novelist*

I think people in America have been spared the worst of the 20th century. They didn't know wars as other countries knew them. They were spared the experience of totalitarianism. Even the least fortunate Americans can scarcely be compared with the Latin-American or Asian poor. So either the gods have spared us or they have shown their contempt for us.

(Interview, August 1980)

Stephen Vincent Benét (1898–1943): *Poet*

American muse, whose strong and diverse heart
So many men have tried to understand
But only made it smaller with their art,
Because you are as various as your land.
(*John Brown's Body*, 1928)

I have fallen in love with American names
The sharp names that never go flat
The snakeskin titles of mining claims
The plumed war bonnet of Medicine Hat
Tucson and Deadwood and Lost Mule Flat
(*Western Star*, 1943)

If two New Hampshiremen aren't a match for the devil, we might as well give the country back to the Indians.
(*The Devil and Daniel Webster*, 1936)

When Daniel Boone goes by, at night,
The phantom deer arise
And all lost, wild America
Is burning in their eyes.
(*Daniel Boone*, 1933)

He toiled not, neither did he spin,
But how he raked the dollars in.

(*A Book of Americans*, 1933)

And those that came were resolved to be Englishmen,
Gone to the world's end but English every one,
And they are the white corn kernels parched in the sun
And they knew it not but they'd not be English again.

(*Western Star*, 1943)

James Gordon Bennett (1841–1918): *Editor and publisher*

It is our manifest destiny to lead and rule all nations.

(*New York Herald*, 3 April 1865)

Thomas Hart Benton (1782–1858): *Senator from Missouri*

They may be devoured by it any moment. They are in the jaws of the monster! A lump of butter in the mouth of a dog! One gulp, one swallow, and all is gone!

(Of western cities and the Bank of the United States, 1819)

You could not look upon the table but there were frogs. You could not sit down at the banquet table but there were frogs, you could not go to the bridal couch and lift the sheets but there were frogs! We can see nothing, touch nothing, have no measures proposed, without having this pestilence thrust before us.

(Speech in Congress, 1848, referring to the introduction of the slavery issue into every debate)

Let us complete the grand design of Columbus, by putting Europe and Asia into communication. Let us give to his ships, converted into cars, a continuous course.

(Advocating the construction of a transcontinental railroad, speech in the Senate, 1849)

George Berkeley (1685–1753): *Anglican Bishop*

Westward the course of empire takes its way;
The first four acts already past,
A fifth shall close the drama with the day:
Time's noblest offspring is the last

("The Prospect of Planitary Arts and Learning in America," 1752)

Sir William Berkeley (1606–1677): *Governor of Virginia colony*

I thank God we have no free schools nor printing; and I hope we shall not have these hundred years. For learning has brought disobedience and heresy and sects into the world; and printing has divulged them and libels against the government. God keep us from both.

(Letter, 1671)

Irving Berlin (1888–   ): *Songwriter*

My brother down in Texas
Can't even write his name.
He signs his cheques with X's,
But they cash 'em just the same.

("Doing What Comes Naturally," *Annie Get Your Gun*, 1946)

Mary McLeod Bethune (1875–1955): *Civil rights activist*

If our people are to fight their way up out of bondage we must arm them with the sword and the shield and the buckler of pride.

(*Journal of Negro History*, January 1938)

For I am my mother's daughter, and the drums of Africa still beat in my heart. They will not let me rest while there is a single Negro boy or girl without a chance to prove his worth.

(*Who*, June 1941)

Albert J. Beveridge (1862–1927): *Senator from Indiana*

The Opposition tells us that we ought not to govern a people without their consent. I answer, The rule of liberty that all just government derives its authority from the consent of the governed, applies only to those who are capable of self-government. We govern the Indians without their consent, we govern our territories without their consent, we govern our children without their consent. How do they know what our government would be without their consent? Would not the people of the Philippines prefer the just, humane, civilizing government of this Republic to the savage, bloody rule of pillage and extortion from which we have rescued them?

(Speech at Indianapolis, 16 September 1898)

God has not been preparing the English-speaking and Teutonic peoples for a thousand years for nothing but vain and idle self-admiration. No. He made us master organizers of the world to establish system where chaos reigned. He has given us the spirit of progress to overwhelm the forces of reaction throughout the earth. He has made us adept in government that we may administer government among savage and senile peoples. Were it not for such a force as this the world would relapse into barbarism and night. And of all our race He has marked the American people as His chosen nation to finally lead in the redemption of the world.

(Speech in the Senate, 9 January 1900)

This party comes from the grass roots. It has grown from the soil of the people's hard necessities.

(Speech to Progressive Party Convention, 1912)

Robert Beverley (1633?–1722): *Colonial Virginia planter and historian*

They have the Happiness to have very few Doctors, as those such as make use only of simple Remedies, of which their Woods afford great Plenty. And indeed, their Distempers are not many, and their Cures are so generally known, that there is not Mystery enough, to make a Trade of Physick there, as the Learned do in other Countries, to the great oppression of Mankind.

(*History and Present State of Virginia*, 1705)

Alexander M. Bickel (1924–   ): *Educator and lawyer*

Wrong and morally wrong in its conduct and consequences, it was nevertheless not evil in intent or origin. What propelled us into this war was a corruption of the generous, idealistic, liberal impulse.

(On the war in Vietnam, *The Morality of Consent*, 1975)

Nicholas Biddle (1786–1844): *Banker*

This worthy President thinks that because he has scalped Indians and imprisoned judges, he is to have his way with the Bank. He is mistaken.

(On President Jackson soon after Jackson's attack on the Bank of the United States, which Biddle headed; attributed, 1831)

Ambrose Bierce (1842–1914?): *Writer and wit*

Bigot, n. One who is obstinately and zealously attached to an opinion that you do not entertain.

(*The Devil's Dictionary*, 1881–1911)

Corporation, n. An ingenious device for obtaining individual profit without individual responsibility.

(Ibid.)

Presidency, n. The greased pig in the field game of American politics.

(Ibid.)

Rebel, n. A proponent of a new misrule who has failed to establish it.

(Ibid.)

Thomas Brigham Bishop (1835–1905): *Songwriter*

John Brown's body lies a-mouldering in the grave, His soul goes marching on.

(*John Brown's Body*, 1861)

Hugo Black (1886–1971): *Supreme Court justice*

It is part of the established tradition in the use of juries as instruments of public justice that the jury be a body truly representative of the community. For racial discrimination to result in the exclusion from jury service of otherwise qualified groups not only violates our Constitution and the laws enacted under it, but is at war with our basic concepts of a democratic society and a representative government.

(*Smith* v. *Texas*, 1940)

No person can be punished for entertaining or professing religious beliefs or disbeliefs, for church attendance or non-attendance.

(*Everson* v. *Board of Education*, 1947)

The First Amendment has erected a wall between church and state. That wall must be kept high and impregnable. We could not approve the slightest breach.

(Ibid.)

There is hope that in calmer times, when the present pressures, passions, and fears subside, this or some later court will restore the First Amendment liberties to the high preferred place where they belong in a free society.

(Dissenting opinion, *Dennis* v. *United States,* 1951)

The interest of the people [lies] in being able to join organizations, advocate causes, and make political "mistakes" without being subjected to government penalties.

(*Dissent, Barenblatt* case, 1959)

Black Hawk (1767–1868): *Sauk chief*

I fought hard. But your guns were well aimed. The bullets flew like birds in the air, and whizzed by our ears like the wind through the trees. My warriors fell around me; it began to look dismal. I saw my evil day at hand. The sun rose dim on us in the morning, and at night it sank in a dark cloud, and looked like a ball of fire. That was the last sun that shone on Black Hawk. His heart is dead, and no longer beats quick in his bosom. He is now a prisoner to the white men; they will do with him as they wish. But he can stand torture and is not afraid of death. He is no coward. Black Hawk is an Indian.

(Upon his surrender, 1832)

I am now an obscure member of a nation, that formerly honored and respected my opinions. The path to glory is rough, and many gloomy hours obscure it. May the Great Spirit shed light on yours— and that you may never experience the humility that the power of the American government has reduced me to is the wish of him, who, in his native forests, was once as proud and bold as yourself.

(In conversation with General H. Atkinson, 1833)

James G. Blaine (1830–1893): *Senator from Maine and secretary of state*

The contempt of that large-minded gentleman is so wilting, his haughty disdain, his grandiloquent swell, his majestic, super-eminent, over-powering turkey-gobbler strut has been so crushing to myself and all the greatest temerity for me to venture upon a controversy with him.

(On his rival for Republican Party leadership, Roscoe Conkling, 1876)

Cole Blease (1868–1942): *Senator from South Carolina*

Whenever the Constitution comes between me and the virtue of white women in South Carolina, I say, "the hell with the Constitution."

(Often-repeated slogan)

Tasker Bliss (1853–1930): *Army chief of staff during World War I*

We ought to get out of Europe, horse, foot and dragoons.

(Attributed, 1917: Bliss insisted that U.S. forces fight as a unit)

Humphrey Bogart (1899–1957):*Film actor*

They'll nail anyone who ever scratched his ass during the national anthem.

(On the House Committee on Un-American Activities, 1947)

Charles E. "Black Bart" Boles (1829–1896): *Notorious stagecoach robber*

I've labored long and hard for bread,
For honor and for riches,
But on my corns too long you've tread,
You fair-haired sons of bitches.

(Note attached to an emptied strongbox, Fort Ross, California, 3 August 1877)

Julian Bond (1940–　　): *Civil rights leader and politician*

The system conceded to black people the right to sit up in the front of the bus—a hollow victory when one's longest trip is likely to be from the feudal South to the mechanized poverty of the North.

(Attributed)

Daniel Boone (1734–1820): *Pioneer and promoter*
I had not been two years at the licks before a d—d Yankee came, and settled down within an hundred miles of me!!
    (Attributed)

All you need for happiness is a good gun, a good horse, and a good wife.
    (Attributed)

Daniel J. Boorstin (1914–   ): *Historian*
Never have people been more the masters of their environment. Yet never has a people felt more deceived and disappointed. For never has a people expected so much more than the world could offer.
    (*The Image*, 1962)

Our most admired national heroes—Franklin, Washington, and Lincoln—are generally supposed to possess the "common touch." We revere them, not because they possess charisma, divine favor, a grace or talent granted them by God, but because they embody popular virtues. We admire them, not because they reveal God, but because they reveal and elevate ourselves.
    (Ibid.)

We expect to eat and stay thin, to be constantly on the move and ever more neighborly . . . to revere God and be God.
    (Interview, *Newsweek*, 26 February 1962)

John Wilkes Booth (1838–1865): *Actor and assassin of Lincoln*
This man's appearance, his pedigree, his coarse low jokes and anecdotes, his vulgar similes and his frivolity, are a disgrace to the seat he holds.
    (Of Lincoln, early 1865, attributed)

I have too great a soul to die like a criminal.
    (Ibid.)

Sic semper tyrannis! The South is avenged!
    (Shouted at Ford's Theater after Booth shot Lincoln, 14 April 1865)

William E. Borah (1865–1940): *Senator from Idaho*

A democracy must remain at home in all matters which affect the nature of her institutions. They are of a nature to call for the undivided energy and devotion of the entire nation. We do not want the racial antipathies or national antagonisms of the Old World translated to this continent, as they will should we become a part of European politics. The people of this country are overwhelmingly for a policy of neutrality.

(Radio address, 22 February 1936)

Gail Borden (1801–1874): *Inventor and industrialist*

I mean to put a potato into a pill box, a pumpkin into a tablespoon, the biggest sort of watermelon into a saucer. . . . The Turks made acres of roses into attar of roses. . . . I intend to make attar of everything.

(*The Meat Biscuit,* 1850)

Thomas K. Bowden (1950–   ): *Soldier, Charlie Company, First Infantry Division, 28th Infantry Regiment*

We are the unwilling working for the unqualified to do the unnecessary for the ungrateful.

(Letter from Vietnam to his father, 1968)

Edward Braddock (1695–1755): *British general*

We shall know better how to do it next time.

(Last words upon having been defeated in battle by French and Indian forces near Pittsburgh, Pennsylvania, 1755)

William Bradford (1590–1657): *Leader of the Plymouth separatists*

Haveing undertaken, for the glorie of God, and advancements of the Christian faith and honour of our king & countrie, a voyage to plant the first colonie in the Northerne parts of Virginia, doe by these presents solemnly & mutualy in the presence of God, and one of another, covenant & combine our selves togeather into a civill body politick; for our better ordering, & preservation & furtherance of the ends aforesaid; and by vertue hearof to enacte, constitute, and frame such just & equall lawes, ordinances, Act, constitutions, &

offices, from time to time, as shall be thought most meete & convenient for the generall good of the Colonie: unto which we promise all due submission and obedience.

(The Mayflower Compact, 1620)

So they left the goodly and pleasant city, which had been their resting-place near twelve years; they knew they were pilgrims, and looked not much on those things, but lift up their eyes to the heavens, their dearest country, and quieted their spirits.

(Of *Plymouth Plantation*, 1647)

So they committed themselves to the will of God and resolved to proceed.

(Ibid.)

Being thus arrived in a good harbor, and brought safe to land, they fell upon their knees and blessed the God of Heaven who had brought them over the vast and furious ocean, and delivered them from all the perils and miseries thereof, again to set their proper element.

(Ibid.)

But it pleased God to visit us then with death daily, and with so general a disease that the living were scarce able to bury the dead.

(Ibid.)

May not and ought not the children of these fathers rightly say: "Our fathers were Englishmen which came over this great ocean, and were ready to perish in this wilderness."

(Ibid.)

Omar Bradley (1893–1981): *General*

We have grasped the mystery of the atom and rejected the Sermon on the Mount. . . . Ours is a world of nuclear giants and ethical infants.

(Armistice Day address, November 1948)

The wrong war, at the wrong place, at the wrong time, and with the wrong enemy.

(On General MacArthur's proposal to carry the Korean conflict into China, May 1951)

The way to win an atomic war is to make certain it never starts.
(Remark to reporters, April 1952)

Ann Bradstreet (1612–1672): *Poetess*

This sinful creature, frail and vain.
This lump of wretchedness, of sin and sorrow.
(*The Tenth Muse*, 1650)

Edward S. Bragg (1827–1912): *Politician*

We love him most for the enemies he has made.
(Of Grover Cleveland, 1896)

John Branch (1782–1863): *Senator from North Carolina, secretary of the navy under Jackson*

If elected, which I trust in God you will be, you will owe your election to the people, Yes Sir, to the unbiased unbought suffrages of the independent, grateful yeomanry of this country. You will come into the Executive chair untrammeled, free to pursue the dictates of your own judgment.
(Letter to Andrew Jackson, 1828)

Louis D. Brandeis (1856–1941): *Supreme Court justice*

Industrial democracy should ultimately attend political democracy.
(*The Employer and Trades Unions*, 1904)

I think we are in a position, after the experience of the last 20 years, to state two things: in the first place, that a corporation may well be too large to be the most efficient instrument of production and of distribution, and, in the second place, whether it has exceeded the point of greatest economic efficiency or not, it may be too large to be tolerated among the people who desire to be free.
(Testimony before the Committee on Interstate Commerce, 1911)

Like the course of the heavenly bodies, harmony in national life is a resultant of the struggle between contending forces. In frank expression of conflicting opinion lies the greatest promise of wisdom in governmental action; and in suppression lies ordinarily the greatest peril.
(*Gilbert* v. *Minnesota*, 1920)

Few laws are of universal application. It is of the nature of our law that it has dealt not with man in general, but with him in relationships.

(*Truax* v. *Corrigan*, 1921)

Nearly all legislation involves a weighing of public needs as against private desires; and likewise a weighing of relative social values.

(Ibid.)

Those who won our independence by revolution were not cowards. They did not fear political change. They did not exalt order at the cost of liberty.

(*Whitney* v. *California*, 1927)

To courageous, self-reliant men, with confidence in the power of free and fearless reasoning applied through the processes of popular government, no danger flowing from speech can be deemed clear and present, unless the incidence of the evil apprehended is so imminent that it may befall before there is opportunity for full discussion. If there be time to expose through discussion the falsehoods and fallacies, to avert the evil by the process of education, the remedy to be applied is more speech, not enforced silence. Only an emergency can justify repression. Such must be the rule if authority is to be reconciled with freedom. Such, in my opinion, is the command of the Constitution.

(Ibid.)

We can have democracy in this country or we can have great wealth concentrated in the hands of a few, but we can't have both.

(*Labor*, 17 October 1941)

The greatest factors making for communism, socialism or anarchy among a free people are the excesses of capital. The talk of the agitator does not advance socialism one step. The great captains of industry and finance . . . are the chief makers of socialism.

(Attributed)

Unlicensed liberty leads necessarily to despotism and oligarchy.

(Ibid.)

Radicals who would take us back to the roots of things often fail because they disregard the fruit Time has produced and preserved. Conservatives fail because they would preserve even what Time has decomposed.

(Ibid.)

Marlon Brando (1924–): *Film actor*

Once you are a star actor, people start asking you questions about politics, astronomy, archaeology and birth control.

(Attributed)

William Cowper Brann (1855–1898): *Journalist*

Boston runs to brains as well as to beans and brown bread. But she is cursed with an army of cranks whom nothing short of a straight-jacket or a swamp-elm club will ever control.

(*Waco, Texas Iconoclast*, 1898)

Arthur Bremer (1950–): *Would-be assassin of George C. Wallace*

How much do you think I'll get for my autobiography?

(To police, shortly after his arrest, May 1972)

William J. Brennan, Jr. (1906–): *Supreme Court justice*

All ideas having even the slightest redeeming social importance—unorthodox ideas, controversial ideas, even ideas hateful to the prevailing climate of opinion—have the full protection of the guaranties, unless excludable because they encroach upon the limited area of more important interests. But implicit in the history of the First Amendment is the rejection of obscenity as utterly without redeeming social importance.

(*Opinion, Roth v. United States*, 1957)

We hold that obscenity is not within the area of constitutionally protected speech or press.

(Ibid.)

Law cannot stand aside from the social changes around it.

(Lecture, Georgetown University, 25 November 1957)

Jimmy Breslin (1930–): *Journalist*

Nixon is a purposeless man, but I have great faith in his cowardice.

(*Observer*, 16 November 1969)

John Bright (1811–1889): *English politician*

In a few years, a very few years, the twenty millions of freemen in the North will be thirty millions, or even fifty millions, a population equal to or exceeding that of this Kingdom. When that time comes, I pray that it may not be said amongst them that, in the darkest hour of their country's trials, England, the land of their fathers, looked on with icy coldness and saw unmoved the perils and calamities of their children.

(Speech on the American Civil War at Rochdale, 4 December 1861)

My opinion is that the Northern States will manage somehow to muddle through.

(On the American Civil War, attributed, 1862)

D. W. Brogan (1900–): *British historian of the United States*

The combination of a profound hatred of war and militarism with an innocent delight in playing soldiers is one of these apparent contradictions of American life that one has to accept.

(*The American Character*, 1944)

Heywood Broun (1888–1939): *Journalist*

The best newspaperman who has ever been President of the United States.

(Of Franklin D. Roosevelt, attributed in conversation)

Hubert Gerold "H. Rap" Brown (1943–): *Black youth leader*

Burn this town down.

(Speech, Cambridge, Maryland, 24 July 1967)

Violence is American as apple pie.

(Speech, Baltimore, 27 July 1967)

You call yourselves revolutionaries? How many white folks you killed today?

(Common conceit in speeches, 1969–1970)

John Brown (1800–1859): *Abolitionist and insurrectionist*

I am quite cheerful in view of my approaching end, being fully persuaded that I am worth inconceivably more to hang than for any other person.

(At his trial for attempting to foment a slave rebellion, 2 November 1859)

Had I interfered in the manner which I admit in behalf of the rich, the powerful, the intelligent, the so-called great, or in behalf of any of their friends, it would have been all right, and every man in this court would have deemed it an act worthy of reward rather than punishment.

(Ibid.)

I am as content to die for God's eternal truth on the scaffold as in any other way.

(Letter to his children on eve of his execution, 2 December 1859)

I, John Brown, am now quite certain that the crimes of this guilty land will never be purged away but with blood.

(Last words, 3 December 1859)

John Mason Brown (1900–1969): *Writer*

The more I observed Washington, the more frequently I visited it, and the more people I interviewed there, the more I understood how prophetic L'Enfant was when he laid it out as a city that goes around in circles.

(*Through These Men*, 1956)

Moses Brown (1738–1836): *Industrialist*

If thou canst do this thing, I invite thee to come to Rhode Island and have the credit of introducing cotton-manufacture into America.

(Letter to Samuel Slater who had smuggled plans for Arkwright textile machinery out of England, 1791)

William Jennings Bryan (1860–1925): *Thrice presidential candidate and secretary of state under President Wilson*

The humblest citizen of all the land, when clad in the armor of a righteous cause, is stronger than all the hosts of error.

> (Speech at the Democratic National Convention, "Cross of Gold," Chicago, 8 July 1896)

Burn down your cities and leave our farms, and your cities will spring up again as if by magic; but destroy our farms and the grass will grow in the streets of every city in the country.

> (Ibid.)

You shall not press down upon the brow of labor this crown of thorns, you shall not crucify mankind upon a cross of gold.

> (Ibid.)

Great has been the Greek, the Latin, the Slav, the Celt, the Teuton, and the Anglo-Saxon, but greater than any of these is the American, in whom are blended the virtues of them all.

> (Speech in Washington, 22 February 1899)

The burning issue of imperialism growing out of the Spanish War involves the very existence of the Republic and the destruction of our free institutions.

> (Speech at the Democratic National Convention, 5 July 1900)

No man can earn $1 million honestly.

> (Attributed, 1906)

Behold a republic gradually but surely becoming the supreme moral factor in disputes.

> (Statement in Washington on his "cooling off" treaties, 1913)

The Bible states it. It must be so.

> (Testimony during the Scopes "Monkey Trial," Dayton, Tennessee, 20 July 1925)

It is better to trust in the Rock of Ages than to know the age of rocks. It is better for one to know that he is close to the Heavenly Father than to know how far the stars in the heavens are apart.

> (Summation in Scopes trial, 21 July 1925, never delivered but published in the press)

William Cullen Bryant (1794–1878): *Poet*

These are the gardens of the Desert, these
The unshorn fields, boundless and beautiful,
For which the speech of England has no name—
The Prairies.

("The Prairies," 1832)

James, Lord Bryce (1838–1922): *British diplomat*

There is a hearty Puritanism in the view of human nature which pervades the instrument of 1787. It is the work of men who believed in original sin, and were determined to leave open for transgressors no door which they could possibly shut.

(*The American Commonwealth,* 1888)

The Americans are a good-natured people, kindly, helpful to one another, disposed to take a charitable view even of wrongdoers. . . . Even a mob lynching a horse thief in the West has consideration for the criminal, and will give him a good drink of whiskey before he is strung up.

(Ibid.)

Scotchmen and Irishmen are more unlike Englishmen, the native of Normandy more unlike the native of Provence, the Pomeranian more unlike the Würtemberger, the Piedmontese more unlike the Neapolitan, the Basque more unlike the Andalusian, than the American from any part of the country is to the American from any other part.

(Ibid.)

The tendency everywhere in America to concentrate power and responsibility in one is unmistakeable.

(Ibid.)

The government of cities is the one conspicuous failure of the United States.

(Ibid.)

After this is may seem a paradox to add that Americans are a conservative people. Yet any one who observes the power of habit among them, the tenacity with which old institutions and usages,

legal and theological formulas, have been clung to, will admit the fact. A love for what is old and established is in their English blood. Moreover, prosperity helps to make them conservative. They are satisfied with the world they live in, for they have found it a good world, in which they have grown rich. . . . They are proud of their history and of their Constitution, which has come out of the furnace of civil war with scarcely the smell of fire upon it.
(Ibid.)

There is in the American government a want of unity. . . . The sailors, the helmsmen, the engineer, do not seem to have one purpose or obey one will, so that instead of making steady way the vessel may pursue a devious or zigzag course, and sometimes merely turn round and round in the water.
(Ibid.)

Zbigniew Brzezinski (1928–   ): *Foreign-policy adviser to President Carter*

What makes America unique in our time is that confrontation with the new is part of the daily American experience. For better or worse, the rest of the world learns what is in store for it by observing what happens in the United States.
(*Between Two Ages*, 1970)

First one up gets to fight the Russians in Ethiopia.
(Racing his Chinese hosts on the Great Wall, 1980)

James Buchanan (1791–1868): *Fifteenth president, 1857–1861*

Let us look the danger fairly in the face. Secession is neither more nor less than revolution. It may or it may not be a justifiable revolution, but still it is a revolution.
(Message to Congress, 3 December 1860)

The fact is that our Union rests upon public opinion, and can never be cemented by the blood of its citizens shed in civil war. If it can not live in the affections of the people, it must one day perish. Congress possesses many means of preserving it by conciliation, but the sword was not placed in their hand to preserve it by force.
(Ibid.)

Whatever the result may be, I shall carry to my grave the consciousness that I at least meant well for my country.

(On his deathbed, 1868)

Art Buchwald (1925–   ): *Newspaper columnist*

Americans are broad-minded people. They'll accept the fact that a person can be an alcoholic, a dope fiend, a wife beater, and even a newspaperman, but if a man doesn't drive there's something wrong with him.

(*Have I Ever Lied to You?*, 1968)

Pearl S. Buck (1892–1973): *Writer*

It is not healthy when a nation lives within a nation, as colored Americans are living inside America. A nation cannot live confident of its tomorrow if its refugees are among its own citizens.

(*What America Means to Me*, 1943)

Race prejudice is not only a shadow over the colored—it is a shadow over all of us, and the shadow is darkest over those who feel it least and allow its evil effects to go on.

(Ibid.)

Samuel D. Burchard (1812–1891): *Presbyterian clergyman and Republican Party politician*

We are Republicans and don't propose to leave our party and identify ourselves with the party whose antecedents are rum, Romanism, and rebellion.

(Speech, New York City, 29 October 1884, said to have contributed to the defeat of the Republican Party in the election of 1884 by alienating Irish-Catholic voters)

Sir John Burgoyne (1722–1792): *British general*

After a fatal procrastination, not only of vigorous measures but of preparations for such, we took a step as decisive as the passage of the Rubicon, and now find ourselves plunged at once in a most serious war without a single requisition, gunpowder excepted, for carrying it on.

(Letter from Boston, after the Battle of Lexington, April 1775)

Edmund Burke (1729–1797): *British member of Parliament and political philosopher*

Reflect how you are to govern a people who think they ought to be free, and think they are not. Your scheme yields no revenue; it yields nothing but discontent, disorder, disobedience; and such is the state of America, that after wading up to your eyes in blood, you could only end just where you begun; that is, to tax where no revenue is to be found, to—my voice fails me; my inclination indeed carries me no farther—all is confusion beyond it.

(Speech in the House of Commons, "On American Taxation," 19 April 1774)

To tax and to please, no more than to love and be wise, is not given to men.

(Ibid.)

By adverting to the dignity of this high calling, our ancestors have turned a savage wilderness into a glorious empire: and have made the most extensive, and the only honourable conquests, not by destroying, but by promoting the wealth, the number, the happiness of the human race.

(Speech in the House of Commons, "On Conciliation with America," 22 March 1775)

All government,—indeed, every human benefit and enjoyment, every virtue and every prudent act,—is founded on compromise and barter.

(Ibid.)

A people who are still, as it were, but in the gristle, and not yet hardened into the bone of manhood.

(Ibid.)

My hold of the colonies is in the close affection which grows from common names, from kindred blood, from similar privileges, and equal protection. These are ties which, though light as air, are as strong as links of iron.

(Ibid.)

All protestantism, even the most cold and passive, is a sort of dissent. But the religion most prevalent in our northern colonies is a

refinement on the principle of resistance: it is the dissidence of dissent, and the protestantism of the Protestant religion.
> (Ibid.)

I do not know a method of drawing up an indictment against a whole people.
> (Ibid.)

A nation is not conquered which is perpetually to be conquered.
> (Ibid.)

Young man, there is America—which at this day serves for little more than to amuse you with stories of savage men, and uncouth manners; yet shall, before you taste of death, show itself equal to the whole of that commerce which now attracts the envy of the world.
> (Ibid.)

I know many have been taught to think that moderation, in a case like this, is a sort of treason.
> (Letter to the Sheriffs of Bristol defending his sympathy for the Americans, 1777)

Arthur Burns (1904–   ): *Chairman of the Federal Reserve System*

Now we have women marching in the streets. If only things would quiet down.
> (Attributed, 1975)

Aaron Burr (1756–1836): *Vice-president, 1801–1805*

When the Constitution was first framed I predicted that it would last fifty years. I was mistaken. It will evidently last longer than that. But I was mistaken only in point of time. The crash will come, but not so quick as I thought.
> (Attributed, c. 1835)

Hugh Butler (1878–1954): *Senator from Nebraska*

I watch his smart-aleck manner and his British clothes and that New Idealism . . . and I want to shout, Get out. You stand for everything that has been wrong with the United States for years.
> (To reporters about Secretary of State Acheson, 1951)

Smedley D. "Old Gimlet Eye" Butler (1881–1940): *Marine Corps general*

I helped make Mexico safe for American oil interests in 1914. I helped make Haiti and Cuba a decent place for the National City Bank boys to collect revenue in. I helped purify Nicaragua for the international banking house of Brown Brothers. . . . I brought light to the Dominican Republic for American sugar interests in 1916. I helped make Honduras "right" for American fruit companies in 1903. Looking back on it, I might have given Al Capone a few hints.

(Interview, *New York Times*, 21 August 1931)

Mather Byles (1706–1788): *Congregationalist minister and Loyalist*

Which is better, to be ruled by one tyrant three thousand miles away, or by three thousand tyrants not a mile away?

(Sermon in Boston, 1776)

William Byrd III (1674–1744): *Colonial Virginia planter and politician*

It was a place free from those 3 great Scourges of Mankind, Priests, Lawyers, and Physicians. . . . The People were yet too poor to maintain these Learned Gentlemen.

(Of early Virginia, *A History of the Dividing Line*, first published 1841)

C

John Cage (1912–): *Composer*

Food, one assumes, provides nourishment; but Americans eat it fully aware that small amounts of poison have been added to improve its appearance and delay its putrefaction.

(*Silence*, 1961)

John C. Calhoun (1782–1850): *Senator from South Carolina and political theorist*

The Government of the absolute majority instead of the Government of the people is but the Government of the strongest interests; and when not efficiently checked, it is the most tyrannical and oppressive that can be devised.

(Speech in the Senate, 15 February 1833)

The very essence of a free government consists in considering offices as public trusts, bestowed for the good of the country, and not for the benefit of an individual or a party.

(Speech in the Senate, 13 February 1835)

A power has risen up in the government greater than the people themselves, consisting of many and various and powerful interests, combined into one mass, and held together by the cohesive power of the vast surplus in the banks.

(Speech, 27 May 1836)

I hold that in the present state of civilization, where two races of different origin, and distinguished by color, and other physical differences, as well as intellectual, are brought together, the relation now existing in the slaveholding States between the two is, instead of an evil, a good—a positive good. I feel myself called upon to speak freely upon the subject where the honor and interests of those I represent are involved. I hold then, that there never has yet existed a wealthy and civilized society in which one portion of the community did not, in point of fact, live on the labor of the other.

(Speech in the Senate, January 1837)

The difficulty is in the diversity of the races. So strongly drawn is the line between the two in consequence, and so strengthened by the force of habit and education, that it is impossible for them to exist together in the community, where their numbers are so nearly equal as in the slaveholding states, under any other relation than that which now exists.

(Ibid.)

It is a great and dangerous error to suppose that all people are equally entitled to liberty.

(Ibid.)

We are not a Nation, but a Union, a confederacy of equal and sovereign States.
(Letter to Oliver Dyer, 1 January 1849)

I have, Senators, believed from the first that the agitation of the subject of slavery would, if not prevented by some timely and effective measure, end in disunion.
(Speech in the Senate, 4 March 1850, read by James M. Mason)

The Union cannot . . . be saved by eulogies on the Union, however splendid or numerous. The cry of "Union, Union, the glorious Union!" can no more prevent disunion than the cry of "Health, health, glorious health!" on the part of the physician, can save a patient lying dangerously ill.
(Ibid.)

Taking the proposition literally, there is not a word of truth in it.
(On the statement in the Declaration of Independence that all men are created equal, attributed)

The South! The poor South! God knows what will become of her.
(Last words, 1850)

Grizzley Calleen (?–?): *Texas panhandle rancher*
Any person caught monkeying with any of my cattle without permission will catch Hell! Yours in Christ, Grizzley Calleen.
(Public notice, *Tascosa (Texas) Pioneer*, September 29, 1886)

Thomas Pratt, Earl of Camden (1714–1794): *British lord high chancellor*
The British parliament has no right to tax the Americans. . . . Taxation and representation are inseparably united. God hath joined them: no British parliament can put them asunder. To endeavour to do so is to stab our very vitals.
(Speech in the House of Lords, December 1765)

Timothy Campbell (1840–1904): *Representative from New York*
What's the Constitution among friends?
(Attributed, 1885)

George Canning (1770–1827): *British foreign minister*

I called the New World into existence, to redress the balance of the Old.

(Speech in the House of Commons, 12 December 1826)

Joseph G. Cannon (1836–1926): *Speaker of the House of Representatives*

I am god-damned tired of listening to all this babble for reform. America is a hell of a success.

(Attributed, 1910)

Robert Canterbury (?–?): *Commanding general, Ohio National Guard*

These students are going to have to find out what law and order is all about.

(Statement minutes before his troops fired on protesting students, killing four, Kent State University, 4 May 1970)

Al Capone (1899–1947): *Bootlegger and gangster*

I don't even know what street Canada is on.

(When asked if he imported bootleg liquor from Canada, attributed)

They call Al Capone a bootlegger. Yes, it's bootleg while it's on the trucks, but when your host at the club, in the locker room, or on the Gold Coast hands it to you on a silver tray, it's hospitality. What's Al Capone done, then? He's supplied a legitimate demand. Some call it bootlegging. Some call it racketeering. I call it a business. They say I violate the prohibition law. Who doesn't?

(Attributed)

I am like any other man. All I do is supply a demand.

(Ibid.)

They talk about me not being on the legitimate. Why, lady, nobody's on the legit., when it comes down to cases; you know that.

(Ibid.)

You can get much farther with a kind word and a gun than you can with a kind word alone.

(Ibid.)

Don't get the idea that I'm one of these goddam radicals. Don't get the idea that I'm knocking the American system.

(Ibid.)

My rackets are run on strictly American lines and they're going to stay that way.

(Ibid.)

Captain Jack (1837–1873): *Modoc Indian war chief*

I am but one man. I am the voice of my people. Whatever their hearts are, that I talk. I want no more war. I want to be a man. You deny me the right of a white man. My skin is red; my heart is a white man's heart; but I am a Modoc. I am not afraid to die. I will not fall on the rocks. When I die, my enemies will be under me. Your soldiers began on me when I was asleep on Lost River. They drove us to these rocks, like a wounded deer. . . .

(Before his defeat at the Battle of the Lava Beds, California, 1873)

Stokely Carmichael (1941–   ): *Leader of Black Power movement*

If we are to proceed toward true liberation, we must cut ourselves off from white people. We must form our own institutions, credit unions, coops, political parties, write our own histories. . . .

(Position Paper, Student Nonviolent Coordinating Committee, 1966)

Take the English language. There are cats who come here from Italy, from Germany, from Poland, from France—in two generations they speak English perfectly—We have never spoken English perfectly, never have we spoken English perfectly, never, never, never. And that is because our people consciously resisted a language that did not belong to us. . . . Anybody can speak the honky's language correctly. Anybody can do it. We have not done it because we have resisted, resisted.

(Speech in Oakland, California, February 1968)

Andrew Carnegie (1835–1919): *Industrialist and philanthropist*

Show me your cost sheet. It is more interesting to know how well and how cheaply you have done this thing than how much money you have made, because the one is a temporary result . . .

but the other means a permanency that will go on with the works as long as they last.

(Standing orders to his employees, 1880s)

I remember that light came as in a flood and all was clear. Not only had I got rid of theology and the supernatural, but I had found the truth of evolution.

(On first reading Herbert Spencer in 1870)

Surplus wealth is a sacred trust which its possessor is bound to administer in his lifetime for the good of the community.

("Wealth," *North American Review*, June 1889)

The man who dies leaving behind him millions of available wealth, which was his to administer during life, will pass away "unwept, unhonored, and unsung," no matter to what uses he leaves the dross which he cannot take with him. Of such as these the public verdict will then be: "The man who dies thus rich dies disgraced."

(Ibid.)

This, then, is held to be the duty of the man of wealth: To set an example of modest, unostentatious living, shunning display or extravagance; to provide moderately for the legitimate wants of those dependent upon him; and, after doing so to consider all surplus revenues which come to him simply as trust funds, which he is called upon to administer, and strictly bound as a matter of duty to administer in the manner which, in his judgment, is best calculated to produce the most beneficial results for the community—the man of wealth thus becoming the mere trustee and agent for his poorer brethren, bringing to their service his superior wisdom, experience, and ability to administer, doing for them better than they would or could do for themselves.

(*The Gospel of Wealth and Other Essays*, 1901)

Pity the poor millionaire, for the way of the philanthropist is hard.

(*Independent*, 26 July 1913)

Rachel Carson (1907–1964): *Environmentalist writer*

The most alarming of all man's assaults upon the environment is the contamination of air, earth, rivers, and sea. . . . This pollution is for the most part irrecoverable.

> (*Silent Spring*, 1962)

Billy Carter (1937–   ): *Celebrated brother of President Jimmy Carter*

I'm not the Carter who'll never tell a lie.

> (Interview, *Newsweek*, 4 November 1977)

Billy Carter is not a buffoon, a boob, or a wacko.

> (Testimony before a Senate Committee, 21 August 1980)

Jimmy Carter (1924–   ): *Thirty-ninth president*

I'm not from Washington and I'm not a lawyer.

> (Introducing himself at the beginning of his campaign for the presidency, 1975)

If I ever tell a lie, if I ever mislead you, if I ever betray a trust or a confidence, I want you to come and take me out of the White House.

> (Speech in Florida, March 1976)

I think the President is the only person who can change the direction or attitude of our nation.

> (Campaign speech, June 1976)

I've looked on a lot of women with lust. I've committed adultery in my heart many times.

> (Interview, *Playboy* magazine, November 1976)

Blessed are the peacemakers.

> (On signing the Middle East peace treaty, September 1978)

For the first time in the history of our country a majority of our people believe that the next five years will be worse than the past five years.

> (Television address, 15 July 1979)

The erosion of our confidence in the future is threatening to destroy the social and political fabric of America.
> (Ibid.)

America did not invent human rights. In a very real sense, human rights invented America.
> (Farewell address, 14 January 1981)

Lillian Carter (1898–1983): *Mother of President Carter*
Sometimes when I look at all my children, I say to myself, "Lillian, you should have stayed a virgin."
> (Statement at Democratic National Convention, August 1980)

Carrie Chapman Catt (1859–1947): *Suffragist*
When a just cause reaches its flood-tide, as ours has done in that country, whatever stands in the way must fall before its overwhelming power.
> ("Is Woman Suffrage Progressing," 1913)

Bennett Cerf (1898–1971): *Publisher*
The Atomic Age is here to stay—but are we?
> (*Observer*, 12 February 1950)

Anton Cermak (1873–1933): *Mayor of Chicago*
I'm glad it was me instead of you.
> (To Franklin D. Roosevelt after the president-elect's intended assassin shot Cermak by mistake. Miami, 15 February 1933)

Neville Chamberlain (1869–1940): *British prime minister*
It is always best and safest to count on nothing from the Americans but words.
> (Remark in Parliament during the Munich debate, October 1938)

Ralph Chaplin (1887–1961): *Radical labor organizer*
When the Union's inspiration through the workers'
  blood shall run,
There can be no power greater anywhere beneath the sun.
Yet what force on earth is weaker than the feeble
  strength of one?

But the Union makes us strong.

It is we who dug the prairies; built the cities where
    they trade;
Dug the mines and built the workshops; endless miles
    of railroad laid.
Now we stand, outcast and starving, 'mid the wonders
    we have made;
But the Union makes us strong.
    Solidarity forever!
    Solidarity forever!
    Solidarity forever!
    For the Union makes us strong.
    ("Solidarity Forever," 1915)

Salmon P. Chase (1808–1873): *Secretary of the treasury and chief justice of the Supreme Court*

No more slave States: no slave Territories.
    (Platform of Free Soil National Convention, 1848)

The only way to resumption is to resume.
    (Letter to Horace Greeley, 1866)

The Constitution, in all its provisions, looks to an indestructible Union composed of indestructible States.
    (Decision in *Texas* v. *White*, 1868)

Stuart Chase (1888–   ): *Writer*

The consequences to our culture of an all-out war abroad are simply told—the liquidation of political democracy, of Congress, the Supreme Court, private enterprise, the banks, free press and free speech; the persecution of German-Americans and Italian-Americans, witch hunts, forced labor, fixed prices, rationing, astronomical debts, and the rest. We would become as a people tough, cruel, and vindictive. With the whole world on our hands, draining our life blood overseas, we would have no time and no desire to plan for the America of the future.
    ("Four Assumptions about the War," Leaflet for the America First
    Committee, January 1941)

G. K. Chesterton (1874–1936): *British author*

There is nothing the matter with Americans except their ideals. The real American is all right; it is the ideal American who is all wrong.

(*New York Times*, 1 February 1931)

Rufus Choate (1799–1859): *Lawyer, Whig politician*

The courage of New England was the "courage of Conscience." It did not rise to that insane and awful passion, the love of war for itself.

(On the Mexican War, 1848)

The final end of Government is not to exercise restraint but to do good.

(Speech in Boston, 26 November 1850)

We join ourselves to no party that does not carry the flag and keep step to the music of the Union.

(Letter to a Worcester Whig convention, 1 October 1855)

David Christy (1802–1859): *Writer*

His majesty, King Cotton, is forced to continue the employment of his slaves; and, by their toil, is riding on, conquering and to conquer.

(*Cotton Is King*, 1855)

Winston Churchill (1874–1965): *British prime minister*

Give us the tools, and we will finish the job.

(Radio broadcast addressed to President Roosevelt, 9 February 1941)

From Stettin in the Baltic to Trieste in the Adriatic, an iron curtain has descended across the Continent.

(Address in Fulton, Missouri, 5 March 1946)

We must build a kind of United States of Europe.

(Speech in Zurich, 19 September 1946)

It was the most unsordid act in history.

(Of the Marshall Plan, attributed)

In Franklin Roosevelt there died the greatest American friend we have ever known, and the greatest champion of freedom who has ever brought help and comfort from the New World to the Old.

(*Triumph and Tragedy*, 1953)

Abraham Clark (1726–1794): *Revolutionary leader*

We set out to oppose Tyranny in all its Strides, and I hope we shall persevere.

(Attributed, 1781)

Champ Clark (1850–1921): *Speaker of the House of Representatives*

I hope to see the day when the American flag will float over every square foot of the British North American possessions clear to the North Pole.

(In the debate on Canadian reciprocity trade bill, June 1911)

In the estimation of Missourians there is precious little difference between a conscript and a convict.

(Remark during Senate debate over draft law, 1917)

William Clark (1770–1838): *Army officer and explorer*

Ocean in view. O the joy!

(Journal, upon completing the first crossing of the North American continent, November 1805)

Paul Claudel (1868–1955): *French ambassador to the United States*

Gentlemen, in the little moment that remains to us between the crisis and the catastrophe, we might as well take a glass of champagne.

(At a Washington party celebrating President Hoover's moratorium on the European war debts, 1932)

Henry Clay (1777–1852): *Whig politician and twice presidential candidate*

If you wish to avoid foreign collision, you had better abandon the ocean.

(Speech in the House, 22 January 1812)

All religions united with government are more or less inimical to liberty. All separated from government are compatible with liberty.
(Speech in the House of Representatives, 24 March 1818)

Government is a trust, and the officers of the government are trustees; and both the trust and the trustees are created for the benefit of the people.
(Speech, Lexington, Kentucky, 16 May 1829)

I had rather be right than be President.
(Speech in the Senate, 7 February 1839)

I am the most unfortunate man in the history of parties: always run by my friends when sure to be defeated, and now betrayed for a nomination when I, or any one, would be sure of an election.
(On failing to win the Whig nomination for the presidency, 1840)

I have heard something said about allegiance to the South. I know no South, no North, no East, no West, to which I owe any allegiance. The Union, sir, is my country.
(Speech in the Senate, 1848)

All oppressed people are authorized, whenever they can, to rise and break their fetters.
(Speech, House of Representatives, 24 March 1818)

Political parties serve to keep each other in check, one keenly watching the other.
(Attributed)

Eldridge Cleaver (1935–): *Black Panther leader, later evangelist*

[Blacks] are asked to die for the System in Vietnam. In Watts they are killed by it. Now—NOW!—they are asking each other, in dead earnest: Why not die right here in Babylon fighting for a better life, like the Viet Cong? If those little cats can do it, what's wrong with big studs like us?

A mood sets in, spreads across America, across the face of Babylon, jells in black hearts everywhere.
(*Soul on Ice*, 1968)

Americans think of themselves collectively as a huge rescue squad on twenty-four-hour call to any spot on the globe where dispute and conflict may erupt.
(Ibid.)

A fabulous new era of progress is opening up to the world, and coping with all of the problems unleashed by Watergate has opened up a creative era for American democracy. . . . With all of its faults, the American political system is the freest and most democratic in the world.
(*New York Times,* 18 November 1975)

Black history began with Malcolm X.
(Attributed)

I saw my former heroes paraded before my eyes . . . Fidel Castro, Mao Tse-tung, Karl Marx, Frederick Engels, passing in review—each one appearing for a moment of time, and then dropping out of sight, like fallen heroes. Finally, at the end of the procession, in dazzling, shimmering light, the image of Jesus Christ appeared.
(*Soul on Fire,* 1978)

Georges Clemenceau (1841–1929): *French prime minister*
God gave us the Ten Commandments and we broke them. Wilson gives us the Fourteen Points. We shall see.
(Attributed, 1918)

America is the only nation in history which miraculously has gone directly from barbarism to degeneration without the usual interval of civilization.
(Attributed)

Grover Cleveland (1837–1908): *Twenty-second president*
I have considered the pension list of the republic a roll of honour.
(Veto of Dependent Pension Bill, 5 July 1888)

The lessons of paternalism ought to be unlearned and the better lesson taught that while the people should patriotically and cheerfully support their government, its functions do not include the support of the people.

(Second inaugural address, March 1893)

If it takes the entire army and navy to deliver a postcard in Chicago, that card will be delivered.

(On the alleged interference with the mails by railwaymen supporting the strike against the Pullman Company, June 1894)

Sensible and intelligent women do not want to vote. The relative positions to be assumed by man and woman in the working out of our civilization were assigned long ago by a higher intelligence than ours.

(Magazine article, 1901)

I have tried so hard to do right.

(Last words, June 1908)

William Cobbett (1762–1835): *British politician*

Never was the memory of any man so cruelly insulted as that of this mild and humane monarch. He was guillotined in effigy, in the capital of the Union, twenty or thirty times every day, during one whole winter and part of the summer. Men, women, and children flocked to the tragical exhibition, and not a single paragraph appeared in the papers to shame them from it.

(On American reaction to the execution of Louis XIV, 1793)

One of the most amiable features in the character of American society is this: that men never boast of their riches, and never disguise their poverty.

(*Advice to Young Men*, 1829)

Cochise (?–1874): *Chiricahua Apache Indian chief*

When I was young I walked all over this country, east and west, and saw no other people than the Apaches. After many summers I walked again and found another race of people had come to take it. How is it? Why is it that the Apaches wait to die—that they carry their lives on their fingernails? They roam over the hills and plains and want the heavens to fall on them. The Apaches were once a great nation; they are now but few, and because of this they so carry their lives on their fingernails. . . .

(On himself, 1873)

George M. Cohan (1878–1942): *Showman*

I'm a Yankee-Doodle Dandy,
Yankee-Doodle do or die,
A real live nephew of my Uncle Sam,
Born on the Fourth of July.

("Yankee Doodle Boy," 1904)

We'll be over, we're coming over,
And we won't come back till it's over, over there.

("Over There," 1917)

From my earliest days I was profoundly impressed with the fact that I had been born under the Stars and Stripes, and that has had a great deal to do with everything I have written. If it had not been for the glorious symbol of Independence, I might have fallen into the habit of writing problem plays, or romantic drama, or questionable farce. Yes, the American flag is in my heart, and it has done everything for me.

(Conversation with John McCabe, 1940)

Many a bum show has been saved by the flag.

(Attributed)

Frank M. Colby (1865–1925): *Author, editor*

If a large city can, after intense intellectual efforts, choose for its mayor a man who merely will not steal from it, we consider it a triumph of the suffrage.

(*The Colby Essays*, 1926)

Charles Colson (1931–   ): *Aide to President Nixon, later evangelist*

If you've got them by the balls, their minds and hearts will follow.

(Motto on office wall, 1969–1973)

Roscoe Conkling (1829–1888): *Senator from New York and corporation lawyer*

This angry man, dizzy with the elevation to which assassination has raised him, frenzied with power and ambition, does not seem to know that not he but the men who made the Constitution placed it in the people's hands. They placed Andrew Johnson in the people's hands also; and when those hands shall drop their votes into the ballot box, Andrew Johnson and his policy of arrogance and usurpation will be snapped like a willow wand.

(Speech in New York, August 1866)

We are told the Republican party is a machine. Yes. A government is a machine; a church is a machine; an army is a machine; an order of Masons is a machine; the common-school system of the State of New York is a machine; a political party is a machine.

(Speech in New York, September 1876)

I do not know how to belong to a party a little.

(Attributed)

He will hew to the line of right, let the chips fall where they may.

(Of President Grant, June 1880)

How can I speak into a grave? How can I battle with a shroud? Silence is a duty and a doom.

(On hearing of the death by assassination of his political rival, President James A. Garfield, September 1881)

I have but one annoyance with the administration of President Arthur, and that is, that, in contrast with it, the Administration of Hayes becomes respectable, if not heroic.

(Attributed, 1883)

Cyril Connolly (1903–1975): *Irish author*

I came to America tourist Third with a cheque for ten pounds and I leave plus five hundred, a wife, a mandarin coat, a set of diamond studs, a state room and bath, and a decent box for the ferret. That's what everybody comes to America to do and I don't think I've managed badly for a beginner.

(Letter to Noel Blakiston, 2 April 1930)

Russell H. Conwell (1843–1925): *Baptist preacher and lecturer*

I say you ought to be rich; you have no right to be poor. To live and not to be rich is a misfortune, and it is doubly a misfortune, because you could have been rich just as well as be poor. You and I know that there are some things more valuable than money, of course we do. . . . Nevertheless the man of common sense also knows that there is not one of those things that is not greatly enhanced by the use of money. Money is power. Love is the grandest thing on God's earth, but fortunate is the lover who has plenty of money. For a man to say "I do not want money," is to say, "I do not wish to do any good to my fellow men."

("Acres of Diamonds," a lecture delivered 4,000 times)

Ninety-eight out of one hundred of the rich men of America are honest. That is why they are rich. That is why they are trusted with money. That is why they carry on great enterprises and find plenty of people to work with them. It is because they are honest men.

(Ibid.)

There is not a poor person in the United States who was not made poor by his own shortcomings.

(Ibid.)

Calvin Coolidge (1872–1933): *Thirtieth president*

There is no right to strike against the public safety by anybody, anywhere, any time.

(Telegram to Samuel Gompers on the Boston police strike, while he was governor of Massachusetts, 14 September 1919)

One with the law is a majority.

(Accepting vice-presidential nomination, July 1920)

I think the American people wants a solemn ass as a President. And I think I'll go along with them.

(In conversation with Ethel Barrymore, quoted some years later in *Time*, 16 May 1955)

Colonel, never go out to meet trouble. If you will just sit still, nine cases out of ten someone will intercept it before it reaches you.

(In conversation with Theodore Roosevelt, Jr., November 1924)

The business of America is business.
> (Speech in Washington, 17 January 1925)

They hired the money, didn't they?
> (Of the Allies' war debt, 1925)

No nation ever had an army large enough to guarantee it against attack in time of peace or insure it victory in time of war.
> (Speech, 6 October 1925)

Prosperity is only an instrument to be used, not a deity to be worshipped.
> (Speech, 11 June 1928)

Civilization and profits go hand in hand.
> (Attributed)

I do not choose to run.
> (On the presidential nomination, 1928)

Perhaps one of the most important accomplishments of my administration has been minding my own business.
> (At a news conference in Washington, 1 March 1929)

When a great many people are unable to find work, unemployment results.
> (Attributed, 1930)

He said he was against it.
> (On being asked what a clergyman had said in a sermon on sin.)

I have noticed that nothing I never said ever did me any harm.
> (Attributed)

You lose.
> (Upon being told by a lady that she had bet she could get him to say three words to her. Attributed)

Gary Cooper (1901–1961): *Film actor*
From what I hear, I don't like it because it isn't on the level.
> (On communism, testifying before the House Committee on Un-American Activities, 1947)

James Fenimore Cooper (1789–1851): *Novelist, historian*

Every advertisement calling assemblies of the young to deliberate on national concerns, ought to be deemed an insult to the good sense, the modesty, and the filial piety of the class to which it is addressed.

(The American Democrat, 1838)

John Singleton Copley (1738–1815): *Painter*

. . . poor America! I hope the best but I fear the worst. Yet certain I am She will finally emerge from her present Callamity and become a Mighty Empire, and it is a pleasing reflection that I shall stand amongst the first of the Artists that shall have led the Country to the knowledge and cultivation of the fine Arts, happy in the pleasing reflection that they will one Day shine with a luster not inferior to what they have done in Greece or Rome in my Native Country.

(Letter to Henry Pelham, 1780)

Gregorio Cortez (1875–1916): *Folk hero on the Texas-Mexico border*

Then said Gregorio Cortez, with his pistol in his hand,
"Ah, so many mounted Rangers just to take one Mexican."
(Ballad of Gregorio Cortez)

Juan Nepomuceno Cortina (1824–1892): *Bandit and revolutionary*

To defend ourselves, and making use of the sacred right of self-preservation, we have assembled in a popular meeting with a view of discussing a means to put an end to our misfortunes. Our personal enemies shall not possess our lands until they have fattened *[them]* with their own gore.

(Speech at Rancho del Carmen, Texas, 30 September 1859)

Thomas Corwin (1794–1865): *Senator from Ohio*

If I were a Mexican I would tell you, "Have you not room enough in your own country to bury your dead?"

(Speech in the Senate, 11 February 1847)

John Cotton (1584–1652): *Puritan divine*

Now God makes room for a people 3 ways.

First, when he casts out the enemies of a people before them by lawfull warre with the inhabitants, which God cals them unto: as in Ps. 44.2. *Thou didst drive out the heathen before them*. But this course of warring against others, & driving them out without provocation, depends upon speciall Commission from God, or else it is not imitable.

Secondly, when he gives a forreigne people favour in the eyes of any native people to come and sit downe with them either by way of purchase, as *Abraham* did obtaine the field of *Machpelah;* or else when they give it in courtesie, as *Pharoah* did the land of *Goshen* unto the sons of *Jacob*.

Thirdly, when hee makes a Countrey though not altogether void of inhabitants, yet voyd in that place where they reside . . . there is liberty for the sonne of *Adam* or *Noah* to come and inhabite, though they neither buy it, nor aske their leaves . . . in a vacant soyle, hee that take possession of it, and bestoweth culture and husbandry upon it, his Right it is. And the ground of this is from the Grand Charter given to *Adam* and his posterity in Paradise, *Gen*. 1. 1. 28. *Multiply, and replenish the earth, and subdue it*. If therefore any sonne of *Adam* come and find a place empty, he hath liberty to come, and fill, and subdue the earth there.

(Sermon justifying the planned Puritan emigration to New England, Saint Botolph's, Boston, England, 1630)

Democracy, I do not conceyve that ever God did ordeyne as a fitt government eyther for church or commonwealth. If the people be governors, who shall be governed?

(Letter to Lord Say and Seal, 1636)

Theocracy [is] the best forme of government in the commonwealth, as well as in the church.

(Ibid.)

When the wrath of God is kindled against a state for corruption of religion, He pours out His judgments against them by degrees; first upon the common sort of people, then upon Church officers, and then upon the principal rulers and lights of that state.

(*Pouring Out of the Seven Vials*, 1642)

A Christian by departing from God may disturb a gentle civil state. And it is no preposterous way for the governors of the state, according to the quality of the disturbance raised by the starting aside of such a Christian, to punish both it and him by civil censure.

    (The Bloudy Tenent Washed, 1647)

It is no impeachment of church liberty, but an enlargement of its beauty and honor, to be bound by strict laws and holy commandments, to observe the pure worship of God, and to be subject unto due punishment for the gross violation of the same.

    (A Brief Exposition, 1655)

Charles E. Coughlin (1891–1979): *Catholic priest and political leader*

The New Deal is Christ's deal.

    (Radio speech, April 1933)

This is the new call to arms—not to be—some cannon fodder for the greedy system of our outworn capitalism nor factory fodder for the slave whip of Communism. This is the call to arms for the establishment of social justice.

    (Proclamation of National Union for Social Justice, 1935)

Democracy is doomed. This is our last election. It is Fascism or Communism. . . . I take the road of Fascism.

    (Union Party pamphlet, 1936)

Harvey Cox (1929–   ): *Theologian*

The real illness of the American city today, and especially of the deprived groups within it, is voicelessness.

    (The Secular City, 1966)

The Negro revolt is not aimed at winning friends but at winning freedom, not interpersonal warmth but institutional justice.

    (Ibid.)

Jacob S. Coxey (1854–1951): *Spokesman for unemployed*

We will send a petition to Washington with boots on.

    (Speech in Massilon, Ohio, launching the "Tramps' March on Washington," 1894)

Stephen Crane (1871–1900): *Novelist*

I was a Socialist for two weeks but when a couple of Socialists assured me I had no right to think differently from any other Socialist and then quarrelled with each other about what Socialism meant, I ran away.

(Attributed, c. 1896)

Alan Cranston (1914–): *Senator from California*

Inflation is not all bad. After all, it has allowed every American to live in a more expensive neighborhood without moving.

(Remark during an interview, 1979)

Crazy Horse (1849?–1877): *Oglala Sioux war chief*

We do not hunt the troops, and never have, they have always hunted us on our own ground. They tell us they want to civilize us. They lie; they want to kill us, and they sneak upon us when we are asleep to do it. I only wish we had the power to civilize them. We would certainly do so; but we would do it fairly, we would not kill their women and children in their own country and in their beds. And if we gave them a home to live in and told them as long as they stayed there they would be safe, they would be safe there. We would not go there the next day and kill them all, as they do us.

(Immediately before his surrender, 1877)

We did not ask you white men to come here. The Great Spirit gave us this country as a home. You had yours. We did not interfere with you. The Great Spirit gave us plenty of land to live on, and buffalo, deer, antelope and other game. But you have come here; you are taking my land from me; you are killing off our game, so it is hard for us to live. Now, you tell us to work for a living, but the Great Spirit did not make us to work, but to live by hunting. You white men can work if you want to. We do not interfere with you, and again you say, why do you not become civilized? We do not want your civilization! We would live as our fathers did, and their fathers before them.

(Upon surrendering, 1877)

Hector St. John de Crèvecoeur (1735–1813): *Farmer and writer*

After a foreigner from any part of Europe is arrived, and become a citizen; let him devoutly listen to the voice of our great parent, which says to him, "Welcome to my shores, distressed European; bless the hour in which thou didst see my verdant fields, my fair navigable rivers, and my green mountains!—If thou wilt work, I have bread for thee; if thou wilt be honest, sober, and industrious, I have greater rewards to confer on thee—ease and independence.

(*Letters from an American Farmer*, 1782)

What then is the American, this new man? He is either an European, or the descendant of an European, hence that strange mixture of blood, which you will find in no other country. I could point out to you a family whose grandfather was an Englishman, whose wife was Dutch, whose son married a French woman, and whose present four sons have now four wives of different nations. He is an American, who leaving behind him all his ancient prejudices and manners, receives new ones from the new mode of life he has embraced, the new government he obeys, and the new rank he holds.

(Ibid.)

John C. Crittenden (1787–1863): *Senator from Kentucky*

I hope to find my country in the right, however, I will stand by her, right or wrong.

(Speech in the House, May 1846)

Davy Crockett (1786–1836): *Frontiersman and politician*

Be always sure you are right—then go ahead.

(Personal motto, *Autobiography*, 1834)

"Gentlemen," says I, "I'm Davy Crockett, the darling branch o' old Kentuck that can eat up a painter, hold a buffalo out to drink, and put a rifle ball through the moon."

(Ibid.)

Fame is like a shaved pig with a greased tail, and it is only after it has slipped through the hands of some thousands, that some fellow, by mere chance, holds on to it!

(Ibid.)

I am at liberty to vote as my conscience and judgment dictates to be right, without the yoke of any party on me, or the driver at my heels, with the whip in his hands, commanding me to "gee-whoa-haw" just at his pleasure.

(Ibid.)

Pierce the heart of the enemy as you would a feller that spit in your face, knocked down your wife, burnt up your houses, and called your dog a skunk! Cram his pesky carcass full of thunder and lightning like a stuffed sassidge and turtle him off with a good hot poller, so that there won't be a piece of him left big enough to give a crow a breakfast, and bite his nose off into the bargain.

(Celebrated war speech, *Crockett Almanac*, 1835)

Walter Cronkite (1916–   ): *Television news reader*

That's the way it is.

(Closing statement of daily newscast, 1956–1981)

The interviews are driving me crazy. I've never read so many boring quotes, all of them from me.

(Interview on the occasion of his retirement, 2 March 1981)

Ernest Howard Crosby (1856–1907): *Reformer*

Onward Christian Soldiers.
'Gainst the heathen crew!
In the name of Jesus
Let us run them through.

(On the declaration of war on Spain, 1898)

Francis "Two Gun" Crowley (1900–1931): *Bank robber and murderer*

You sons of bitches. Give my love to Mother.

(Last words before his electrocution, 1931)

Edward E. Cummings (1894–1962): *Poet*

next to of course god america i
Love you land of the pilgrims and so forth oh

("Next to of course God")

To like an individual because he's black is just as insulting as to dislike him because he isn't white.

(Attributed)

Samuel R. Curtis (1805–1866): *Civil and Indian Wars general*
I want no peace till the Indians suffer more.
> (To his troops, Council Bluffs, Iowa, 1866)

George Armstrong Custer (1839–1876): *General*
If I were an Indian, I often think I would greatly prefer to cast my lot among those of my people who adhered to the free open plains, rather than submit to the confined limits of a reservation, there to be the recipient of the blessed benefits of civilization.
> (*My Life on the Plains*, 1874)

We've got them.
> (Upon being attacked by Sioux Indians at the Little Big Horn, June 1876)

Leon Czolgosz (1873–1901): *Assassin of President McKinley*
I didn't believe one man should have so much service and another man should have none.
> (Upon shooting the president, Buffalo, September 1901)

I killed the President because he was the enemy of the good people, the good working people. I am not sorry for my crime.
> (On the eve of his execution, 1902)

D

Richard E. Daley (1902–1976): *Mayor and boss of Chicago*
You motherfucker Jew bastard, get your ass out of Chicago.
> (Shouted at Senator Abraham Ribicoff on national television at the Democratic National Convention, 27 August 1968)

The police are not here to create disorder. The police are here to preserve disorder.
> (To reporters, 29 August 1968)

Charles E. Dana (1819–1897): *Editor*

When a dog bites a man that is not news, but when a man bites a dog, that is news.

(*New York Sun*, 1882)

Alvin Dark (1922–   ): *Baseball player and manager*

Any pitcher who throws at a batter and deliberately tries to hit him is a Communist.

(Attributed)

Clarence S. Darrow (1857–1938): *Attorney*

With all their faults, trade-unions have done more for humanity than any other organization of men that ever existed. They have done more for decency, for honesty, for education, for the better-ment of the race, for the developing of character in man, than any other association of men.

(*The Railroad Trainman*, November 1909)

When I was a boy I was told that anybody could become President; I'm beginning to believe it.

(On the nomination of Warren G. Harding, 1920, attributed)

Do you think you can cure the hatreds and the maladjustments of the world by hanging them? You simply show your ignorance and your hate when you say it.

(Summation in the Leopold and Loeb murder trial, 1924)

Harry M. Daugherty (1860–1941): *Republican Party political strategist and attorney-general under President Harding*

Well, boys, I'll tell you what I think. The convention will be deadlocked. After the other candidates have failed, we'll get to-gether in some hotel room, oh, about 2:11 in the morning, and some 15 men, bleary-eyed with lack of sleep, will sit down around a big table and when that time comes Senator Harding will be selected.

(To reporters on the eve of the Republican National Convention, July 1920. The "smoke-filled room," the scene of the fulfillment of Daugherty's prophecy, was in the Blackstone Hotel, Chicago)

He looked like a president.

(To reporters who asked him why he sponsored Harding's candidacy, 1923)

David Davis (1815–1886): *Supreme Court justice*

The Constitution of the United States is a law for rulers and people, equally in war and peace, and covers with the shield of its protection all classes of men, at all times, and under all circumstances. No doctrine, involving more pernicious consequences, was ever invented by the wit of men than that any of its provisions can be suspended during any of the great exigencies of government.

(Decision in *Ex parte Milligan*, 1866)

Jefferson Davis (1808–1889): *President of the Confederacy*

Through the portal of slavery alone has the descendant of the graceless son of Noah ever entered the temple of civilization.

(Speech in the Senate, 1850)

All we ask is to be let alone.

(Inaugural address, 18 February 1861)

Now, there, I Jefferson Davis, President of the Confederate States of America, and in their name do pronounce and declare the said Benjamin Butler to be a felon deserving of capital punishment. I do order that he shall no longer be considered or treated simply as a public enemy of the Confederate States of America, but as an outlaw and common enemy of mankind, and that, in the event of his capture, the officer of the capturing force do cause him to be immediately executed by hanging.

(Proclamation, 23 December 1862, because of Butler's alleged insult to southern womanhood)

Richard Harding Davis (1864–1916): *War correspondent*

Marines have landed and the situation is well in hand.

(Cablegram from Panama, 1885)

Dorothy Day (1897–   ): *Catholic pacifist leader*

Christ is being martyred today in Vietnam, in Santo Domingo and in all places where men are taking to the sword in this world crisis.

(*Catholic Worker*, July–August 1965)

J. D. B. DeBow (1820–1867): *Southern editor and publisher*

We have a destiny to perform, a "manifest destiny" over all Mexico, over South America, over the West Indies, and Canada. The Sandwich Islands is as necessary to our eastern, as the isles of the gulf to our western commerce. The gates of the Chinese empire must be thrown down by the men from the Sacramento and the Oregon, and the haughty Japanese tramplers upon the cross be enlightened in the doctrines of republicanism and the ballot box. The eagle of the republic shall poise itself over the field of Waterloo, after tracing its flight among the gorges of the Himalaya or the Ural mountains, and a successor of Washington ascend the chair of universal empire.

(*DeBow's Review*, 1850)

Eugene V. Debs (1855–1926): *Socialist presidential nominee*

The issue is Socialism versus Capitalism. I am for Socialism because I am for humanity.

(Speech, 1 January 1897)

I am not a labor leader. I don't want you to follow me or anything else. If you are looking for a Moses to lead you out of the wilderness, you will stay right where you are. I would not lead you into this promised land if I could, because if I could lead you in, someone else could lead you out.

(Campaign speech, 1912)

I have no country to fight for; my country is the earth, and I am a citizen of the world.

(Speech, 1914)

While there is a lower class I am in it; while there is a criminal element I am of it; while there is a soul in prison, I am not free.

(In his own defense, sedition trial, 12 September 1918)

When great changes occur in history, when great principles are involved, as a rule the majority are wrong.

(Ibid.)

It is he, not I, who needs a pardon. If I had it in my power I would give him the pardon which would set him free.

(On President Wilson, statement from Atlanta Penitentiary upon receiving the news that Wilson had rejected a suggestion Debs be pardoned, February 1921)

The American people can have anything they want; the trouble is they don't know what they want.

(Attributed)

Stephen Decatur (1779–1820): *Naval officer*

Our country! In her intercourse with foreign nations, may she always be in the right; but our country, right or wrong.

(Toast at Norfolk, Virginia, April 1816)

Charles de Gaulle (1890–1970): *French president*

I predict that you will sink step by step into a bottomless military and political quagmire, however much you spend in men and money.

(Remark to President Kennedy on the subject of Vietnam, 31 May 1961)

America returns to its ancient demons.

(On hearing of Kennedy's assassination, November 1963)

Chauncey Depew (1834–1928): *Railroad president and senator from New York*

The government of the United States is and always has been a lawyer's government.

(Speech at a dinner for the British ambassador, New York, 5 November 1898)

Thomas Roderick Dew (1802–1846): *President of the College of William and Mary and proslavery theorist*

The slave of Italy or France could be emancipated or escape to the city, and soon all records of his former state would perish, and he would gradually sink into the mass of freemen around him. But, unfortunately, the emancipated black carries a mark which no time can erase; he forever wears the indelible symbol of his inferior condition; the Ethiopian cannot change his skin nor the leopard his spots.

(*Review of the debate in the Virginia Legislature*, 1832)

The slaves, in both an economical and moral point of view, are entirely unfit for a state of freedom among the whites.

(Ibid.)

George Dewey (1837–1917): *Naval officer*
You may fire when you are ready, Gridley.

(At the Battle of Manila Bay, 1 May 1898)

Since studying this subject I am convinced that the office of the President is not such a very difficult one to fill, his duties being mainly to execute the laws of Congress. Should I be chosen for this exalted position I would execute the laws of Congress as faithfully as I have always executed the orders of my superiors.

(Responding to and thereby destroying a movement to nominate him for the presidency, April 1900)

Thomas E. Dewey (1902–1971): *Governor of New York and presidential nominee*
It's time for a change.

(Campaign slogan, speech, 21 September 1944)

Porfirio Díaz (1830–1915): *Mexican dictator*
Poor Mexico, so far from God and so near to the United States!

(Attributed)

Charles Dickens (1812–1870): *English novelist*
There is no other country on earth which in so short a time has accomplished so much.

(*American Notes*, 1843)

I believe that the heaviest blow ever dealt at liberty's head will be dealt by this nation in the ultimate failure of its example to the earth.

(Ibid.)

John Dickinson (1732–1808): *Revolutionary leader*

Then join hand in hand, brave Americans all! By uniting we stand, by dividing we fall.

> *(The Liberty Song, 1768)*

Here then, let my countrymen, ROUSE yourselves, and behold the ruin hanging over their heads. If they ONCE admit, that Great Britain *for the purpose of levying money on us only,* may lay duties upon her exportations to us, she then will have nothing to do, but to lay those duties on the articles which she prohibits us to manufacture—and the tragedy of American liberty is finished.

> *(Letters from a Farmer in Pennsylvania, 1767–1768)*

Our cause is just. Our Union is perfect. Our internal resources are great, and, if necessary, foreign assistance is undoubtedly obtainable.

> *(Declaration of the Causes for Taking Up Arms, 6 July 1775)*

Martin Dies (1901–1972): *Congressman from Texas*

Never participate in anything without consulting the American Legion or your local Chamber of Commerce.

> (At hearings of House Committee on Un-American Activities, which he chaired, 1939)

John Dillinger (1902–1934): *Bank robber and folk hero*

A jail is just like a nut with a worm in it. The worm can always get out.

> (Attributed)

Dorothea Dix (1802–1887): *Reformer*

Confined within this Commonwealth in cages, closets, cellars, stalls, pens! Chained, naked, beaten with rods, and lashed into obedience.

> (On the insane, memorial to the Massachusetts state legislature, 1843)

Thomas Dixon (1864–1946): *Methodist minister and writer*

No amount of education of any kind, industrial, classical, or religious, can make a Negro a white man or bridge the chasm of the centuries which separate him from the white man in the evolution of human civilization.

(*Saturday Evening Post*, 19 August 1905)

Ignatius Donnelly (1831–1901): *Populist agitator and author*

The Democratic Party is like a mule—without pride of ancestry or hope of posterity.

(Speech to the Minnesota legislature, 13 September 1860)

We meet in the midst of a nation brought to the verge of moral, political, and material ruin. Corruption dominates the ballot-box, the legislatures, the Congress, and touches even the ermine of the bench. The newspapers are largely subsidized or muzzled, public opinion silenced, business prostrated, our homes covered with mortgages, labor impoverished, and the land concentrated in the hands of the capitalists.

(Populist Party platform, February 1892)

We put him to school and he wound up by stealing the school-books.

(Of William Jennings Bryan, attributed)

John Dos Passos (1896–1970): *Novelist*

Rumors of peace talks worried him. Peace would ruin his plans for an American army.

(Of General Pershing, *Mr. Wilson's War*, 1962)

Stephen A. Douglas (1813–1861): *Senator from Illinois and presidential candidate*

I could travel from Boston to Chicago by the light of my own effigies.

(On himself in 1854 and the reaction to his Kansas-Nebraska Act)

In my opinion the people of a territory can, by lawful means, exclude slavery from their limits prior to the formation of a State constitution. . . . It matters not what way the Supreme Court may hereafter decide as to the abstract question whether slavery may or may not go into a territory under the constitution; the people have the lawful means to introduce it or exclude it as they please, for the reason that slavery cannot exist a day or an hour anywhere, unless it is supported by local police regulations.

(Debate with Lincoln at Freeport, Illinois, 17 June 1858)

Between the Negro and the crocodile, he took the side of the Negro. But between the Negro and the white man, he would go for the white man.

(On himself in *New York Tribune*, 6 December 1858)

William O. Douglas (1898–1980): *Supreme Court justice*

Men may believe what they cannot prove. They may not be put to the proof of their religious doctrines or beliefs. Religious experiences which are as real as life to some may be incomprehensible to others.

(*U.S.* v. *Ballard*, 1944)

The command of the First Amendment is so clear that we should not allow Congress to call a halt to free speech except in the extreme case of peril from the speech itself. The First Amendment makes confidence in the common sense of our people and in their maturity of judgment the great postulate of our democracy. Its philosophy is that violence is rarely, if ever, stopped by denying civil liberties to those advocating resort to force.

(Dissenting opinion, *Dennis* v. *U.S.*, 1951)

The political censor has no place in our public debates.

(Ibid.)

The press will commonly reflect (or even try to create) the view that the end justifies the means. Those of us dedicated to the law must stand before those gales.

(Speech to the American Law Institute, 1953)

Government should be concerned with anti-social conduct, not with utterances.

(Dissenting opinion, *Roth* v. *U.S.*, 1957)

The great and invigorating influences in American life have been the unorthodox; the people who challenge an existing institution or way of life, or say and do things that make people think.

(Interview, Fund for the Republic, 1958)

Power that controls the economy should be in the hands of elected representatives of the people, not in the hands of an industrial oligarchy.

(Dissenting opinion, *U.S. v. Columbia Steel Company*, 1948)

Frederick Douglass (1817?–1895): *Abolitionist and supporter of feminism*

I have often been utterly astonished, since I came to the North, to find persons who could think of the singing among slaves, as evidence of their contentment and happiness. It is impossible to conceive of a greater mistake. Slaves sing most when they are most unhappy. The songs of the slave represent the sorrows of his heart.

(*Narrative of the Life of Frederick Douglass*, 1845)

Everybody in the South wants the privilege of whipping somebody else.

(Ibid.)

Having despised us, it is not strange that Americans should seek to render us despicable; having enslaved us, it is natural that they should strive to prove us unfit for freedom; having denounced us as indolent, it is not strange that they should cripple our enterprises.

(Colored National Convention, Rochester, New York, 6–8 July 1853)

Lorenzo Dow (1777–1834): *Revivalist preacher*

You can and you can't
You shall and you shan't;
You will and you won't
You'll be damned if you do,
And you'll be damned if you don't.

(Denouncing orthodox Calvinism, early nineteenth century)

Theodore Dreiser (1871–1945): *Novelist*

Our civilization is still in a middle stage, scarcely beast, in that it is no longer wholly guided by instinct; scarcely human, in that it is not yet wholly guided by reason.

(*Sister Carrie*, 1900)

It would be an excellent thing for Europe and the world if the despicable British aristocracy were smashed and a German viceroy sat in London.

(Attributed, September 1914)

God will save the good American, and seat him at His right hand on the Golden Throne.

(*Life Art, and America*, 1917)

William Driver (1803–1886): *Naval officer*
I name thee Old Glory.

(Of the American flag, as it was hoisted to the masthead of his brig, 1831)

W. E. B. Du Bois (1868–1963): *Historian and Negro leader*
Would America have been America without her Negro people?
(*The Souls of Black Folk*, 1903)

The problem of the Twentieth Century is the problem of the color-line.

(Ibid.)

Cannot the nation that has absorbed ten million foreigners into its political life without catastrophe absorb ten million Negro Americans into that same political life at less cost than their unjust and illegal exclusion will involve?

(Ibid.)

Little of beauty has America given the world save the rude grandeur God himself stamped on her bosom; the human spirit in this new world has expressed itself in vigor and ingenuity rather than in beauty.

(Ibid.)

We must lay at the soul of this man a heavy responsibility for the consummation of Negro disenfranchisement, the decline of the Negro college and public school, and the firmer establishment of color caste in this land.

(On the death of Booker T. Washington, *The Crisis*, 1915)

The spell of Africa is upon me. The ancient witchery of her medicine is burning in my drowsy, dreamy blood.

(On his residence in Ghana, 1960)

Francis P. Duffy (1871–1932): *Catholic priest*

No soldier starts a war—they only give their lives to it. Wars are started by you and me, by bankers and politicians, excitable women, newspaper editors, clergymen who are ex-pacifists, and Congressmen with vertebrae of putty. The youngsters yelling in the streets, poor kids, are the ones who pay the price.

(Sermon, New York, 1931)

John Foster Dulles (1888–1959): *Secretary of state*

Our capacity to retaliate must be, and is, massive in order to deter all forms of aggression.

(Speech at Chicago, 8 December 1955)

The ability to get to the verge of war without getting into war is the necessary art. If you cannot master it, you inevitably get into wars. If you try to run away from it, if you are scared to go to the brink, you are lost. We've had to look it square in the face—on the question of enlarging the Korean War, on the question of getting into the Indo-China war, on the question of Formosa. We walked to the brink and we looked it in the face.

(*Life Magazine*, 11 January 1956)

An obsolete conception, and except under very exceptional circumstances it is an immoral and short-sighted conception.

(On neutralism, speech in Iowa, 9 June 1956)

The world is divided into two groups of people: the Christian anti-Communists, and the others.

(Attributed)

Isadora Duncan (1878–1927): *Dancer*

You were once wild here. Don't let them tame you.

(Speech on behalf of the Bolsheviks, Boston, 1922)

Finley Peter Dunne (1867–1936): *Humorist*

Whin a man gets to be my age, he ducks pol-itical meetin's, an' r-reads th' papers an' weighs th' ividence an' th' argymints,—pro-argymints an' con-argymints,—an' makes up his mind ca'mly, an' votes th' Dimmycratic ticket.

(*Mr. Dooley in Peace and in War,* 1898)

Rayformers, Hinnissy, is in favor iv suppressin' ivrything, but rale pollyticians believes in supressin' nawthin' but ividince.

(Ibid.)

Pierpont Morgan calls in wan iv his office boys, th' presidint iv a national bank, an' says he, "James," he says, "take some change out iv th' hamper an' r-run out an' buy Europe f'r me," he says. "I intind to re-organize it an' put it on a paying basis," he says. "Call up the Czar an' th' Pope an' th' Sultan an' th' Impror Willum, an' tell thim we won't need their savices afther nex' week," he says. "Give thim a year's salary in advance."

(Ibid.)

No matter whether th' constitution follows th' flag or not, th' supreme court follows th' iliction returns.

(Ibid.)

Th' Turkey bur-rd's th' rale cause iv Thanksgivin'. He's th' naytional air. Abolish th' Turkey an' ye destroy th' tie that binds us as wan people.

(Ibid.)

We march through life an' behind us marches th' phottygrafter an' th' rayporther. There are no such things as private citizens.

(*Observations by Mr. Dooley,* 1902)

What does a woman want iv rights whin she has priv'leges?

(Ibid.)

"Th' American nation in th' Sixth Ward is a fine people," he says. "They love th' eagle," he says, "on th' back iv a dollar."

(Ibid.)

I don't know what to do with the Ph'lippeens. . . . We can't seel thim, we can't ate thim, an' we can't throw thim into th' alley whin no wan is lookin'.

(Ibid.)

Th' modhren idee iv governmint is "Snub th' people, buy th' people, jaw th' people."

(*Mr. Dooley's Philosophy,* 1900)

Behold, th' land iv freedom, where ivry man's as good as ivry other man, on'y th' other man don't know it.

(*Mr. Dooley's Opinions,* 1901)

A man that'l expict to thrain lobsters to fly in a year is called a loonytic; but a man that thinks men can be tur-rned into angels by an iliction is called a rayformer an' remains at large.

(Ibid.)

A prince is a gr-reat man in th' ol' counthry, but he niver is as gr-reat over there as he is here.

(Ibid.)

He don't undherstand that people wud rather be wrong an' comfortable thin right in jail.

(On "rayformers," ibid.)

Th' prisidincy is th' highest office in th' gift iv th' people. Th' vice-prisidincy is th' next highest an' the lowest. It isn't a crime exactly. Ye can't be sint to jail f'r it, but it's a kind iv a disgrace.

(*Dissertations by Mr. Dooley,* 1906)

Sthrikes are a great evil f'r th' wurrukin' man, but so are picnics an' he acts th' same at both.

(*Mr. Dooley Says,* 1910)

I don't know what a chamber of commerce is unless 'tis a place where business men go to sleep.

(Ibid.)

When we Americans are done with the English language, it will look as if it had been run over by a musical comedy.

(Ibid.)

Enrique Dupuy de Lome (1851–1904): *Spanish ambassador to the United States*

McKinley is weak and a bidder for the admiration of the crowd, besides being a would-be politician who tries to leave a door open behind himself while keeping on good terms with the jingoes of his party.

(Letter to a colleague in Havana, intercepted and published by Hearst newspapers, 1898)

Jimmy Durante (1893–1980): *Comedian*

Don't put no constrictions on da people. Leave 'em ta hell alone.
(Attributed)

Leo Durocher (1906–   ): *Baseball player and manager*

Nice guys finish last.
(Attributed)

Timothy Dwight (1752–1817): *Clergyman, educator*

If Jefferson be elected we may see our wives and daughters the victims of legal prostitution, soberly dishonored, speciously polluted, the outcasts of delicacy and virtue, the loathing of God and man.

(Election sermon, 1800)

No American has within my knowledge been willing to inhabit a garret, for the sake of becoming an author.

(Attributed)

E

Mary Baker Eddy (1821–1910): *Religious teacher*

Matter does not express Spirit. God is infinite omnipresent Spirit. If Spirit is all and is everywhere, what and where is matter?

Remember that truth is greater than error, and we cannot put the greater into the less. Soul is Spirit, and Spirit is greater than body. If Spirit were once within the body, Spirit would be finite, and therefore could not be Spirit.

(*Science and Health*, 1875)

Christian Science explains all cause and effect as mental, not physical.

(Ibid.)

Thomas A. Edison (1847–1931): *Inventor*

Genius is one percent inspiration and ninety-nine percent perspiration.

(Commonly attributed)

I never did anything worth doing by accident, nor did any of my inventions come by accident; they came by work.

(Ibid.)

I speak without exaggeration when I say that I have constructed three thousand different theories in connection with the electric light. . . . Yet in only two cases did my experiments prove the truth of my theory.

(Interview, 1878)

I am proud of the fact that I never invented weapons to kill.

(*New York Times*, 8 June 1915)

Jonathan Edwards (1703–1758): *Calvinist theologian and philosopher*

The God that holds you over the pit of hell, much as one holds a spider or some loathesome insect over the fire, abhors you, and is dreadfully provoked. His wrath toward you burns like fire; he looks upon you as worthy of nothing else but to be cast into the fire.

("Sinners in the Hands of an Angry God," 1741)

The material universe exists only in the mind.

("On Mind," c. 1720)

John Ehrlichman (1925– **):** *Assistant to President Nixon*
When the President says "Jump" they only ask "How high?"
(Attributed, 1974)

Albert Einstein (1879–1955): *Physicist and philosopher*
Some recent work by E. Fermi and L. Szilard, which has been communicated to me in manuscript, leads me to expect that the element uranium may be turned into a new and important source of energy in the immediate future. Certain aspects of the situation seem to call for watchfulness and, if necessary, quick action on the part of the Administration.
(Handwritten letter to Franklin D. Roosevelt, 1939)

Since I do not foresee that atomic energy is to be a great boon for a long time, I have to say that for the present it is a menace. Perhaps it is well that it should be. It may intimidate the human race into bringing order into its international affairs, which without the pressure of fear, it would not do.
(Speech to the National Commission of Nuclear Scientists, May 1946)

The release of atom power has changed everything except our way of thinking, and thus we are being driven unarmed towards a catastrophe. . . . The solution of this problem lies in the heart of humankind.
(Ibid.)

If I had known, I should have become a watchmaker.
(On his role in making possible the atomic bomb, attributed)

Dwight D. Eisenhower (1890–1969): *General and thirty-fourth president*
The eyes of the world are upon you. The hopes and prayers of liberty-loving people everywhere march with you.
(Order to his troops for D-Day, 6 June 1944)

I have full confidence in your courage, devotion to duty and skill in battle. We will accept nothing less than full victory.
(Ibid.)

A landing was made this morning on the coast of France by the troops of the Allied Expeditionary Force. This landing is part of the concerted United Nations plan for the liberation of Europe.
(Radio broadcast, 6 June 1944)

The necessary and wise subordination of the military to civilian power will be best sustained when life-long professional soldiers abstain from seeking high political office.
(Statement refusing to be a candidate for president, April 1948)

The middle of the road is all of the usable surface. The extremes, right and left, are in the gutters.
(Attributed, 1952)

You're my boy.
(To Richard M. Nixon after the "Checkers" speech, September 1952)

I shall go to Korea.
(Speech in Detroit, 24 October 1952)

Whatever America hopes to bring to pass in the world must first come to pass in the heart of America.
(Inaugural address, 20 January 1953)

History does not long entrust the care of freedom to the weak or the timid.
(Ibid.)

There is one thing about being President—nobody can tell you when to sit down.
(In conversation, August 1953)

Some of my medical advisors believe that adverse effects on my health will be less in the Presidency than in any other position I might hold.
(Announcing he would run for reelection, June 1956)

Don't worry, Jim. If that comes up, I'll just confuse them.
(To his press secretary before meeting reporters, c. 1956)

In the councils of government, we must guard against the acquisition of unwarranted influence, whether sought or unsought, by the military-industrial complex. The potential for the disastrous rise of misplaced power exists and will persist. We must never let the weight of this combination endanger our liberties or democratic processes. We should take nothing for granted. . . .

(Farewell address, 17 January 1961)

In holding scientific research and discovery in respect, as we should, we must also be alert to the equal and opposite danger that public policy could itself become the captive of a scientific-technological elite.

(Ibid.)

Berlin is not so much a beleaguered city or threatened city as it is a symbol—for the West, of principle, of good faith, of determination, for the Soviets, a thorn in their flesh, a wound to their pride, an impediment to their designs.

(*Saturday Evening Post*, 9 December 1961)

No *easy* problems ever come to the President of the United States. If they are easy to solve, somebody else has solved them.

(Quoted by John F. Kennedy, 8 April 1962)

I've always loved my wife, my children, and my grandchildren, and I've always loved my country.

(Last words, 1969)

Ralph Ellison (1914–   ): *Writer*

When American life is most American it is apt to be most theatrical.

(*Shadow & Act*, 1964)

Oliver Ellsworth (1745–1807): *Chief justice*

Apostles of anarchy, bloodshed, and atheism.

(On Thomas Jefferson and his followers, 1800)

Ralph Waldo Emerson (1803–1882): *Lecturer and philosopher*

The word *liberty* in the mouth of Mr. Webster sounds like the word *love* in the mouth of a courtesan.

(Journal, 20 December 1822)

The Yankee is one who, if he once gets his teeth set on a thing, all creation can't make him let go.
(Journals, 1842)

The spirit of our American radicalism is destructive and aimless: it is not loving, it has no ulterior and divine ends; but is destructive only out of hatred and selfishness.
(Essays: Second Series, 1844)

Europe stretches to the Alleghanies; America lies beyond.
(Essays, 1844)

The United States will conquer Mexico but it will be as the man who swallows the arsenic which brings him down in turn. Mexico will poison us.
(Lecture, 1845)

I do not see how a barbarous community and a civilized community can constitute a state. I think we must get rid of slavery or we must get rid of freedom.
(Ibid.)

We are a puny and a fickle folk. Avarice, hesitation, and following are our diseases.
(The Method of Nature, 1849)

By God, I will not obey this filthy enactment!
(1850, of the Fugitive Slave Law)

The American is only the continuation of the English genius into new conditions, more or less propitious.
(English Traits, 1856)

That new saint, than whom nothing purer or more brave was ever led by love of men into conflict and death . . . will make the gallows glorious like the cross.
(Of John Brown's execution, December 1859)

In America the geography is sublime, but the men are not: the inventions are excellent, but the inventors one is sometimes ashamed of.

(*The Conduct of Life*, 1860)

The German and Irish millions, like the Negro, have a great deal of guano in their destiny. They are ferried over the Atlantic, and carted over America, to ditch and to drudge, to make corn cheap, and to lie down prematurely to make a spot of green grass on the prairie.

(Ibid.)

The value of a dollar is social, as it is created by society.

(Ibid.)

We go to Europe to be Americanized.

(Ibid.)

Who makes and keeps the Jew or the Negro base, who but you, who exclude them from the rights which others enjoy?

(*Journals*, 1867)

This country is filling up with thousands and millions of voters, and you must educate them to keep them from our throats.

(Lecture, 1870s)

America is a country of young men.

(*Society and Solitude*, "Old Age," 1870)

Here once the embattled farmers stood,
And fired the shot heard round the world.

(Hymn sung at the completion of the Concord Monument)

Daniel D. Emmett (1815–1904): *Showman, songwriter*

I wish I was in de land ob cotton,
Old times dar am not forgotten,
Look away, look away,
Look away, Dixie Land!
In Dixie land I'll take my stand,
To lib and die in Dixie;
Away, away,
Away down south in Dixie.

("Dixie's Land," 1859)

Erik H. Erickson (1902–   ): *Psychologist and writer*

The American feels so rich in his opportunities for free expression that he often no longer knows what he is free from. Neither does he know where he is not free; he does not recognize his native autocrats when he sees them.

(*Childhood and Society*, 1950)

In America nature is autocratic, saying, "I am not arguing, I am telling you."

(Ibid.)

Sam Ervin (1896–   ): *Senator from North Carolina*

That is not executive privilege. It is executive poppycock.

(At Watergate hearings, 1973)

There are two ways to indicate a horse. One is to draw a picture that is a great likeness. The other is to draw a picture that is a great likeness and write underneath it, "This is a horse." We just drew the picture.

(To reporters upon releasing the report of his Watergate investigation, 1973)

St. John Ervine (1884–1971): *Irish playwright*

American motion pictures are written by the half-educated for the half-witted.

(*New York Mirror*, 6 June 1963)

Bergen Evans (1904–   ): *Writer*

While the car may limit the size of the family, it is certainly instrumental in getting one started. There is no more irresistible mating call than the imperious horn at the kerb.

(*The Spoor of Spooks*, 1954)

Hiram Wesley Evans (1881–1945): *Imperial Wizard of the Ku Klux Klan*

There are three great racial instincts, vital elements in both the historic and the present attempts to build an America which shall fulfill the aspirations and justify the heroism of the men who made the nation. These are the instincts of loyalty to the white race, to the traditions of America, and to the spirit of Protestantism, which has been an essential part of Americanism ever since the days of Roanoke and Plymouth Rock. They are condensed into the Klan slogan: "Native, white, Protestant supremacy!"

("The Gospel of the KKK," 1926)

William M. Evarts (1818–1901): *Lawyer, diplomat*

The pious ones of Plymouth, who, reaching the Rock, first fell upon their own knees and then upon the aborigines.

(Attributed)

Edward Everett (1794–1865): *Politician and orator*

The faithful marble may preserve their image; the graven brass may proclaim their worth; but the humblest sod of Independent America, with nothing but the dew-drops of the morning to gild it, is a prouder mausoleum than kings or conquerers can boast. The country is their monument. Its independence is their epitaph.

(Memorial address honoring John Adams and Thomas Jefferson, July 1826)

F

Henry P. Fairchild (1880–1956): *Social scientist*

The only way to become a part of America is to live in America for an extended period of time. But the immigrant does not live in America . . . at all, but, from the point of view of nationality, in Italy, Poland, Czecho-Slovakia, or some other foreign country.

(*The Melting Pot Mistake,* 1926)

Lucius Fairchild (1831–1896): *Governor of Wisconsin and commander of the Grand Army of the Republic*

May God palsy the hand that wrote that order. May God palsy the brain that conceived it, and may God palsy the tongue that dictated it.

> (Upon hearing that President Cleveland had ordered captured Confederate battle flags returned to southern states, 1887)

Jerry Falwell (1933–   ): *Fundamentalist preacher and political organizer*

They should be registered and we'll stamp it on their foreheads.

> (On Communists, interview, *Penthouse* magazine, February 1981)

James A. Farley (1888–1976): *Democratic Party politician, postmaster-general under Franklin D. Roosevelt*

As Maine goes, so goes Vermont.

> (Quip to reporters when Maine voted Republican in 1936; Franklin D. Roosevelt carried every state except Maine and Vermont.)

David Farragut (1801–1870): *Naval commander*

Damn the torpedoes! Captain Drayton, go ahead!

> (Battle of Mobile Bay, 5 August 1864)

James T. Farrell (1904–1979): *Novelist*

America is so vast that almost everything said about it is likely to be true, and the opposite is probably equally true.

> (Introduction to Mencken, *Prejudices*, 1958)

William Faulkner (1897–1962): *Novelist*

If you could just be a nigger one Saturday night, you wouldn't want to be a white man again as long as you live.

> (Attributed)

To live anywhere in the world today and be against equality because of race or color, is like living in Alaska and being against snow.

> (*Essays*, 1965)

The last sound on the worthless earth will be two human beings trying to launch a homemade space ship and already quarreling about where they are going next.

(Address, Denver, 2 October 1959)

William J. Fetterman (1833–1866): *Army captain*

Give me 80 men and I'll ride through the whole Sioux nation.

(Said before riding into an ambush in which he and eighty-one men were killed, 21 December 1866)

Stephen J. Field (1816–1899): *Supreme Court justice*

The present assault upon capital is but the beginning. It will be but the stepping-stone to others, larger and more sweeping, 'til our political contests will become a war of the poor against the rich; a war constantly growing in intensity and bitterness.

(Declaring a 2 percent income tax unconstitutional, *Pollock* v. *Farmers' Loan and Trust Co.*, 1895)

Adolf Fischer (1859–1887): *German-born anarchist*

This is the happiest moment of my life.

(At his hanging after conviction for the Haymarket bombing, 1886)

James Fisk (1834–1872): *Financier*

Nothing is lost save honor.

(After an unsuccessful attempt to corner the nation's gold supply, September 1869)

Bradley A. Fiske (1854–1942): *Admiral*

Long, continuous periods of peace and prosperity have always brought about the physical, mental, and moral deterioration of the individual.

(Attributed)

F. Scott Fitzgerald (1896–1940): *Writer*

There are no second acts in American lives.

(*The Last Tycoon*, 1953, published posthumously)

George Fitzhugh (1806–1881): *Lawyer and proslavery writer*

A southern farm is the beau ideal of Communism: it is a joint concern, in which the slave consumes more than the master, of the coarse products, and is far happier, because . . . he is always sure of a support.

(*Sociology for the South*, 1854)

The negro slaves of the South are the happiest, and, in some sense, the freest people in the world. The children and the aged and infirm work not at all, and yet have all the comforts and necessaries of life provided for them. They enjoy liberty, because they are oppressed neither by care nor labor. The women do little hard work, and are protected from the despotism of their husbands by their masters. The negro men and stout boys work, on the average, in good weather, not more than nine hours a day. . . . Besides, they have their Sabbaths and holidays. White men, with so much of license and liberty, would die of ennui, but negroes luxuriate in corporeal and mental repose. With their faces upturned to the sun, they can sleep at any hour; and quiet sleep is the greatest of human enjoyments. . . . The free laborer must work or starve. He is more of a slave than the negro, because he works longer and harder for less allowance than the slave, and has no holiday, because the cares of life with him begin when its labors end. He has no liberty, and not a single right.

(*Cannibals All!*, 1857)

Some are born with saddles on their backs, and others booted and spurred to ride them—and the riding does them good.

(Ibid.)

Arthur "Dutch Schultz" Flegensheimer (?–1935): *Gangster*
Don't make no bull moves, George.

(Advice to an associate after his mortal wounding by gangster enemies, 23 October 1935)

Mother is the best bet.

(Last words)

Gerald R. Ford (1913–   ): *Thirty-seventh president*
I am a Ford, not a Lincoln.

(On becoming vice-president, 6 December 1973)

Truth is the glue that holds our government together. . . . Our long national nightmare is over. Our constitution works.
> (On being sworn in as president after the resignation of Nixon, 9 August 1974)

I guess it just proves that in America anyone can be president.
> (Remark after his inaugural address, 9 August 1974)

Instead of addressing the image of America, I prefer to consider the reality of America. It is true that we have launched our bicentennial celebration without having achieved human perfection. But we have attained a remarkable self-governed society that possesses the flexibility and dynamism to grow and undertake an entirely new agenda—agenda for America's third century.
> (Speech in Washington, April 1975)

I did not take the sacred oath of office to preside over the decline and fall of the United States of America.
> (Speech, September 1975)

Break out the flag, strike up the band, light up the sky.
> (Proclamation to the American people, 3 July 1976)

There is no Soviet domination of Eastern Europe and there never will be under a Ford administration.
> (Third television debate with Jimmy Carter, October 1976)

I've had a lifelong ambition to be a professional baseball player, but nobody would sign me.
> (To reporters, 4 December 1976)

Ronald Reagan doesn't dye his hair—he's just prematurely orange.
> (On his rival for the Republican presidential nomination, 1976)

I managed to rank in the top twenty-five per cent of our class. How that happened I can't explain.
> (A Time to Heal, 1979)

Henry Ford (1863–1947): *Industrialist*

The car of the future must be a car for the people . . . the market for a low-priced car is unlimited.

> (Conversation, 1909)

I am going to democratize the automobile. When I'm through everybody will be able to afford one, and about everyone will have one.

> (Ibid.)

We want to get the boys out of the trenches.

> (Upon sailing on the "peace ship," November 1915)

History is more or less bunk. It's tradition. We don't want tradition. We want to live in the present and the only history that is worth a tinker's dam is the history we make today.

> (Quoted in the *Chicago Tribune*, 25 May 1916)

I did not say it was bunk. It was bunk to me. . . . I did not need it very bad.

> (Testimony in a libel suit against the *Chicago Tribune*, Mt. Clemens, Illinois, July 1919)

These really are good times, but only a few know it.

> (Newspaper interview, 15 March 1931)

Howell Forgy (1908–   ): *Army chaplain*

Praise the Lord and pass the ammunition.

> (On the U.S. cruiser *New Orleans* during the Japanese attack on Pearl Harbor, 7 December 1941. It became the title of a popular song by Frank Loesser, 1942)

Nathan Bedford Forrest (1821–1877): *Confederate cavalry commander*

I git there the fustest with the mostest men.

> (Explaining his formula for success in battle, attributed)

Charles Foster (1828–1904): *Congressman and governor from Ohio*

Isn't this a billion dollar country?

> (Retorting to a gibe about "a billion-dollar Congress," 1891)

Stephen Foster (1826–1864): *Popular songwriter*

Weep no more, my lady,
Oh! weep no more to-day!
We will sing one song for the old Kentucky Home,
For the old Kentucky Home far away.
("My Old Kentucky Home," 1853)

'Way down upon de Swanee Ribber,
    Far, far away,
Dere's where my heart is turning
    ebber:
Dere's where de old folks stay.
All up and down de whole creation
    Sadly I roam,
Still longing for de old plantation,
    And for de old folks at home.
("Old Folks at Home," 1851)

Dere's no more hard work for poor
    old Ned,
He's gone whar de good niggers go.
("Uncle Ned," 1848)

Down in de cornfield
Hear dat mournful sound!
All de darkies am a weeping
Massa's in de cold, cold ground.
("Massa's in de Cold, Cold Ground," 1852)

Oh! darkies, how my heart grows weary,
    Far from the old folks at home.
(Ibid.)

Where are the hearts once so happy and free?
The children so dear that I held upon my knee?
Gone to the shore where my soul has longed to go,
I hear their gentle voices calling, "Old Black Joe!"
("Old Black Joe," 1860)

Gone are the days when my heart was young and gay,
Gone are my friends from the cotton fields away,
Gone from the earth to a better land I know.
(Ibid.)

George Fox (1624–1691): *English Quaker*

My friends going over to plant, and make outward plantations in America, keep your own plantations in your hearts, with the spirit and power of God, that your own vines and lilies be not hurt.

(Message to emigrants to Pennsylvania, 1681)

Felix Frankfurter (1882–1965): *Supreme Court justice*

Freedom of the press is not an end in itself but a means to the end of a free society.

(*New York Times,* 28 November 1954)

Benjamin Franklin (1706–1790): *Printer, colonial and Revolutionary leader*

God works wonders now and then: Behold! a lawyer, an honest man!

(*Poor Richard's Almanack,* 1732–1757)

> The greatest monarch on the proudest throne
> is obliged to sit upon his own arse.
> (Ibid.)

Leisure is the time for doing something useful.

(Ibid.)

> He that by the plow would thrive
> Himself must either hold or drive.

(Ibid.)

A ploughman on his legs is higher than a gentleman on his knees.

(Ibid.)

Handle your tools without mittens.

(Ibid.)

Remember, that time is money.

("Advice to Young Tradesman," 1748)

Join or die.

(Caption on cartoon showing colonies as parts of a snake, 1754)

A little neglect may breed mischief, . . . for want of a nail, the shoe was lost; for want of a shoe the horse was lost; and for want of a horse the rider was lost.

("Maxims," *Poor Richard's Almanack,* 1758)

The grand leap of the whale up the Fall of Niagara is esteemed, by all who have seen it, as one of the finest spectacles in nature.

(To the editor of a London newspaper, intended to chaff the English for their ignorance of America, 1765)

A disposition to abolish Slavery prevails in North America.

(Letter, 1773)

There never was a good war or a bad peace.

(Letter to Josiah Quincy, 11 September 1773)

We must indeed all hang together, or most assuredly, we shall all hang separately.

(At the signing of the Declaration of Independence, July 1776)

George Washington, Commander of the American armies, who, like Joshua of old, commanded the sun and the moon to stand still, and they obeyed him.

(A toast at a dinner in Versailles, 1778)

It cannot be worth any Man's while, who has a means of Living at home, to expatriate himself, in hopes of obtaining a profitable civil office in America; and, as to military Offices, they are at an end with the War, the Armies being disbanded. Much less is it adviseable for a Person to go thither, who has no other quality to recommend him but his Birth. In Europe it has indeed its Value; but it is a Commodity that cannot be carried to a worse Market than that of America, where people do not inquire concerning a Stranger, What is he? but, What can he do?

(*Information to Those Who Would Remove to America,* pamphlet, 1782)

The Husbandman is in honor there, and even the Mechanic, because their Employments are useful. The People have a saying, that God Almighty is himself a Mechanic, the greatest in the Universe; and he is respected and admired more for the Variety, Inge-

nuity, and Utility of his Handyworks, than for the Antiquity of his Family.
> (Ibid.)

I am persuaded that he means well for his Country, is always an honest Man, often a wise one, but sometimes, and in some things, absolutely out of his senses.
> (On John Adams, letter to Robert R. Livingston, 22 July 1783)

I wish the bald eagle had not been chosen as the representative of our country; he is a bird of bad moral character; like those among men who live by sharping and robbing, he is generally poor, and often very lousy.

The turkey is a much more respectable bird, and withal a true original native of America.
> (Letter to Sarah Bache, his daughter, 26 January 1784)

A republic, if you can keep it.
> (When asked after the Constitutional Convention, "Well, Doctor, what have we got, a republic or a monarchy?" 1787)

Our Constitution is in actual operation; everything appears to promise that it will last; but in this world nothing is certain but death and taxes.
> (Letter to Jean Baptiste LeRoy, 13 November 1789)

No nation was ever ruined by trade.
> (*Thoughts on Commercial Subjects*, 1791)

Those who govern, having much business on their hands, do not generally like to take the trouble of considering and carrying into execution new projects. The best public measures are therefore seldom adopted from previous wisdom, but forced by the occasion.
> (*Autobiography*, 1791)

When men are employed, they are best contented; for on the days they worked they were good-natured and cheerful, and, with the consciousness of having done a good day's work, they spent the evening jollily; but on our idle days they were mutinous and quarrelsome.
> (Ibid.)

A Bible and a newspaper in every house, a good school in every district—all studies and appreciated as they merit—are the principal support of virtue, morality and civil liberty.

(Ibid.)

Edward A. Freeman (1823–1892): *English historian*

The best remedy for whatever is amiss in America would be if every Irishman should kill a negro and be hanged for it.

(Lecture in the United States, 1881)

Sigmund Freud (1856–1939): *Austrian psychoanalyst*

America is a mistake, a giant mistake!

(After visiting the United States, attributed)

Henry C. Frick (1849–1919): *Industrialist*

I am very sorry for President Harrison, but I cannot see that our interests are going to be affected one way or another by the change in administration.

(Letter to Andrew Carnegie, December 1892)

Edgar Z. Friedenburg (1921–   ): *Popular psychologist of the 1960s*

Our culture impedes the clear definition of any faithful self-image—indeed, of any clear image whatever. We do not break images; there are few iconoclasts among us. Instead, we blur and soften them.

(*The Vanishing Adolescent*, 1959)

The growing American characteristically defends himself against anxiety by learning not to become too involved.

(Ibid.)

We are an obsessively moral people, but our morality is a team morality.

(Ibid.)

So much of learning to be an American is learning not to let your individuality become a nuisance.

(Ibid.)

The "teen-ager" seems to have replaced the Communist as the appropriate target for public controversy and foreboding.
(Ibid.)

Erich Fromm (1900–): *Psychologist and philosopher*
Women are equal because they are not different any more.
(*The Art of Loving,* 1956)

Lynette "Squeaky" Fromme (1950–): *Would-be assassin of President Ford*
Anybody can kill anybody.
(In conversation shortly before her attempt to assassinate President Ford, Sacramento, September 1975)

Robert Frost (1874–1963): *Poet*
Americans are like a rich father who wishes he knew how to give his sons the hardships that made him rich.
(Attributed)

J. William Fulbright (1905–): *Senator from Arkansas*
The truth is, Mr. President, that our foreign policy is inadequate, outmoded and misdirected. It is based in part on a false conception of our real long-term national interests, and in part on an erroneous appraisal of the state of the world in which we live.
(Speech in the Senate, 6 August 1958)

Margaret Fuller (1810–1850): *Writer*
Women could take part in the processions, the songs, the dances, of old religions; no one fancied their delicacy was impaired by appearing in public for such a cause.
(*Women in the Nineteenth Century,* 1845)

In order that she may be able to give her hand with dignity, she must be able to stand alone.
(Ibid.)

It does not follow because many books are written by persons in America that there exists an American literature. Books which imitate or represent the thoughts and life of Europe do not constitute an American literature. Before such can exist, an original idea must animate this nation and fresh currents of life must call into life such fresh thoughts along its shores.

(*New York Tribune*, 1846)

I now know all the people worth knowing in America, and I find no intellect comparable to my own.

(Attributed)

'Tis an evil lot to have a man's ambition and woman's heart.

(Attributed)

Robert Fulton (1765–1815): *Inventor*

My steamboat voyage to Albany and back has turned out rather more favourable than I had calculated. The distance from New York to Albany is 150 miles; I ran it up in thirty-two hours, and down in thirty hours; the latter is just five miles an hour. I had a light breeze against me the whole way going and coming, so that no use was made of my sails, and the voyage has been performed wholly by the power of the steam engine, I overtook many sloops and schooners beating to windward, and passed them as if they had been at anchor.

(Letter to Joel Barlow, August 1907)

G

Gabriel (?–1800): *Rebel slave leader*

I have nothing more to offer than what General Washington would have had to offer, had he been taken by the British and put to trial by them. I have adventured my life in endeavoring to obtain the liberty of my countrymen, and am a willing sacrifice to their cause. . . .

(Statement before his execution in Richmond, 1800)

John Kenneth Galbraith (1908–): *Economist and ambassador to India under President Kennedy*

Wealth is not without its advantages and the case to the contrary, although it has often been made, has never proved widely persuasive.

(*The Affluent Society,* 1958)

The urge to consume is fathered by the value system which emphasizes the ability of the society to produce.

(Ibid.)

More die in the United States of too much food than of too little.

(Ibid.)

Politics is not the art of the possible. It consists in choosing between the disastrous and the unpalatable.

(*Ambassador's Journal,* 1969)

Augustus P. Gardner (1865–1918): *Congressman from Massachusetts*

Wake up, America.

(Speech in Congress, 16 October 1916)

James A. Garfield (1831–1881): *Twentieth president*

You and I know that teaching is not the work in which a man can live and grow.

(To a friend while teaching at Hiram College, 1859)

Fellow citizens! God reigns, and the government at Washington still lives.

(Speech in New York upon the death of Lincoln, 15 April 1865)

A pine bench, with Mark Hopkins at one end of it and me at the other, is a good enough college for me!

(Speech, 1871)

All free governments are party-governments.

(Speech in the House of Representatives, 18 January 1878)

All free governments are managed by the combined wisdom and folly of the people.
(Attributed, 1880)

My God! What is there in this place that a man should ever want to get into it?
(On the flood of office-seekers, June 1881)

The last person in the world to know what the people really want and think.
(On the presidency, attributed)

John Nance Garner (1868–1967): *Vice-president under Franklin D. Roosevelt*
The trouble today is that we have too many laws.
(Speech during 1932 election campaign)

Not worth a pitcher full of warm spit.
(On the vice-presidency, attributed)

Henry Highland Garnet (1815–1882): *Black abolitionist*
Strike for your lives and liberties. . . . You cannot be more oppressed than you have been—you cannot suffer greater cruelties than you have already. Rather die freemen than live to be slaves. Remember that you are FOUR MILLIONS.
(Speech to National Negro Convention, 1843)

William Lloyd Garrison (1805–1879): *Abolitionist editor*
Our country is the world—our countrymen are all mankind.
(Prospectus for *The Liberator*, 15 December 1830)

I am aware that many object to the severity of my language; but is there not cause for severity? I will be as harsh as truth, and as uncompromising as justice. On this subject, I do not wish to think, or speak, or write with moderation. No! No! Tell a man whose house is on fire, to give a moderate alarm; tell him to moderately rescue his wife from the hands of the ravisher; tell the mother to gradually extricate her babe from the fire into which it has fallen;—but urge me not to use moderation in a cause like the present. I am in earnest—I will not equivocate—I will not excuse—I will not retreat a single inch—AND I WILL BE HEARD.

(Inaugural issue of *The Liberator*, 1 January 1831)

Let Southern oppressors tremble—let their secret abettors tremble—let their Northern apologists tremble—let all the enemies of the persecuted blacks tremble.

(Ibid.)

The compact which exists between the North and the South is "a covenant with death and an agreement with hell."

(Resolution adopted by Massachusetts Anti-Slavery Society, 27 January 1843)

Was John Brown justified in his attempt? Yes, if Washington was in his, if Warren and Hancock were in theirs. If men are justified in striking a blow for freedom, when the question is one of a three penny tax on tea, then, I say, they are a thousand times more justified, when it is to save fathers, mothers, wives and children from the slave-coffle and the auction block, and to restore them their God-given rights.

(*The Liberator*, 16 December 1859)

Wherever there is a human being, I see God-given rights inherent in that being, whatever may be the sex or complexion.

(*Life of William Lloyd Garrison*, 1885–1889)

With reasonable men, I will reason; with humane men, I will plead; but to tyrants I will give no quarter, nor waste arguments where they will certainly be lost.

(Ibid.)

The success of any great moral enterprise does not depend upon numbers.

(Ibid.)

Marcus Garvey (1887–1940): *Jamaican-born black separatist leader*

I asked, "Where is the black man's Government?" "Where is his King and his kingdom?" "Where is his President, his country, and his ambassador, his army, his navy, his men of big affairs?" I could not find them, and then I declared, "I will help to make them."

(Speech in Harlem, 1923)

Eugene D. Genovese (1930–): *Historian*

Those who find America an especially violent and oppressive country ("Amerika") have apparently never read the history of England or France, Germany or Russia, Indonesia or Burundi, Turkey or Uganda.

(New York Times, 18 June 1978)

George III (1738–1820): *King of England during the Revolution*

Experience has thoroughly convinced me that the Country gains nothing by granting to Her Dependencies indulgencies, for opening the Door encourages a desire for more which if not complied with causes discontent, and the former benefit is obliterated.

(Letter to Lord North, 12 November 1778)

I cannot conclude without mentioning how sensibly I feel the dismemberment of America from this empire, and that I should be miserable indeed if I did not feel that no blame on that account can be laid at my door, and did I not also know that knavery seems to be so much the striking feature of its inhabitants that it may not in the end be an evil that they will become aliens to this kingdom.

(Letter to the Earl of Shelburne, 10 November 1782)

I was the last to consent to the separation, but the separation having been made and having become inevitable, I have always said that I would be the first to meet the friendship of the United States as an independent power.

(To John Adams, ambassador to England, 1 June 1785)

Henry George (1839–1897): *Journalist and social critic*

The Single Tax

(Title given his program for national reform, 1879)

The association of poverty with progress is the enigma of our times.

(Progress and Poverty, 1879)

Our boasted freedom necessarily involves slavery, so long as we recognize private property in land. Until that is abolished, Declarations of Independence and Acts of Emancipation are in vain. So long as one man can claim the exclusive ownership of the land from which other men must live, slavery will exist, and as material progresses on, must grow and deepen.

(Ibid.)

So long as all the increased wealth which modern progress brings goes but to build up great fortunes, to increase luxury, and make sharper the contrast between the House of Have and the House of Want, progress is not real and cannot be permanent.

(Ibid.)

Capital is the result of labor, and is used by labor to assist it in further production. Labor is the active and initial force, and labor is therefore the employer of capital.

(Ibid.)

For as labor cannot produce without the use of land, the denial of the equal right to use of land is necessarily the denial of the right of labor to its own produce.

(Ibid.)

Geronimo (1829–1909): *Chiricahua Apache warrior chief*

Once I moved about like the wind. Now I surrender to you and that is all.

(On surrendering, 1886)

Elbridge Gerry (1744–1814): *Revolutionary War politician, diplomat*

Confederations are a mongrel kind of government, and the world does not afford a precedent to go by.

(Speech in the Contintental Congress, 1780)

The evils we experience flow from the excess of democracy. The people do not want virtue, but are the dupes of pretended patriots.

(Attributed)

James Gibbons (1834–1921): *Roman Catholic cardinal*

Our country has liberty without license and authority without despotism.

> (Speech in Rome, 25 March 1887)

American Catholics rejoice in our separation of Church and State, and I can conceive no combination of circumstances likely to arise which would make a union desirable for either Church or State.

> (*North American Review,* March 1909)

James Sloan Gibbons (1810–1892): *Banker, abolitionist*

We are coming, Father Abraham, three hundred thousand
  more,
From Mississippi's winding stream and from New England's
  shore;
We leave our ploughs and workshops, our wives and
  children dear,
With hearts too full for utterance, with but a single
  tear.

> ("We are Coming, Father Abraham," 1862)

Frank Gibney (1924–   ): *British grammarian*

At the center of the linguistic realm stands the inarticulate American, his speech a mix of canned phrases and slang, awash with breathless parentheses punctuated by repetitions and obscenities. The ability to use language threatens to become a memory among us.

> (*Britannica Book of English Usage,* 1980)

Charlotte Perkins Gilman (1860–1935): *Social reformer and writer*

The woman's movement rests not alone on her larger personality, with its tingling sense of revolt against injustice, but on the wide, deep sympathy of women for one another. It is a concerted movement, based on the recognition of a common evil and seeking a common good.

> (*Women and Economics,* 1898)

Hermione Gingold (1899–   ): *British actress*

What we at home call draught, Americans refer to as cross-ventilation.

(*Observer*, 2 October 1958)

Allen Ginsberg (1926–   ): *Poet and peace movement leader*

I saw the best minds of my generation destroyed by madness.

(*Howl*, 1956)

America I'm putting my queer shoulder to the wheel.

(*America*, 1973)

Tom Girdler (1877–1965): *Industrialist*

I never knew a steel plant that didn't have guns and ammunition to protect its property.

(*Time*, 14 January 1937)

I won't have a contract, verbal or written, with an irresponsible, racketeering, violent, communistic body like the CIO, and until they pass a law making me do it, I am not going to do it.

(Interview, April 1938)

Valéry Giscard d'Estaing (1926–   ): *French president*

It is not for us to predict what role you will actually play in the future. That answer . . . remains to be heard. I assure you of this: We are all listening.

(Bicentennial congratulations, 4 July 1976)

William E. Gladstone (1809–1898): *British prime minister*

There is no doubt that Jefferson Davis and other leaders of the South have made an army; they are making it appears, a navy; and they have made what is more than either, they have made a nation.

(Speech at Newcastle-upon-Tyne, 7 October 1862)

John Glenn (1921–   ): *Astronaut and senator from Ohio*

Cape is go and I am go.

(Remark launching first American orbital flight in space, 20 February 1962)

Martin H. Glynn (1891–1924): *New York governor and Democratic Party politician*

He kept us out of war!

(On Woodrow Wilson, Saint Louis, 15 June 1916)

Emma Goldman (1869–1940): *Russian-born American anarchist*

All wars are wars among thieves who are too cowardly to fight and who therefore induce the young manhood of the whole world to do the fighting for them.

(Address to the jury at her sedition trial, July 1917)

The government will go on in the highly democratic method of conscripting American manhood for European slaughter.

(Ibid.)

Barry Goldwater (1909–   ): *Senator from Arizona and Republican presidential candidate, 1964*

We ought to saw off the Eastern seaboard and float it out to sea.

(Attributed, 1962)

We now have a President who tries to save money by turning off lights in the White House, even as he heads toward a staggering addition to the national debt. "L.B.J." should stand for Light Bulb Johnson.

(Speech in Chicago, 10 April 1964)

I would remind you that extremism in the defense of liberty is no vice. And let me remind you also that moderation in the pursuit of justice is no virtue.

(Speech accepting Republican nomination for president, 16 July 1964)

A government that is big enough to give you all you want is big enough to take it all away.

(Speech, West Chester, Pennsylvania, 21 October 1964)

You've got to forget about this civilian. Whenever you drop bombs, you're going to hit civilians.

(Speech in New York, 23 January 1967)

Samuel Gompers (1850–1924): *President of the American Federation of Labor*

Caucasians are not going to let their standard of living be destroyed by Negroes, Japs, or any others.

(*American Federationist*, 1900)

The intelligent, comprehensive, common-sense workmen prefer to deal with the problems of today, the problem which confronts them today, with which they are bound to contend if they want to advance, rather than to deal with a picture and a dream which has never had, and I am sure never will have, any reality in the affairs of humanity.

("Debate" with socialist Morris Hillquit, Commission on Industrial Relations, 22 May 1914)

Does it require much discernment to know that a wage of $3 a day and a workday of 8 hours a day in sanitary workshops are all better than $2.50 a day and 12 hours a day and under perilous conditions of labor? It does not require much conception of a social philosophy to understand that.

(Ibid.)

God bless our American institutions. They grow better day by day.

(Last words, San Antonio, Texas, 1924)

Paul Goodman (1911–1972): *Social critic and philosopher*

American society has tried so hard and so ably to defend the practice and theory of production for profit and not primarily for use that now it has succeeded in making its jobs and products profitable and useless.

(*Growing Up Absurd*, 1960)

Where there is official censorship it is a sign that speech is serious. Where there is none, it is pretty certain that the official spokesmen have all the loud-speakers.

(Ibid.)

The stultifying effect of the movies is not that the children see them but that their parents do, as if Hollywood provided a plausible adult recreation to grow up into.

(Ibid.)

In the modern world, we Americans are the old inhabitants. We first had political freedom, high industrial production, an economy of abundance.
(Ibid.)

The young have the right to power because they are numerous and are directly affected by what goes on, but especially because their new point of view is indispensable to cope with changing conditions. This is why Jefferson urged us to adopt a new constitution every generation.
(Ibid.)

The organization of American society is an interlocking system of semi-monopolies notoriously venal, an electorate notoriously unenlightened, misled by mass media notoriously phony.
(Community of Scholars, 1962)

John B. Gough (1817–1886): *Temperance propagandist*
Crawl from the slimy ooze, ye drowned drunkards, and with suffocation's blue and livid lips speak out against the drink.
(Sermon, 1842)

Jay Gould (1836–1892): *Financier*
I can hire one-half of the working class to kill the other half.
(Newspaper interview, 1886)

Anybody can make a fortune. It takes genius to hold on to one.
(Attributed)

Henry W. Grady (1850–1889): *Southern editor*
When the Negro was enfranchised, the South was condemned to solidity as surely as self-preservation was the first law of nature.
(Speech, November 1888)

Billy Graham (1918–   ): *Baptist revivalist*
I have asked you for a moral and spiritual restoration in the land and give thanks that in Thy sovereignty Thou has permitted Richard M. Nixon to lead us at this momentous hour of our history.
(Prayer at breakfast in Washington, 1969)

Ulysses S. Grant (1822–1885): *Union general and eighteenth president*

No terms except unconditional and immediate surrender can be accepted. I propose to move immediately upon your works.

> (To Confederate general Simon Buckner, during the siege of Fort Donelson, 16 February 1862)

There was nothing left to be done but to go forward to a decisive victory.

> (Of his Vicksburg campaign, May 1863)

I propose to fight it out on this line, if it takes all summer.

> (Dispatch to Washington from the front before Richmond, 11 May 1864)

The arms, artillery and public property to be parked and stacked, and turned over to the officer appointed by me to receive them. This will not embrace the sidearms of the officers, nor their private horses or baggage. This done, each officer and man will be allowed to return to their homes, not to be disturbed by United States authority so long as they observe their paroles and laws in force where they may reside.

> (Terms of surrender for the Army of Northern Virginia, 9 April 1865)

Let us have peace.

> (Accepting presidential nomination, 29 May 1868)

I know no method to secure the repeal of bad or obnoxious laws so effective as their stringent execution.

> (Inaugural Address, 4 March 1869)

Let no guilty man escape, if it can be avoided. No personal considerations should stand in the way of performing a public duty.

> (On the corrupt "Whiskey Ring," 29 July 1875)

Leave the matter of religion to the family altar, the church, and the private school, supported entirely by private contributions. Keep the Church and the State forever separate.

> (Speech, 1875)

Labor disgraces no man; unfortunately you occasionally find men disgrace labor.

(Farewell address, Washington, March 1877)

What General Lee's feelings were I do not know. . . . My own feelings, which had been quite jubilant . . . were sad and depressing. I felt like anything rather than rejoicing at the downfall of a foe who had fought so long and gallantly. . . . The much talked of surrendering of Lee's sword and my handing it back, this and much more that has been said about it is the purest romance.

(*Memoirs*, 1885)

William J. Grayson (1788–1863): *Planter from South Carolina*

Secure they toil, uncursed their peaceful life,
With labor's hungry broils and wasteful strife.
No want to goad, no faction to deplore.
The slave escapes the perils of the poor.

("The Hireling and the Slave," 1856)

Horace Greeley (1811–1872): *Editor and reformer*

Go West, young man, and grow up with the country.

(*Hints toward Reform*, 1850)

The best business you can go into you will find on your father's farm or in his workshop. If you have no family or friends to aid you, and no prospect opened to you there, turn your face to the Great West, and there build up a home and fortune.

(Ibid.)

We could not retard the great forward movement of humanity if we would. But each of us may decide for himself whether to share in the glory of promoting it or incur the shame of having looked coldly and indifferently on.

(Ibid.)

North and South are eager to clasp hands across the bloody chasm which has so long divided them.

(Speech in Baltimore, 1872)

Dick Gregory (1932–   ): *Comedian and civil rights activist*
In America, with all of its evils and faults, you can still reach through the forest and see the sun. But we don't know yet whether that sun is rising or setting for our country.
>(*Nigger,* 1964)

Just being a Negro doesn't qualify you to understand the race situation any more than being sick makes you an expert on medicine.
>(Ibid.)

Joseph C. Grew (1880–1965): *Ambassador to Japan*
Until such time as there is a complete regeneration of thought in this country, a show of force, together with a determination to employ it if need be, can alone contribute effectively to the achievement of such an outcome and to our own future security.
>(Communiqué from Tokyo, September 1940)

Sir Edward Grey (1826–1933): *British statesman*
The United States is like a gigantic boiler. Once the fire is lighted under it there is no limit to the power it can generate.
>(Attributed)

Angelina Grimké (1805–1879): *Abolitionist*
If a law commands me to sin *I will break it;* if it calls me to suffer, I will let it take its course *unresistingly.* The doctrine of blind obedience and unqualified submission to any human power, whether civil or ecclesiastical, is the doctrine of despotism, and ought to have no place 'mong Republicans and Christians.
>("Appeal to the Christian Women of the South," 1836)

Philip Guedalla (1889–1944): *British historian*
The twentieth century is only the nineteenth speaking with a slight American accent.
>(Attributed)

Texas Guinan (1884–1933): *Notorious speakeasy operator*
Never give a sucker an even break.
>(Attributed, 1920s)

Hello, sucker!
> (Said to customers entering her nightclub)

Fifty million Frenchmen can't be wrong.
> (*New York World-Telegram,* 21 March 1931)

Charles Guiteau (1841–1882): *Assassin of President Garfield*

I am a stalwart. Now Arthur is President.
> (On shooting President Garfield, attributed, July 1881)

My inspiration is a godsend to you, and I presume you appreciate it. It raises you from $8,000 to $50,000 a year. It raises you from a political cipher to President of the United States with all its power and honors. For the Cabinet I would suggest as follows. . . .
> (Letter to President Arthur, 20 September 1881)

Glory hallelujah! I am with the Lord, Glory, ready, go!
> (Last words on the scaffold, 30 June 1882)

John Gunther (1901–1970): *Writer*

Ours is the only country founded on a good idea.
> (*Inside U.S.A.,* 1951)

Walter K. Gutman (1903–   ): *Writer*

There is nothing like the ticker tape except a woman—nothing that promises, hour after hour, day after day, such sudden developments; nothing that disappoints so often or occasionally fulfills with such unbelievable, passionate magnificence.
> (*Coronet,* March 1960)

H

Thomas J. Hagerty (1862?–1920): *Catholic priest and labor organizer*

The working class and the employing class have nothing in common. There can be no peace so long as hunger and want are found among millions of working people and the few, who make up the employing class, have all the good things of life.

(Preamble to the Constitution of the Industrial Workers of the World, June 1905)

Frank Hague (1876–1956): *Political boss of Jersey City*

You hear about constitutional rights, free speech, and the free press. Every time I hear these words I say to myself, "That man is a Red, that man is a Communist." You never hear a real American talk like that.

(Speech in Jersey City, 12 January 1938)

Alexander Haig (1924–   ): *General and secretary of state under President Reagan*

There are worse things than war.

(Testimony during his confirmation hearings before the Senate, 12 January 1981)

Mistakes were made, but I didn't make them. I wasn't there when they were made. I inherited them. I never willingly, consciously or unconsciously participated in any actions that I considered wrong, immoral, or illegal.

(Ibid., 13 January 1981, on his role as chief of the White House staff during President Nixon's Watergate scandal)

H. R. Haldeman (1927–   ): *Adviser to President Nixon*

We have tried to keep a spread of opinion on the staff so that no one is to the left of the president at his most liberal, or to the right of the president at his most conservative. . . . We do act as a screen because there is a real danger of some advocate of an idea rushing into the president . . . and actually managing to convince him in a burst of emotion or argument.

(Interview, 1971)

Nathan Hale (1755–1776): *Revolutionary War spy*

I only regret that I have but one life to lose for my country.

(On being hanged as a spy, 22 September 1776)

Alexander Hamilton (1755–1804): *First secretary of the Treasury*

Self-preservation is the first principle of our nature.

(*A Full Vindication*, 15 December 1774)

A national debt, if it is not excessive, will be to us a national blessing.

(Letter to Robert Morris, 30 April 1781)

I believe the British government forms the best model the world ever produced. . . . This government has for its object public strength and individual security.

(Speech to the Constitutional Convention, 18 June 1787)

Even to observe neutrality you must have a strong government.

(Speech to the Constitutional Convention, 29 June 1787)

All communities divide themselves into the few and the many. The first are the rich and wellborn, the other the mass of the people. . . . The people are turbulent and changing; they seldom judge or determine right. Give therefore to the first class a distinct, permanent share in the government. They will check the unsteadiness of the second, and as they cannot receive any advantage by change, they therefore will ever maintain good government.

(Ibid.)

The voice of the people has been said to be the voice of God; and however generally this maxim has been quoted and believed, it is not true in fact. The people are turbulent and changing; they seldom judge or determine right.

> (Ibid.)

Let Americans disdain to be the instruments of European greatness. Let the Thirteen States, bound together in a strict and indissoluble union, concur in erecting one great American system, superior to the control of all trans-atlantic force or influence, and able to dictate the terms of the connection between the old and the new world!

> (*Federalist Papers, XI*, November 1787)

Constitutions should consist only of general provisions; the reason is that they must necessarily be permanent, and that they cannot possibly calculate for the possible change of things.

> (Ibid.)

Your people, sir, is a great beast.

> (During a debate at a cabinet meeting with Thomas Jefferson, 1792)

Learn to think continentally.

> (Attributed)

Andrew Hamilton (?–1741): *Colonial attorney*

The question before the court and you, gentlemen of the jury, is not of small nor private concern. It is not the cause of a poor printer, nor of New York alone, which you are now trying. No! It may, in its consequences, affect every freeman that lives under a British government on the main of America. It is the best cause. It is the cause of liberty.

> (Summation in the Zenger case, 1735)

James H. "Mudsill" Hammond (1807–1864): *Senator from South Carolina*

You dare not make war on cotton. Cotton is King!

> (Speech in the Senate, March 1858)

John Hancock (1736–1797): *Merchant and revolutionary leader*

There, King George will be able to read that without his spectacles.

(Upon signing the Declaration of Independence in an outsize script, 2 August 1776)

Learned Hand (1872–1961): *Jurist*

Liberty lies in the hearts of men and women; when it dies there, no constitution, no law, no court can save it; no constitution, no law, no court can even do much to help it. While it lies there, it needs no constitution, no law, no court to save it.

(Speech in New York, 21 May 1944)

The public official must pick his way nicely, must learn to placate though not to yield too much, to have the art of honeyed words but not to seem neutral, and above all to keep constantly audible, visible, likable, even kissable.

(Speech, Washington, D.C., 8 March 1932)

The hand that rules the press, the radio, the screen and the far-spread magazine, rules the country.

(Speech, 21 December 1942)

Marcus A. Hanna (1837–1904): *Senator and Republican Party boss*

I told William McKinley it was a mistake to nominate that wild man at Philadelphia. I asked him if he realized what would happen if he should die. Now, look, that damned cowboy is president of the United States.

(In conversation at President McKinley's funeral, September 1901)

Mr. Roosevelt is an entirely different man today from what he was a few weeks since. He has now acquired all that was needed to round out his character—equipoise and conservatism.

(Interview, October 1901)

Yip Harburg (1896–   ): *Songwriter*

Brother, can you spare a dime.

(Title of a song, 1930, unofficial theme of the early depression)

Warren G. Harding (1865–1923): *Twenty-ninth president, 1921–1923*

I don't know much about Americanism, but it's a damned good word with which to carry an election.

(Attributed, 1916)

Stabilize America first, prosper America first, think of America first, exalt America first.

(Speech accepting presidential nomination, 22 July 1920)

America's present need is not heroism but healing, not nostrums but normalcy, not agitation but adjustment, not surgery but serenity, not the dramatic but the dispassionate, not experiment but equipoise, not submergence in internationality but sustainment in triumphant nationality.

(Speech in Boston, August 1920)

Talk to God about me every day by name, and ask Him somehow to give me strength for my great task.

(To a clergyman on the day of his inauguration, 4 March 1921)

I can't make a damn thing out of this tax problem. I listen to one side and they seem right, and then—God!—I talk to the other side and they seem to be right. . . . I know somewhere there is a book that will give me the truth but I couldn't read the book. I know somewhere there is an economist who knows the truth, but I don't know where to find him and haven't the sense to know him and trust him when I find him. God! what a job.

(Conversation, 1922)

I have no trouble with my enemies but my goddam friends, White, they are the ones who keep me walking the floor nights.

(In conversation with William Allen White, 1923)

I am a man of limited talents from a small town. I don't seem to grasp that I am President.

(Ibid.)

John Marshall Harlan (1833–1911): *Supreme Court justice*

But in view of the Constitution in the eye of the law, there is in this country no superior, dominant, ruling class of citizens. There is no caste here. Our Constitution is color-blind, and neither knows nor tolerates classes among citizens. In respect of civil rights, all citizens are equal before the law. The humblest is the peer of the most powerful. The law regards man as man, and takes no account of his surroundings or of his color when his civil rights as guaranteed by the supreme law of the land are involved.

(Dissenting opinion, *Plessy* v. *Ferguson,* 1896)

Michael Harrington (1928–): *Socialist writer*

America has the best-dressed poverty the world has ever known.
(The Other America, 1962)

For the middle class, the police protect property, give directions, and help old ladies. For the urban poor, the police are those who arrest you.
(Ibid.)

Our affluent society contains those of talent and insight who are driven to prefer poverty, to choose it, rather than to submit to the desolation of an empty abundance.
(Ibid.)

The American economy, the American society, the American unconscious are all racist.
(Ibid.)

To be a Negro is to participate in a culture of poverty and fear that goes far deeper than any law for or against discrimination.
(Ibid.)

Joel Chandler Harris (1848–1980): *Southern writer*

Bred en bawn in a brier-patch!
(Uncle Remus, 1880)

Benjamin Harrison (1833–1901): *Twenty-third president, 1889–1893*

I would a thousand times rather march under the bloody shirt, stained with the lifeblood of a Union soldier, than to march under the black flag of treason or the white flag of compromise.

(Campaign speech, 1883)

Honorable party service will certainly not be esteemed by me a disqualification for public office.

(Speech during the election campaign of 1888)

We Americans have no commission from God to police the world.

(Campaign speech, September 1888)

The President is a good deal like the old camp horse that Dickens described; he is strapped up so he can't fall down.

(Letter to William McKinley, 4 February 1892)

William Henry Harrison (1773–1841): *Ninth president, 1841*

Some folks are silly enough as to have formed a plan to make a President of the United States out of this Clerk and Clodhopper.

(Letter to Stephen Van Rensselaer, 1836)

The delicate duty of devising schemes of revenue should be left where the Constitution has placed it—with the immediate representatives of the people.

(Inaugural address, 4 March 1841)

If parties in a republic are necessary to secure a degree of vigilance to keep the public functionaries within the bounds of law and duty, at that point their usefulness ends.

(Ibid.)

Bret Harte (1836–1902): *Writer*

> Which I wish to remark,
> And my language is plain,
> That for ways that are dark
> And for tricks that are vain,
> The heathen Chinee is peculiar.

(*Plain Language from Truthful James*, 1871)

We are ruined by Chinese cheap labour.

(Ibid.)

Paul Harvey (1918–): *Radio commentator*

In the 200 years since we weaned ourselves, every other nation in the world has been turned upside down, and ours is still right side up.

(Radio broadcast, 4 July 1976)

Henry T. Havemeyer (1804–1874): *Mayor of New York*

Let the buyer beware; that covers the whole business. You cannot wet-nurse people from the time they are born until the time they die. They have to wade in and get stuck, and that is the way men are educated.

(Attributed)

Nathaniel Hawthorne (1804–1864): *Novelist*

No author, without a trial, can conceive of the difficulty of writing a romance about a country where there is no shadow, r. antiquity, no mystery, no picturesque and gloomy wrong, not any thing but a commonplace prosperity, in broad and simple daylight, as is happily the case with my dear native land. . . . Romance and poetry, ivy, lichens and wallflowers need ruin to make them grow.

(Preface to *The Marble Faun*, 1860)

John Hay (1838–1905): *Secretary of state*

A halfbaked glib little briefless jack-leg lawyer, grasping with anxiety to collar that $50,000 salary, promising the millennium to everybody with a hole in his pants and destruction to everybody with a clean shirt.

(On William Jennings Bryan, 1896)

A splendid little war.

(Describing the war with Spain, 1898)

Tom Hayden (1940–): *New Left leader and Democratic Party politician*

We are people of this generation, bred in at least modest comfort, housed now in universities, looking uncomfortably to the world we inherit.

(Port Huron statement, June 1962)

We would replace power rooted in possession, privilege, or circumstance by power and uniqueness rooted in love, reflectiveness, reason, and creativity. As a *social system* we seek the establishment of a democracy of individual participation, governed by two central aims: that the individual share in those social decisions determining the quality and direction of his life; that society be organized to encourage independence in men and provide the media for their common participation.

(Ibid.)

We will not bury you; we will just outlive you.

(Slogan, late 1960s)

Rutherford B. Hayes (1822–1893): *Nineteenth president, 1877–1881*

He serves his party best who serves the country best.

(Inaugural address, 4 March 1877)

Party leaders should have no more influence in appointments than other equally respectable citizens. No assessments for political purposes, of officers or subordinates, should be allowed. No useless officer or employee should be retained. No officer should be required to take part in the management of political organizations, caucuses, conventions, or political campaigns.

(Ibid.)

Many, if not most, of our Indian wars have had their origin in broken promises and acts of injustice on our part.

(Message to Congress, 4 December 1877)

Robert Y. Hayne (1791–1840): *Senator from South Carolina*

We deal in no abstractions. We will not look to enquire whether our fathers were guiltless in introducing slaves into the country. If an inquiry should ever be instituted in these matters, however, it will be found that the profits of the slave trade were not confined to the South. Southern ships and Southern sailors were not the instruments of bringing slaves to the shores of America, nor did our merchants reap the profits of the "accursed traffic." But, Sir, we will pass over all this.

(Speech in the Senate, 21 June 1830)

Sir, there does not exist on the face of the whole earth, a population so poor, so wretched, so vile, so loathsome, so utterly destitute of all the comforts, conveniences, and decencies of life, as the unfortunate blacks of Philadelphia and New York and Boston. Liberty has been to them the greatest of calamities, the heaviest of curses.

(Ibid.)

Will H. Hays (1879–1954): *Film industry "czar"*

This industry must have toward that sacred thing, the mind of a child, toward that clean virgin thing, that unmarked slate, the same responsibility, the same care about the impressions made upon it, that the best clergyman or the most inspired teacher of youth would have.

(Speech promulgating "Hays Code," 1934)

William D. Haywood (1869–1928): *Radical labor organizer*

Fellow workers, this is the Continental Congress of the working class.

(Greeting the Organizing Convention of the Industrial Workers of the World, 27 June 1905)

We are going down into the gutter to get at the mass of workers and bring them up to a decent plane of living.

(Ibid.)

The manager's brains are under the workman's cap.

(*International Socialist Review*, 1910)

To the working class there is no foreigner but the capitalist.

(Ibid.)

The IWW is socialism with its working clothes on.

(Testimony before the Industrial Relations Commission, 12 May 1915)

Can you conceive of anything that labor can not do if they were organized in one big union? If labor were organized and self-disciplined it could stop every wheel in the United States tonight— every one—and sweep off your capitalists and State legislatures and politicians into the sea.

(Ibid.)

These Russians attach the hell of a lot to *ideelogical* theory, and marking words, if they're not careful they'll come to blows about it one of these days. Don't you know that most of them would sooner talk than work, or even eat?

(Attributed by Walter Duranty, 1920s)

The barbarous gold barons. They did not find the gold, they did not mine the gold, they did not mill the gold, but by some weird alchemy all the gold belonged to them.

(Autobiography, 1927)

George Hearst (1820–1891): *Gold-mining magnate, senator from California*

I do not know much about books; I have not read very much; but I have travelled a good deal and have observed men and things and I have made up my mind after my experiences that the members of the Senate are the survivors of the fittest.

(Speech in the Senate, March 1887)

Here's to low-grade ore, and plenty of it.

(Toast at a banquet, San Francisco, 1890)

Patricia Hearst (1954–   ): *Heiress-kidnap victim-revolutionist-heiress*

Greetings to the People. This is Tania. . . . I'm a soldier in the People's army. *Patria o muerte . . . Venceremos.*

(Tape-recorded message to the world, April 1974)

William Randolph Hearst (1863–1951): *Newspaper publisher and politician*

Please remain. You furnish the pictures and I'll furnish the war.

(Cable to artist Frederic Remington, who asked to be recalled from Cuba because "There is no trouble here. There will be no war." March 1898)

Lillian Hellman (1905–   ): *Writer*

I cannot and will not cut my conscience to fit this year's fashions.

(Letter to House Un-American Activities Committee, 1952)

Ernest Hemingway (1898–1961): *Novelist*

All modern American literature comes from one book by Mark Twain called *Huckleberry Finn*.

(*The Green Hills of Africa*, 1935)

David Hendin (1945–   ): *Writer*

Death is simply un-American. Its inevitability is an affront to our inalienable rights to "life, liberty, and the pursuit of happiness."

(*Death as a Fact of Life*, 1973)

O. Henry (W. S. Porter) (1862–1910): *Short-story writer*

Made by a Dago . . . on behalf of the French . . . for the purpose of welcomin' Irish immigrants into the Dutch city of New York.

(On the Statue of Liberty, "The Lady Higher Up," *Sixes and Sevens*, 1911)

I guess I must have had New England ancestors away back and inherited some of their staunch and rugged fear of the police.

(Ibid.)

East is East, and West is San Francisco, according to Californians. Californians are a race of people; they are not merely inhabitants of a State.

(*A Municipal Report*, 1909)

If there ever was an aviary over-stocked with jays it is that Yap-town-on-the-Hudson called New York.

(*The Gentle Grafter*, 1920)

Patrick Henry (1736–1799): *Lawyer, revolutionary agitator*

Caesar had his Brutus: Charles the First, his Cromwell: and George III . . . ("Treason," the Speaker intervened) . . . may profit by their example. If *this* be treason, make the most of it.

(Speech to the Virginia House of Delegates, 1765)

Is life so dear or peace so sweet, as to be purchased at the price of chains and slavery? Forbid it, Almighty God! I know not what course others may take, but as for me, give me liberty or give me death!

(Speech to the Virginia House of Delegates, 23 March 1775)

I am not a Virginian, but an American.
>   (Speech to the First Continental Congress, 5 September 1774)

Brewster Higley (1823–1911): *Physician and songwriter*

> Oh, give me a home where the buffalo roam,
> Where the deer and the antelope play.
> Where seldom is heard a discouraging word
> And the skies are not cloudy all day.

("Home on the Range," 1873)

Joe Hill (Joel Haaglund) (1879–1915): *Swedish-born songwriter and labor martyr*

> Long haired preachers come out every night,
> Try to tell you what's wrong and what's right;
> But when asked 'bout something to eat
> They will answer with voices so sweet:
>   You will eat, bye and bye,
>   In that glorious land above the sky;
>   Work and pray, live on hay,
>   You'll get pie in the sky when you die.
>
> Workingmen of all countries, unite,
> Side by side we for freedom will fight;
> When the world and its wealth we have gained
> To the grafters we'll sing this refrain:
>   You will eat, bye and bye,
>   When you've learned how to cook and to fry.
>   Chop some wood, t'will do you good,
>   And you'll eat in the sweet bye and bye.

("The Preacher and the Slave," from *Songs to Fan the Flames of Discontent*, [The *Little Red Songbook*], 1911)

The workers said to Casey: "Won't you help us win this strike?"
But Casey said: "Let me alone, you'd better take a hike."
Then someone put a bunch of railroad ties across the track,
And Casey hit the river bottom with an awful crack.

Casey Jones went to Hell a-flying.
"Casey Jones," the devil said, "Oh fine:
Casey Jones get busy shoveling sulphur;
That's what you get for scabbing on the S.P. line."

>   ("The Union Scab," from *Songs to Fan the Flames of Discontent* [the
>   *Little Red Songbook*], 1912)

Goodbye Bill: I die like a true rebel. Don't waste
any time mourning—organize! It is a hundred miles
from here to Wyoming. Could you arrange to have my
body hauled to the state line to be buried? I don't
want to be found dead in Utah.

(Telegram to Big Bill Haywood, on the eve of his execution, 18
November 1915)

David Hilliard (1942–   ): *Black youth leader*

Everyone knows that pigs are depraved traducers that violate the
lives of human beings and that there ain't nothing wrong with taking
the life of a motherfucking pig.

(Speech at Yale University, 21 April 1970)

Sidney Hillman (1887–1946): *Labor leader*

Politics is the science of who gets what, when, and why.

(*Political Primer for All Americans*, 1944)

Morris Hillquit (1869–1933): *Socialist leader*

The Socialist Party of the United States in the present great crisis solemnly reaffirms its allegiance to the principle of interna-
tionalism and working class solidarity the world over, and proclaims
its unalterable opposition to the war just declared by the government of the United States.

(Resolution adopted at Saint Louis, April 1917)

Hirohito (1901–   ): *Emperor of Japan*

We have resolved to endure the unendurable and suffer what is
insufferable.

(After the atomic attack on Hiroshima, August 1945)

Adolf Hitler (1889–1945): *German Nazi dictator*

I can only be grateful to Providence that it entrusted me with
the leadership in this historic struggle, which, for the next five hundred or a thousand years, will be described as decisive, not only for
the history of Germany but for the whole of Europe and indeed the
whole world. A historical revision on a unique scale has been im-
posed on us by the Creator.

(Speech declaring war on the United States, December 1941)

George Frisbie Hoar (1826–1904): *Senator from Massachusetts*

The men who do the work of piety and charity in our churches . . . the men who own and till their own farms . . . the men who went to war . . . and saved the nation's honor . . . by the natural law of their being find their place in the Republican Party. While the old slave owner and slave driver, the saloon keeper, the ballot box stuffer . . . the criminal class of the great cities, the men who cannot read or write, by the natural law of their being find their congenial place in the Democratic Party.

(Speech in Boston, 1888)

Harold Hobson (1904–   ): *British critic*

The United States, I believe, are under the impression that they are twenty years in advance of this country; whilst, as a matter of actual verifiable fact, of course, they are just about six hours behind it.

(*The Devil in Woodford Wells,* 1948)

James "Jimmy" Hoffa (1913–?): *Labor leader*

I do unto others what they do unto me, only worse.

(Interview with reporters, 1957)

Eric Hoffer (1902–   ): *Popular philosopher*

To the intellectual, America's unforgivable sin is that it has revolutions without revolutionaries, and achieves the momentous in a matter-of-fact way.

(Syndicated newspaper column, 9 February 1968)

Eisenhower sat on his ass and we were a thousand times better off.

(Interview in *People,* 16 January 1978)

Abbott "Abbie" Hoffman (1936–   ): *Leader of "the Yippies"*

They nominate a president and he eats the people. We nominate a president and the people eat him.

(On the nomination of a pig as Youth International Party presidential candidate, Chicago, August 1968)

You're a disgrace to the Jews.

> (Shouted at Judge Julius Hoffman at the "Chicago Seven" trial, September 1969)

Oliver Wendell Holmes (1809–1894): *Physician, poet, and wit*

One flag, one land, one head, one hand,
One Nation, evermore!

> ("Voyage of the Good Ship Union," 1862)

Thou, O my country, hast thy foolish ways,
Too apt to purr at every stranger's praise!

> ("An After-Dinner Poem," 1843)

It is a very curious fact that, with all our boasted "free and equal" superiority over the communities of the Old World, our people have the most enormous appetite for Old World titles of distinction.

> (*Over the Teacups*, 1891)

He comes from the Brahmin caste of New England. This is the harmless, inoffensive, untitled aristocracy.

> (Ibid.)

Boston State-house is the hub of the solar system. You couldn't pry that out of a Boston man if you had the tire of all creation straightened out for a crow-bar.

> (Ibid.)

Oliver Wendell Holmes, Jr. (1841–1935): *Supreme Court justice*

The law is the witness and external deposit of our moral life. Its history is the history of the moral development of the race.

> (Speech, Boston, 8 January 1897)

It would need more than the 19th Amendment to convince me that there are no differences between men and women, or that legislation cannot take those differences into account.

> (*Dissent in the Adkins Case*, 1922)

Herbert Hoover (1874–1964): *Thirty-first president*

We, through free and universal education, provide the training of the runners; we give to them an equal start; we provide in government the umpire in the race.

(*American Individualism*, 1922)

Our country has deliberately undertaken a great social and economic experiment, noble in motive and far-reaching in purpose.

(On Prohibition, letter to W. H. Borah, 28 February 1928)

We are challenged with a peacetime choice between the American system of rugged individualism and a European philosophy of diametrically opposed doctrines—doctrines of paternalism and state socialism.

(Speech in New York, 22 October 1928)

We are nearer today to the ideal of the abolition of poverty and fear from the lives of men and women than ever before in any land.

(Ibid.)

In no nation are the fruits of accomplishment more secure. . . . I have no fears for the future of our country. It is bright with hope.

(Inaugural address, 4 March 1929)

What our country needs is a good big laugh. If someone could get off a good joke every ten days, I think our troubles would be over.

(To newspapermen, 1931)

Older men declare war. But it is youth that must fight and die.

(Speech, Republican National Convention, Chicago, 27 June 1944)

There are no rules in such a game. Hitherto acceptable norms of human conduct do not apply.

(Hoover Commission Report on the Intelligence Community, 4 July 1954)

When we get sick, we want an uncommon doctor. If we have a construction job, we want an uncommon engineer. When we get into a war, we dreadfully want an uncommon admiral and an uncommon general. Only when we get into politics are we content with the common man.

(Attributed in his obituary, *New York Times*, 21 October 1964)

J. Edgar Hoover (1895–1972): *Director of the Federal Bureau of Investigation*

Justice is merely incidental to law and order.

(Attributed)

Edward House (1858–1938): *Confidant and adviser to President Woodrow Wilson*

Saturday was a remarkable day. . . . We actually got down to work at half past ten and finished remaking the map of the world as we would have it, at half past twelve o'clock.

(Diary, 1918)

Sam Houston (1793–1863): *President of the Republic of Texas, later governor*

There is not an American on earth but what loves land.

(Speech, 1848)

He is as cold as a lizard and as proud as Lucifer. What he touches shall not prosper.

(On Jefferson Davis, attributed)

Edgar Watson Howe (1853–1937): *Editor*

Americans detest all lies except lies spoken in public or printed lies.

(*Ventures in Common Sense*, 1919)

Julia Ward Howe (1819–1910): *Poet, reformer*

Mine eyes have seen the glory of the coming of the Lord;
He is trampling out the vintage where the grapes of
    wrath are stored;
He hath loosed the fateful lightning of His terrible swift
sword:
        His truth is marching on.
In the beauty of the lilies Christ was born across the sea,
With a glory in his bosom that transfigures you and me:

As he died to make men holy, let us die to make men free,
While God is marching on.
("The Battle Hymn of the Republic," 1861)

Elbert Hubbard (1859–1915): *Popular inspirational writer*

It is not book learning young men need, nor instruction about this and that, but a stiffening of the vertebrae which will cause them to be loyal to a trust, to act promptly, concentrate their energies, do a thing—"carry a message to Garcia."
("A Message to Garcia," 1899)

Charles Evans Hughes (1862–1948): *Chief justice of the Supreme Court*

We are under a Constitution, but the Constitution is what the judges say it is.
(Speech in Elmira, New York, 3 May 1907)

Hubert H. Humphrey (1911–1978): *Vice-president, 1965–1969*

There are not enough jails, not enough policemen, not enough courts to enforce a law not supported by the people.
(Speech at Williamsburg, Virginia, 1 May 1965)

Bunker Hunt (1926–   ): *Son of oilman millionaire*

A billion dollars is not what it used to be.
(Remark after failing to corner the world's silver, March 1980)

Robert Hutchins (1899–1977): *Educator*

We can put television in its proper light by supposing that Gutenberg's great invention had been directed at printing only comic books.
(Attributed)

Jesse Hutchinson, Jr. (1813–1853): *Forty-niner*

Then, ho, brothers, ho
To California go;
There's plenty of gold in the world we're told
On the banks of the Sacramento.
("Ho for California," 1848)

Thomas Hutchinson (1711–1780): *Governor of colonial Massachusetts*

A thirst for liberty seems to be the ruling passion not only of America but of the present age. In governments under arbitrary rule it may have a salutary effect but in governments where as much freedom is enjoyed as can consist with the ends of government it must work anarchy and confusion.

(Letter to John H. Hutchinson, 18 January 1769)

I am sensible that your favorite doctrine is received in all parts of the colonies, and in some of your writers we find positions as these: no act of Parliament can deprive us of the liberties of men, citizens, and British subjects; the supreme power cannot take from any man any part of his property without his consent in person or by representation. It seems to have been the grand point which some of these writers have had in view to captivate their readers with big sounding words. Examine these positions. Does not every change from a state of nature into government more or less deprive us of the rights we enjoyed as men? In Europe, governments in general breathe more of the spirit of Liberty. In Asia the climate or some other cause inclines to despotism. No prince in Asia has a right to deprive me of my natural liberty by compelling me to become his subject, but if for the sake of his protection I become or continue his subject, I have as much submitted my natural rights to his government there although I have parted with more of them as I should have done in Europe in what we call free governments. What this writer means by rights of citizens is very uncertain seeing you will scarce find any two cities in which they are just the same, and the rights of British subjects vary in every age and perhaps in every session of Parliament.

(On Locke's Second Treatise, Dialogue Between a European and an American Englishman, 1769)

I shall never see that there were just grounds for this revolt.

(Attributed, 1780)

I

John J. Ingalls (1833–1900): *Senator from Kansas*

The purification of politics is an iridescent dream. Government is force.

(Attributed, 1890)

Robert G. Ingersoll (1833–1899): *Republican orator and agnostic lecturer*

Like an armed warrior, like a plumed knight, James G. Blaine marched down the halls of the American Congress and threw his shining lance full and fair against the brazen foreheads of the defamers of his country and the maligners of his honor.

(Speech nominating James G. Blaine for the presidency, 15 June 1876)

In all ages, hypocrites, called priests, have put crowns upon the heads of thieves, called kings.

(*Prose-Poems and Selections*, 1844)

An honest God is the noblest work of man.

(Ibid.)

I am the inferior of any man whose rights I trample under foot.

(Ibid.)

In the republic of mediocrity, genius is dangerous.

(Ibid.)

Washington Irving (1783–1859): *Writer*

There was one species of government under which he had long groaned, and that was petticoat government.

(*Rip Van Winkle*, 1819)

Jemmy Madison—Oh, poor Jemmy, he is but a withered little applejohn.

(In conversation, 1812)

The almighty dollar, that great object of universal devotion throughout our land.

(*Creole Village*, 1837)

Speculation is the romance of trade, and casts contempt upon all its sober realities. It renders the stock-jobber a magician, and the exchange a region of enchantment.

(*Wolfert's Roost*, 1855)

J

Andrew Jackson (1767–1845): *Seventh president, 1829–1837*

The individual who refuses to defend his rights when called by his Government, deserves to be a slave, and must be punished as an enemy of his country and friend to her foe.

(Proclamation to the people of Louisiana, 21 September 1814)

The brave man inattentive to his duty, is worth little more to his country, than the coward who deserts her in the hour of danger.

(To troops at the battle of New Orleans, 8 January 1815)

In a country where offices are created solely for the benefit of the People, no one man has any more intrinsic right to official station than another. Offices were not established to give support to paticular men, at the public expense. No individual wrong is therefore done by removal, since neither appointment to, nor continuance in, office, is matter of right.

(April 1829)

I do not dislike your Bank any more than all banks. But ever since I read the history of the South Sea Bubble I have been afraid of banks.

(In conversation with Nicholas Biddle, 1829)

Our Federal Union: it must be preserved.

(Toast at Jefferson birthday celebration, in defiance of the nullifier, John C. Calhoun, 13 April 1830)

Humanity has often wept over the fate of the aborigines of this country, and Philanthropy has been busily employed in devising means to avert it, but its progress has never for a moment been arrested, and one by one have many powerful tribes disappeared from the earth. To follow to the tomb the last of his race and to tread on the graves of extinct nations excites melancholy reflections. But true philanthropy reconciles the mind to these vicissitudes as it does to the extinction of one generation to make room for another.

(Second annual address, 1830)

The bank, Mr. Van Buren, is trying to kill me, but I will kill it.

(To Martin Van Buren, 1832)

There are no necessary evils in government. Its evils exist only in its abuses.

(Veto of the Bank Bill, 10 July 1832)

Every man is equally entitled to protection by law; but when the laws undertake to add . . . artificial distinctions, to grant titles, gratuities, and exclusive privileges, to make the rich richer and the potent more powerful, the humble members of society—the farmers, mechanics, and laborers—who have neither the time nor the means of securing like favors to themselves, have a right to complain of the injustice of their government.

(Ibid.)

The wisdom of man never yet contrived a system of taxation that would operate with perfect equality.

(Proclamation to the people of South Carolina, 10 December 1832)

I consider, then, the power to annul a law of the United States, assumed by one State, incompatible with the existence of the

Union, contradicted expressly by the letter of the Constitution, unauthorized by its spirit, inconsistent with every principle on which it was founded, and destructive of the great object for which it was formed.

(Ibid.)

Helen Hunt Jackson (1830–1885): *Writer*

It makes little difference, however, where one opens the record of the history of the Indians; every page and every year has its dark stain. The story of one tribe is the story of all, varied only by differences of time and place; but neither time nor place makes any difference in the main facts. Colorado is as greedy and unjust in 1880 as was Georgia in 1830, and Ohio in 1795; and the United States Government breaks promises now as deftly as then, and with added ingenuity from long practice.

(*A Century of Dishonor*, 1881)

Thomas J. "Stonewall" Jackson (1824–1863): *Confederate general*

Let us cross over the river and rest under the shade of the trees.

(Last words, 4 May 1863)

James I (1566–1625): *King of England*

A custom loathsome to the eye, harmful to the brain, dangerous to the lungs, and in the black stinking fume thereof, nearest resembling the horrible Stygian smoke of the pit that is bottomless.

(*Counterblaste to Tobacco*, 1604)

Henry James (1843–1916): *American-born novelist*

We are Americans born–*il faut en prendre son parti*. I look upon it as a great blessing; and I think that to be an American is an excellent preparation for culture. We have exquisite qualities as a race, and it seems to me that we are ahead of the European races in the fact that more than either of them we can deal freely with forms of civilization not our own, can pick and choose and assimilate and in short claim our property wherever we find it.

(Letter to Thomas Perry, 20 September 1867)

One might enumerate the items of high civilization, as it exists in other countries, which are absent from the texture of American life, until it should become a wonder to know what was left. No State, in the European sense of the word, and indeed barely a significant national name. No sovereign, no court, no personal loyalty, no aristocracy, no church, no clergy, no army, no diplomatic service, no country gentlemen, no palaces, no castles . . . nor ivied ruins; no cathedrals, nor abbeys, nor little Norman churches; no great Universities nor public schools—no Oxford, nor Eton, nor Harrow, no literature, no novels, no museums, no pictures, no political society, no sporting class—No Epsom nor Ascot!
(Life of Nathaniel Hawthorne, 1879)

It takes a great deal of history to produce a little literature.
(Ibid.)

He was unperfect, unfinished, inartistic; he was worse than provincial—he was parochial.
(On Thoreau, ibid.)

William James (1842–1910): *Philosopher*
A symptom of the moral flabbiness born of the exclusive worship of the bitch-goddess SUCCESS.
(Letter to H. G. Wells, 1906)

Randall Jarrell (1914–1965): *British writer*
To Americans English manners are far more frightening than none at all.
(Pictures from an Institution, 1954)

European and Americans are like men and women: they understand each other worse, and it matters less, than either of them suppose.
(Ibid.)

You Americans do not rear children: you incite them; you give them food and shelter and applause.
(Ibid.)

Thomas Jefferson (1743–1826): *Third president, 1801–1809*

We hold these truths to be sacred and undeniable; that all men are created equal and independent, that from that equal creation they derive rights inherent and inalienable, among which are the preservation of life, and liberty, and the pursuit of happiness.

(Original draft for the Declaration of Independence, June 1776)

When, in the course of human events, it becomes necessary for one people to dissolve the political bands which have connected them with another, and to assume among the powers of the earth the separate and equal station to which the laws of nature and of nature's God entitle them, a decent respect to the opinions of mankind requires that they should declare the causes which impel them to the separation. We hold these truths to be self-evident; that all men are created equal; that they are endowed by their creator with certain unalienable rights; that among these are life, liberty, and the pursuit of happiness; that to secure these rights, governments are instituted among men, deriving their just powers from the consent of the governed; that whenever any form of government becomes destructive to these ends, it is the right of the people to alter or to abolish it, and to institute new government, laying its foundation on such principles, and organizing its powers in such form, as to them shall seem most likely to effect their safety and happiness.

(Declaration of Independence, 4 July 1776)

The whole commerce between master and slave is a perpetual exercise of the most boisterous passions, the most unremitting despotism on the one part, and degrading submissions on the other. Our children see this, and learn to imitate it; for man is an imitative animal. . . . The parent storms, the child looks on, catches the lineaments of wrath, puts on the same airs in the circle of smaller slaves, gives a loose to the worst of passions, and thus nursed, educated and daily exercised in tyranny, cannot but be stamped by it with odious peculiarities. The man must be a prodigy who can retain his manners and morals undepraved by such circumstances.

(Notes on the State of Virginia, 1784)

I tremble for my country when I reflect that God is just; that his justice cannot sleep forever; that considering numbers, nature and natural means only, a revolution of the wheel of fortune, an ex-

change of situation is among possible events; that it may become probable by super-natural interference.
(Ibid.)

Those who labor in the earth are the chosen people of God, if He ever had a chosen people, whose breasts He has made His peculiar deposit for substantial and genuine virtue.
(Ibid.)

While we have land to labor then, let us never wish to see our citizens occupied at a work-bench, or twirling a distaff. . . . For the general operations of manufacture, let our workshops remain in Europe. . . . The mobs of great cities add just so much to the support of pure government, as sores do to the strength of the human body.
(Ibid.)

Every government degenerates when trusted to the rulers of the people alone. The people themselves therefore are its only safe depositories.
(Ibid.)

The genius of architecture seems to have shed its maledictions over this land.
(Ibid.)

I hold it, that a little rebellion, now and then, is a good thing, and as necessary in the political world as storms in the physical.
(Letter to James Madison, 30 January 1787)

State a moral case to a ploughman and a professor. The former will decide it as well, and often better than the latter, because he has not been led astray by artificial rules.
(Letter to Peter Carr, 10 August 1787)

The tree of liberty must be refreshed from time to time with the blood of patriots and tyrants. It is its natural manure.
(Letter to W. S. Smith, 13 November 1787)

What country can preserve its liberties, if its rulers are not warned from time to time, that this people preserve the spirit of resistance?
(Ibid.)

There shall be neither slavery nor involuntary servitude in the said territory, otherwise than in the punishment of crimes whereof the party shall have been duly convicted.

(Northwest Ordinance, 1787)

There is not a single crowned head in Europe whose talents or merits would entitle him to be elected a vestryman by the people of any parish in America.

(Letter to George Washington, from Paris, 2 May 1788)

The republican is the only form of government which is not eternally at open or secret war with the rights of mankind.

(Letter to William Hunter, 11 March 1790)

Offices are as acceptable here as elsewhere, and whenever a man has cast a longing eye on them, a rottenness begins in his conduct.

(Letter to Tench Coxe, 21 May 1799)

I have sworn upon the altar of God, eternal hostility against every form of tyranny over the mind of men.

(Letter to Benjamin Rush, 23 September 1800)

Sometimes it is said that man can not be trusted with the government of himself. Can he, then, be trusted with the government of others? Or have we found angels in the forms of kings to govern him? Let history answer this question.

(First inaugural address, 4 March 1801)

We are all Republicans—we are all Federalists. If there be any among us who would wish to dissolve this Union or to change its republican form, let them stand undisturbed as monuments of the safety with which error of opinion may be tolerated where reason is left free to combat it.

(Ibid.)

Error of opinion may be tolerated when reason is left free to combat it.

(Ibid.)

Peace, commerce and honest friendship with all nations, entangling alliances with none.

(Ibid.)

A respectable minority is useful as censors.
(Letter to Joel Barlow, 3 May 1802)

Though written constitutions may be violated in moments of passion or delusion, yet they furnish a text to which those who are watchful may again rally and recall the people; they fix too for the people the principles of their political creed.
(Letter to Joséph Priestley, 19 July 1802)

General Washington set the example of voluntary retirement after eight years. I shall follow it, and a few more precedents will oppose the obstacle of habit to anyone after a while who shall endeavor to extend his term. Perhaps it may beget a disposition to establish it by an amendment to the Constitution.
(1805)

The man who never looks into a newspaper is better informed than he who reads them; inasmuch as he who knows nothing is nearer to truth than he whose mind is filled with falsehood and errors.
(Letter to John Norvell, 11 June 1807)

When a man assumes a public trust, he should consider himself as public property.
(Remark to Baron von Humboldt, 1807)

The care of human life and happiness, and not their destruction, is the first and only legitimate object of good government.
(To the Republican citizens of Washington County, Maryland, 1809)

The only orthodox object of the institution of government is to secure the greatest degree of happiness possible to the general mass of those associated under it.
(Letter to F. A. Van Der Kamp, 22 March 1812)

There is a natural aristocracy among men. The grounds of this are virtue and talent.
(Letter to John Adams, 28 October 1813)

Merchants have no country. The mere spot they stand on does not constitute so strong an attachment as that from which they draw their gains.

(Letter to Horatio G. Spafford, 17 March 1814)

Enlighten the people generally, and tyranny and oppressions of body and mind will vanish like evil spirits at the dawn of day.

(Letter to Du Pont de Nemours, 24 April 1816)

Some men look at constitutions with sanctimonious reverence and deem them like the ark of the covenant, too sacred to be touched.

(Letter to Samuel Kercheval, 12 July 1816)

Laws and institutions must go hand in hand with the progress of the human mind.

(Ibid.)

I thank you for your information on the progress and prospects of the Missouri question. It is the most portentous one which ever yet threatened our Union. In the gloomiest moment of the revolutionary war I never had any apprehension equal to what I feel from this source.

(Letter to John Adams, 22 April 1820)

But this momentous question, like a firebell in the night awakened and filled me with terror. I considered it the knell of the Union.

(On the introduction of the morality of slavery into the congressional debate on the admission of Missouri, Letter to John Holmes, 22 April 1820)

Our first and fundamental maxim should be never to entangle ourselves in the broils of Europe. Our second, never to suffer Europe to intermeddle with cis-Atlantic affairs.

(Letter to James Monroe, 24 October 1823)

The sickly, weakly, timid man fears the people, and is a Tory by nature.

(Letter to Lafayette, 4 November 1823)

Men by their constitutions are naturally divided into two parties: 1) Those who fear and distrust the people, and wish to draw all powers from them into the hands of the higher classes. 2) Those who identify themselves with the people, have confidence in them, cherish and consider them as the most honest and safe, although not the most wise depository of the public interests. In every country these two parties exist; and in every one where they are free to think, speak, and write, they will declare themselves.

(Letter to Henry Lee, 10 August 1824)

Is this the Fourth?

(Last words, 4 July 1826)

Rebellion to tyrants is obedience to God.

(Motto on his seal)

William Jenner (1908–1962): *Senator from Indiana*

General Marshall is not only willing, he is eager to play the role of a front man, for traitors.

The truth is this is no new role for him, for Gen. George C. Marshall is a living lie . . . unless he himself was desperate, he could not possibly agree to continue as an errand boy, a front man, a stooge, or a co-conspirator for this administration's crazy assortment of collectivist, cutthroat crackpots and Communist fellow-traveling appeasers. . . .

(Speech in the Senate opposing George Marshall's nomination as secretary of defense, 1947)

Arthur Jensen (1923–   ): *Scientist and educational theorist*

The orthodox environmental theories have been accepted not because they have stood up under proper scientific investigations but because they harmonize so well with our democratic belief in human equality.

(*Educational Differences*, 1973)

Andrew Johnson (1808–1875): *Seventeenth president, 1865–1869*

Damn the negroes. I am fighting these traitorous aristocrats, their masters.

(Remark in conversation, 1863)

What will the aristocrats do, with a railsplitter for President, and a tailor for Vice President.

> (Attributed, November 1864)

It is not promulgating anything that I have not heretofore said that traitors must be made odious, that treason must be made odious, that traitors must be punished and impoverished.

> (Speech in Washington, 21 April 1865)

We are swinging 'round the circle.

> (Describing his disastrous speaking tour in opposition to the Radical Republicans, August 1866)

Let them impeach and be damned.

> (On hearing that the House had voted to impeach him, 24 February 1868)

Lyndon B. Johnson (1908–1973): *Thirty-sixth president, 1963–1969*

I hate war. And if the day ever comes when my vote must be cast to send your boy to the trenches, that day Lyndon Johnson will leave his Senate seat to go with him.

> (Speech during unsuccessful campaign for the Senate from Texas, September 1941)

Boys, I may not know much, but I know chicken shit from chicken salad.

> (On Richard M. Nixon's "Checkers" Speech, 24 September 1952)

In this age when there can be no losers in peace and no victors in war—we must recognize the obligation to match national strength with national restraint.

> (Address to Congress, 26 November 1963)

I don't believe the President of the United States ought to debate with anybody.

> (Speech, Washington, 15 December 1963)

Well, it's probably better to have him inside the tent pissing out than outside pissing in.

> (On deciding to retain J. Edgar Hoover as director of the FBI, 1964)

On every continent and in every land to which Mrs. Johnson and I travelled, we found faith and hope toward this land of America and toward our people.

(Speech, Washington, 8 January 1964)

For the first time in our history it is possible to conquer poverty.

(Speech, March 1964)

Every night when I go to bed I ask myself: what did we do today that we can point to for generations to come, to say that we laid the foundation for a better and more peaceful and more prosperous world?

(Speech, Washington, 21 April 1964)

I'm the only President you've got.

(Press conference, 27 April 1964)

So I ask you tonight to join me and march along the road to the future, the road that leads to the Great Society.

(Speech, New York, 28 May 1964)

Our one desire—our one determination—is that the people of Southeast Asia be left in peace to work out their own destinies in their own way.

(Statement, Washington, 10 August 1964)

The Congress approves and supports the determination of the President, as Commander in Chief, to take all necessary measures to repel any armed attack against the forces of the United States and to prevent further aggression.

(Tonkin Gulf Resolution, August 1964)

We don't want our American boys to do the fighting for Asian boys. We don't want to get involved in a nation with 700 million people and get tied down in a land war in Asia.

(Speech, Eufaula, Oklahoma, 25 September 1964)

But we are not about to send American boys nine or ten thousand miles away from home to do what Asian boys ought to be doing for themselves.

(Speech, Akron, 21 October 1964)

I just knew in my heart that it was not right for Dick Nixon to ever be President of this country.

> (Speech, Pittsburgh, 27 October 1964)

I've been kissing asses all my life and I don't have to kiss them any more.

> (In conversation with George Ready after his decisive election as president, November 1964)

I am going to build the kind of nation that President Roosevelt hoped for, President Truman worked for and President Kennedy died for.

> (Speech, December 1964)

A President's hardest task is not to do what is right, but to know what is right.

> (State of the Union Message, 4 January 1965)

Poverty has many roots, but the tap root is ignorance.

> (Message to Congress, 12 January 1965)

The guns and the bombs, the rockets and the warships, are all symbols of human failure. They are necessary symbols. They protect what we cherish. But they are witness to human folly.

> (Speech in Baltimore, 7 April 1965)

Their cause must be our cause too. Because it is not just Negroes, but really it is all of us, who must overcome the crippling legacy of bigotry and injustice. And we shall overcome.

As a man whose roots go deeply into Southern soil I know how agonizing racial feelings are. I know how difficult it is to reshape the attitudes and the structure of our society.

But a century has passed, more than a hundred years, since the Negro was freed. And he is not fully free tonight.

> (Address on voting rights, 6 August 1965)

The vote is the most powerful instrument ever devised by man for breaking down injustice and destroying the terrible walls which imprison men because they are different from other men.

> (Ibid.)

Until justice is blind to color, until education is unaware of race, until opportunity is unconcerned with the color of men's skins, emancipation will be a proclamation but not a fact.
> (Ibid.)

I do not genuinely believe that there's any single person in the world that wants peace as much as I want it.
> (Speech, Chicago, 17 May 1966)

There will be some Nervous Nellies and some who will become frustrated and bothered and break ranks under the strain. And some will turn on their leaders and on their country and on our fighting men.
> (Ibid.)

Come home with that coonskin on the wall.
> (Speech to troops, Cam Ranh Bay, Vietnam, 1966)

That's the ugliest thing I ever saw.
> (To painter Peter Hurd on his official presidential portrait, 6 January 1967)

Your daddy may go down in history as having started World War III.
> (To his daughter, May 1967)

When a great ship cuts through the sea, the waters are always stirred and troubled. And our ship is moving—moving through troubled new waters, toward new and better shores.
> (State of the Union Message, 17 January 1968)

I seldom think of politics more than eighteen hours a day.
> (In conversation, attributed)

While you're trying to save your face, you're losing your ass.
> (Ibid.)

Eisenhower told me never to trust a Communist.
> (Ibid.)

I never trust a man unless I've got his pecker in my pocket.
>   (Ibid.)

I am the king. I am the king.
>   (Striding down the aisle of the presidential plane, attributed)

I'll never get credit for anything I do in foreign policy because I didn't go to Harvard.
>   (Attributed)

Jerry Ford is so dumb that he can't fart and chew gum at the same time.
>   (Attributed)

Samuel Johnson (1709–1784): *English writer*
How is it that we hear the loudest yelps for liberty among the drivers of negroes?
>   ("Taxation No Tyrrany," 1775)

They are a race of convicts, and ought to be thankful for anything we allow them short of hanging.
>   (On Americans, attributed by Boswell, 21 March 1775)

I am willing to love all mankind, except an American.
>   (Ibid., 15 April 1778)

A nation scattered in the boundless regions of America resembles rays diverging from a focus. All the rays remain but the heat is gone.
>   (Ibid., 1783)

Al Jolson (1886–1950): *Entertainer*
You ain't heard nothin' yet, folks.
>   (Remark in the first talking film, *The Jazz Singer*, July 1927)

Jenkin Lloyd Jones (1911–   ): *Newspaper columnist*
We are drowning our youngsters in violence, cynicism and sadism piped into the living room and even the nursery. The grandchildren of the kids who used to weep because the Little Match Girl

froze to death now feel cheated if she isn't slugged, raped and thrown into a Bessemer converter.

Jim Jones (1931–1978): *Religious leader, self-styled revolutionary*

It is beautiful to die.

(Sermon to cult members, Jonestown, Guiana, November 1978)

John Paul Jones (1747–1792): *Scotland-born naval commander*

I have not yet begun to fight!

(To Captain Pearson of H.M.S. *Serapis* when asked if he was prepared to surrender at the battle off Flamborough, 25 September 1779)

I have not drawn my sword in our glorious cause for hire, but in support of the dignity of human nature and the divine feelings of philanthropy. I hoisted with my own hands the flag of freedom the first time it was displayed on board the *Alfred* in the Delaware; and I have attended it ever since with veneration on the ocean.

(Remark to Samuel Huntington, 1780)

I hope you will be convinced that in the British prints I have been censured unjustly. I was, indeed, born in Britain, but I do not inherit the degenerate spirit of that fallen nation, which I at once lament and despise. It is far beneath one to reply to their hirely invectives. They are strangers to the inward approbation that greatly . . . rewards the man who draws his sword only in support of the dignity of freedom.

(Attributed)

LeRoi Jones (1934–   ): *Writer and agitator*

If you are black the only roads into the mainland of American life are through subservience, cowardice, and loss of manhood. These are the white man's roads.

(*Home*, 1966)

A rich man told me recently that a liberal is a man who tells other people what to do with their money.

(Ibid.)

Chief Joseph (c. 1840–1904): *Nez Percé chieftan*

I am tired of fighting. Our chiefs are killed. Looking Glass is dead. The old men are all killed. It is the young men who say yes or no. He who led the young men is dead. The little children are freezing to death. My people, some of them, have run away to the hills and have no blankets, no food; no one knows where they are, perhaps freezing to death. I want time to look for my children and see how many of them I can find. Hear me, my chiefs, I am tired; my heart is sick and sad. From where the sun now stands, I will fight no more forever.

(To his beleaguered band before he surrendered, 5 October 1877)

I have carried a heavy load on my back ever since I was a boy. I learned then that we were but few, while the white men were many, and that we could not hold our own with them. We were like deer. They were like grizzly bears. We had a small country. Their country was large. We were contented to let things remain as the Great Spirit Chief made them. They were not; and would change the rivers and mountains if they did not suit them.

(Quoted in the *North American Review*, 1879)

K

Peter Kalm (1716–1779): *Swedish naturalist*

I have been told by Englishmen . . . that the English colonies in North America, in the space of thirty or fifty years, would be able to form a state by themselves, entirely independent of Old England. But as the whole country which lies along the sea-shore is unguarded, and on the land side is harassed by the French, in times of war these dangerous neighbors are sufficient to prevent the connection of the colonies with their mother country from being quite broken off. The English government has therefore sufficient reason to consider the French in North America as the best means of keeping their colonies in due submission.

(*En Resa til Norra Amerika*, 1749)

Kenneth B. Keating (1901–1975): *Senator from New York*

Roosevelt proved a man could be president for life; Truman proved anybody could be president; Eisenhower proved you don't need to have a president.

(Speech, 1955)

Too often our Washington reflex is to discover a problem and then throw money at it, hoping it will somehow go away.

(Interview with reporters, *New York Times,* 24 December 1961)

John Keats (1920–   ): *Writer*

The automobile changed our dress, manners, social customs, vacation habits, the shape of our cities, consumer purchasing patterns, common tastes, and positions in intercourse.

(*The Insolent Chariots*, 1958)

Walt Kelly (1913–1973): *Cartoonist*

We have met the enemy and they are us.

(In his comic strip, "Pogo," 1953)

Murray Kempton (1918–   ): *Journalist*

It is a measure of the Negro's circumstance that, in America, the smallest things usually take him so very long, and that, by the time he wins them, they are no longer little things: they are miracles.

(*Part of Our Time*, 1955)

A neighborhood is where, when you go out of it, you get beat up.

(*America Comes of Middle Age*, 1963)

The faces in New York remind me of people who played a game and lost.

(Ibid.)

There are things a man must not do even to save a nation.

(Ibid.)

As an organized political group, the Communists have done nothing to damage our society a fraction as much as what their enemies have done in the name of defending us against subversion.

(Ibid.)

The genius of our politics is the art of distracting the resentments of a cheated middle class and letting them fall upon a worse-cheated lower class.

(*New York Review of Books*, 19 February 1981)

John Kendrick (?–?): *Radical journalist*

Onward Christian soldiers! Duty's way is plain;
Slay your Christian neighbors, or by them be slain.
Pulpiteers are spouting effervescent swill,
God above is calling you to rob and rape and kill,
All your acts are sanctified by the Lamb on high;
If you love the Holy Ghost, go murder, pray and die.

("Christians at War," 1915)

Kenneth Keniston (1930–   ): *Psychologist*

I see little likelihood of American students ever playing a radical role, much less a revolutionary one, in our society.

(*The Uncommitted*, 1962)

George Kennan (1904–   ): *Diplomat*

The main element of any United States policy toward the Soviet Union must be that of a long-term, patient but firm and vigilant containment of Russian expansive tendencies.

("Sources of Soviet Conduct," the "X article," *Foreign Affairs*, July 1947)

It is clear that the United States cannot expect in the foreseeable future to enjoy political intimacy with the Soviet regime. It must continue to regard the Soviet Union as a rival, not a partner, in the political arena. It must continue to expect that Soviet policies will reflect no abstract love of peace and stability, no real faith in the possibility of a permanent happy coexistence of the Socialist and capitalist worlds.

(Ibid.)

Andrew Kennedy (1810–1847): *Congressman from Indiana*

Where shall we find room for all our people, unless we have Oregon? What shall we do with all those little white-headed boys and girls—God bless them!—that cover the Mississippi Valley, as the flowers cover the western prairies?

(Speech in Congress, 1844)

Edward M. Kennedy (1932–   ): *Senator from Massachusetts*

Like my brothers before me, I pick up a fallen standard. Sustained by the memory of our priceless years together, I shall try to carry forward that special commitment to justice, to excellence, and to courage that distinguished their lives.

(Speech, 21 August 1968)

What is striking about America today is that regardless of income, all of us are losing control over the quality of our lives. None of us can run away from air pollution, water pollution, and noise pollution. None of us can escape shoddy and unsafe products.

(Speech, 24 September 1970)

One of the saddest ironies in the worldwide movement for social justice in the twentieth century is that America now stands virtually alone in the international community on national health insurance. It seems that every nation is out of step but Uncle Sam. With the sole exception of South Africa, no other industrial nation in the world leaves its citizens in fear of financial ruin because of illness.

(Speech, 9 December 1978)

John F. Kennedy (1917–1963): *Thirty-fifth president, 1961–1963*

Only in the case of the Negro has the melting pot failed to bring a minority into the full stream of American life.

(*A Nation of Immigrants*, 1958)

When written in Chinese, the word "crisis" is composed of two characters—one represents danger and the other represents opportunity.

(Address, United Negro College Fund Convocation, 12 April 1959)

The American, by nature, is optimistic. He is experimental, an inventor and a builder who builds best when called upon to build greatly.

> (Speech in Washington announcing candidacy for the presidency, 1 January 1960)

We stand today on the edge of a new frontier—the frontier of the 1960s—a frontier of unknown opportunities and perils—a frontier of unfulfilled hopes and threats.

> (Speech accepting Democratic presidential nomination, Los Angeles, 13 July 1960)

It is an unfortunate fact that we can secure peace only by preparing for war.

> (Speech in Seattle, 6 September 1960)

We hold the view that the people make the best judgment in the long run.

> (Speech in Greensboro, North Carolina, 17 September 1960)

We cannot be satisfied with things as they are. We cannot be satisfied to drift, to rest on our oars, to glide over a sea whose depths are shaken by subterranean upheavals.

> (Speech in Syracuse, New York, 29 September 1960)

If men and women are in chains, anywhere in the world, then freedom is endangered everywhere.

> (Pulaski Day statement, 2 October 1960)

Let the word go forth from this time and place, to friend and foe alike, that the torch has been passed to a new generation of Americans, born in this century, tempered by war, disciplined by a hard and bitter peace, proud of our ancient heritage, and unwilling to witness or permit the slow undoing of those human rights to which this nation has always been committed, and to which we are committed today at home and around the world.

> (Inaugural address, 20 January 1961)

Let every nation know, whether it wishes us well or ill, that we shall pay any price, bear any burden, meet any hardship, support any friend, oppose any foe, in order to assure the survival and the success of liberty.

> (Ibid.)

To those nations who would make themselves our adversary, we offer not a pledge but a request; that both sides begin anew the quest for peace, before the dark powers of destruction unleashed by science engulf all humanity in planned or accidental self-destruction.

So let us begin anew—remembering on both sides that civility is not a sign of weakness, and sincerity is always subject to proof. Let us never negotiate out of fear. But let us never fear to negotiate.

And so, my fellow Americans: ask not what your country can do for you—ask what you can do for your country. My fellow citizens of the world: ask not what America will do for you, but what together we can do for the freedom of man.

(Ibid.)

I believe that this nation should commit itself to achieving the goal, before this decade is out, of landing a man on the Moon and returning him safely to earth.

(Message to Congress, 25 May 1961)

When we got into office, the thing that surprised me most was to find that things were just as bad as we'd been saying they were.

(Speech at Washington, 27 May 1961)

Today every inhabitant of this planet must contemplate the day when this planet may no longer be habitable. Every man, woman and child lives under a nuclear sword of Damocles, hanging by the slenderest of threads, capable of being cut at any moment by accident or miscalculation or madness.

(Address to the United Nations, New York, 25 September 1961)

Mankind must put an end to war or war will put an end to mankind.

(Ibid.)

Conformity is the jailer of freedom and the enemy of growth.

(Ibid.)

We will neglect our cities to our peril, for in neglecting them we neglect the nation.

(Message to Congress, 30 January 1962)

Washington is a city of Southern efficiency and Northern charm.

(Attributed in William Manchester, *Portrait of a President*, 1962)

We believe that when men reach beyond this planet, they should leave their national differences behind them.
(News conference, Washington, 21 February 1962)

I know that when things don't go well they like to blame the Presidents, and that is one of the things which Presidents are paid for.
(News conference, 14 June 1962)

We will not act prematurely or unnecessarily risk the costs of worldwide nuclear war in which even the fruits of victory would be ashes in our mouth. But neither will we shrink from that risk at any time it must be faced.
(Television address, 22 October 1962)

We shall be judged more by what we do at home than what we preach abroad.
(State of the Union Message, 14 January 1963)

Peace and freedom walk together. In too many of our cities to-day, the peace is not secure because freedom is incomplete.
(Speech at American University, Washington, 10 June 1963)

We seek not the worldwide victory of one nation or system but a worldwide victory of men.
(Ibid.)

There are no "white" or "colored" signs on the foxholes or grave-yards of battle.
(Message to Congress, 19 June 1963)

All free men, wherever they may live, are citizens of Berlin. And therefore, as a free man, I take pride in the words, *"Ich bin ein Berliner."*
(Speech in Berlin, June 1963)

The United States has to move very fast to even stand still.
(Remark at a press conference, July 1963)

We have the power to make this the best generation of mankind in the history of the world—or to make it the last.
(Speech to the United Nations, 20 September 1963)

In the final analysis it is their war. They are the ones who have to win it or lose it . . . the people of Vietnam.

(Remark at a press conference, September 1963)

I look forward to a great future for America—a future in which our country will match its military strength with our moral restraint, its wealth with our wisdom, its power with our purpose.

(Speech at Amherst College, Massachusetts, 26 October 1963)

It has recently been observed that whether I serve one or two terms in the Presidency, I will find myself at the end of that period at what might be called an awkward age—too old to begin a new career and too young to write my memoirs.

(Attributed)

If someone is going to kill me, they will kill me.

(Shortly before his final trip to Dallas, Texas, November 1963)

I don't think the intelligence reports are all that hot. Some days I get more out of the *New York Times*.

(Ibid.)

Joseph P. Kennedy (1889–1969): *Ambassador to Great Britain*

I do not want to see this country go to war under any conditions whatsoever unless we are attacked. . . . England is not fighting our battle. This is not our war.

(Speech in New York, 1940)

Robert F. Kennedy (1925–1968): *Attorney-general under President Kennedy and senator from New York*

Progress is a nice word. But change is its motivator. And change has its enemies.

(*The Pursuit of Justice,* 1964)

Justice delayed is democracy denied.

(Ibid.)

One fifth of the people are against everything all the time.

(Speech, 10 May 1964)

Mayor Daley is the ball game.

(On Chicago mayor Richard Daley's key role in Democratic Party politics, April 1968)

Jack Kerouac (1922–1969): *Writer*

Where we going, man?
I don't know, but we gotta go.

(*On the Road*, 1957)

Clark Kerr (1911–   ): *University and foundation president*

I find the three major administrative problems on a campus are sex for the students, athletics for the alumni, and parking for the faculty.

(Speech, November 1958)

Francis Scott Key (1779–1843): *Lawyer*

Oh, say can you see by the dawn's early light
  What so proudly we hailed at the twilight's last
    gleaming?
Whose broad stripes and bright stars, thro' the perilous
  fight,
  O'er the ramparts we watched were so gallantly
    streaming?
And the rockets' red glare, the bombs bursting in air,
  Gave proof thro' the night that our flag was still there.

Oh, say, does that star-spangled banner yet wave,
O'er the land of the free and the home of the brave?

(The national anthem, 1814)

Nikita Khrushchev (1894–1971): *Soviet political leader*

Whether or not you like it, history is on our side. We will bury you.

(Speech to Western diplomats, Kremlin, Moscow, 26 November 1956)

They talk about who won and who lost. Human reason won. Mankind won.

(On the Cuban crisis, November 1962)

Martin Luther King, Jr. (1929–1968): *Clergyman, civil rights leader*

I want to be the white man's brother, not his brother-in-law.
(Newspaper interview, 10 September 1962)

I have a dream that one day on the red hills of Georgia, the sons of former slaves and the sons of former slave-owners will be able to sit together at the table of brotherhood. I have a dream that one day even the State of Mississippi, a state sweltering with the heat of oppression, will be transformed into an oasis of freedom and justice. I have a dream that my four little children will one day live in a nation where they will not be judged by the color of their skin but by the content of their character. I have a dream . . .
(Speech to 200,000 civil rights demonstrators, Washington, 28 August 1963)

The church must be reminded that it is not the master or the servant of the state, but rather the conscience of the state.
(*Strength to Love*, 1963)

Success, recognition, and conformity are the bywords of the modern world where everyone seems to crave the anesthetizing security of being identified with the majority.
(Ibid.)

Morality cannot be legislated, but behavior can be regulated. Judicial decrees may not change the heart, but they can restrain the heartless.
(Ibid.)

Segregation is on its deathbed—the question now is, how costly will the segregationists make the funeral?
(Address, Villanova University, 20 January 1965)

Everyone is worrying about the long hot summer with its threat of riots.
(Speech, June 1967)

Probably the most destructive feature of Black Power is its unconscious and often conscious call for retaliatory violence. . . . The problem with hatred and violence is that they intensify the fears of the white majority and leave them less ashamed of their prejudices toward Negroes. In the guilt and confusion confronting our society, violence only adds to the chaos. It deepens the brutality of the oppressor and increases the bitterness of the oppressed. Violence is the antithesis of creativity and wholeness. It destroys community and makes brotherhood impossible.

(Where Do We Go From Here?, 1967)

Henry M. Kissinger (1923–): *Secretary of state under President Nixon*

Nothing is more difficult for Americans to understand than the possibility of tragedy.

(Quoted in *New York Times,* 28 October 1973)

We are all the President's men.

(Remark on the much-criticized invasion of Cambodia, April 1975)

The longer I am out of office, the more infallible I appear to myself.

(Remark to reporters, July 1979)

The superpowers often behave like two heavily armed blind men feeling their way around a room, each believing himself in mortal peril from the other, whom he assumes to have perfect vision.

(Observer, 30 September 1979)

I've always acted alone. Americans admire that enormously. Americans admire the cowboy leading the caravan alone on his horse, the cowboy entering a village or city alone on his horse.

(Interview with Oriana Fallaci, 1972)

Richard G. Kleindienst (1923–): *Attorney-general under President Nixon*

If people demonstrate in a manner to interfere with others, they should be rounded up and put in a concentration camp.

(Remark to reporters, 1972)

Louis Kronenberger (1904–   ): *Writer*

The compelling fact about art in America is that it is not organic. It has almost no share in shaping our life; it offers, rather, compensation for the shapelessness.

(*Company Manners*, 1954)

It is one of the sublime provincialities of New York that its inhabitants lap up trivial gossip about essential nobodies they've never set eyes on, while continuing to boast that they could live somewhere for twenty years without so much as exchanging pleasantries with their neighbors across the hall.

(Ibid.)

The trouble with us in America isn't that the poetry of life has turned to prose, but that it has turned to advertising copy.

(Ibid.)

Ours is the country where, in order to sell your product, you don't so much point out its merits as you first work like hell to sell yourself.

(Ibid.)

The American Way is so restlessly creative as to be essentially destructive; the American Way is to carry common sense itself almost to the point of madness.

(Ibid.)

Joseph Wood Krutch (1893–1970): *Popular philosopher*

Technology made large populations possible; large populations now make technology indispensable.

(*Human Nature and the Human Condition*, 1959)

The typical American believes that no necessity of the soul is free and that there are precious few, if any, which cannot be bought.

(*If You Don't Mind My Saying So*, 1964)

Stanley Kubrick (1928–   ): *Film producer*

The great nations have always acted like gangsters, and the small nations like prostitutes.

(Newspaper interview, 5 June 1963)

L

Marquis de Lafayette (1757–1834): *French revolutionary and officer in the Continental Army*
> The play is over. The fifth act has come to an end.
> (On British surrender at Yorktown, October 1783)

Fiorello La Guardia (1882–1947): *Mayor of New York City*
> Ticker tape ain't spaghetti.
> (Speech to United Nations, 29 March 1946)

Walter Savage Landor (1775–1864): *English writer*
> I detest the American character as much as you do.
> (Letter to Robert Southey, 1812)

Ralph Lane (1584–1650): *Governor of Virginia Colony*
> . . . we have discovered the maine to be the goodliest soile under the cope of heaven, so abounding with sweete trees, that bring such sundry rich and most pleasant gummes, grapes of such greatnes, yet wild, as France, Spaine nor Italy hath no greater. . . . Besides that, it is the goodliest and most pleasing territorie of the world (for the soile is of an huge and unknowen greatnesse, and very wel peopled and towned, though savagelie) and the climate so wholesome, that we have not had one sicke, since we touched the land here. To conclude, if Virginia had but Horses and Kine in some reasonable proportion, I dare assure my self being inhabited with English, no realme in Christendome were comparable to it.
> (Letter to Richard Hakluyt, 3 September 1585)

Sidney Lanier (1842–1881): *Poet*
> Long as thine art shall love true love,
> Long as they science truth shall know,

Long as thine eagle harms no dove,
   Long as they law by law shall grow,
Long as they God is God above,
   Thy brother every man below,
So long, dear land of all my love,
   Thy name shall shine, thy fame shall glow!
("The Centennial Meditation of Columbia," 1876)

Robert Cavelier, Sieur de La Salle (1643–1687): *French explorer*

I do now take, in the name of his Majesty and of his successors to the crown, possession of this country of Louisiana, the seas, harbours, ports, bays, adjacent straits, and all the nations, peoples, provinces, cities, towns, villages, mines, minerals, fisheries, streams and rivers, within the extent of the said Louisiana, from the mouth of the great river St. Louis, otherwise called the Ohio . . . as also along the river Colbert or Mississippi.

(Proclamation on reaching the mouth of the Mississippi, 9 April 1682)

James Lawrence (1781–1813): *Naval commander*

Don't give up the ship.

(Legendary orders as captain of U.S.S. *Chesapeake* in battle with H.M.S. *Shannon* when mortally wounded, 1 June 1813. In fact, his last words were, "Tell the men to fire faster and not give up the ship. Fight her till she sinks.")

Emma Lazarus (1849–1887): *Russian-born poet*

"Keep, ancient lands, your storied pomp!" cries she
With silent lips. "Give me your tired, your poor,
Your huddled masses yearning to breathe free,
The wretched refuse of your teeming shore.
Send these, the homeless, tempest-tost to me,
I lift my lamp beside the golden door!"

("The New Colossus," 1883; the final five lines are inscribed on the Statue of Liberty)

Timothy Leary (1920–   ): *Mind-expanding drugs advocate*

Tune in, turn on, drop out.

(Advice to the nation, late 1960s)

Mary Elizabeth "Mother" Lease (1853–1933): *Populist orator*
Raise less corn and more hell.
> (Advice to the farmers of Kansas, in many speeches, 1890–1896)

The people are at bay, let the bloodhounds of money beware.
> (Campaign speech, Wichita, Kansas, October 1894)

Henry Lee (1756–1818): *Revolutionary politician and soldier*
First in war, first in peace, first in the hearts of his countrymen.
> (Resolution in House of Representatives on the death of Washington, 26 December 1799)

Richard Henry Lee (1732–1794): *Revolutionary politician*
That these United Colonies are, and of right ought to be, free and independent states.
> (Motion in the Continental Congress, 7 June 1776)

Robert E. Lee (1807–1870): *Confederate commander*
Secession is nothing but revolution. . . . Still, a union that can only be maintained by swords and bayonets, and in which strife and civil war are to take the place of brotherly love and kindness, has no charm for me. If the Union is dissolved, the government disrupted, I shall return to my native state and share the miseries of my people. Save in her defense, I will draw my sword no more.
> (Letter to his son, January 1861)

It is well that war is so terrible, or we should grow too fond of it.
> (Remark to General James Longstreet at the Battle of Fredericksburg, 14 December 1862)

I have lost my right arm.
> (Upon hearing of the death of General Thomas J. "Stonewall" Jackson after the Battle of Chancellorsville, 10 May 1862)

Go home, all you boys who fought with me, and help to build up the shattered fortunes of our old state.
> (Address to Confederate troops after his surrender at Appomattox, 9 April 1865)

I should be trading on the blood of my men.
> (Refusing to write his memoirs, 1868)

Strike the tent.
> (Last words, 1870)

Curtis E. LeMay (1906–   ): *Air force chief of staff*

My solution? Tell the Vietnamese they've got to draw in their horns . . . or we're going to bomb them back into the Stone Age.
> (Remark to reporters, 6 May 1964)

Aldo Leopold (1886–1948): *Ecologist*

We abuse land because we regard it as a commodity belonging to us. When we see land as a community to which we belong, we may begin to use it with love and respect.
> (*Sand County Almanac*, published 1966)

Max Lerner (1902–   ): *Newspaper columnist*

In our culture we make heroes of the men who sit on top of a heap of money, and we pay attention not only to what they say in their field of competence, but to their wisdom on every other question in the world.
> (*Actions and Passions*, 1949)

There is no crime in the cynical American calendar more humiliating than to be a sucker.
> (Ibid.)

Some of the more fatuous flag-waving Americans are in danger of forgetting that you can't extract gratitude as you would extract a tooth; that unless friendship is freely given, it means nothing and less than nothing.
> (Ibid.)

If you mean by capitalism the God-given right of a few big corporations to make all the decisions that will affect millions of workers and consumers and to exclude everyone else from discussing and examining those decisions, then the unions are threatening capitalism.
> (Ibid.)

Action, swiftness, violence, power: these are native, homegrown American qualities, derived from the vast continent that has been ours to open up, and the big prizes that have made our economy into a jungle where the law is eat or be eaten.

(Ibid.)

America is a passionate idea or it is nothing. America is a human brotherhood or it is a chaos.

(Ibid.)

A world technology means either a world government or world suicide.

(Ibid.)

John L. Lewis (1880–1969): *Labor leader*

I'm not interested in classes. . . . Far be it from me to foster inferiority complexes among the workers by trying to make them think they belong to some special class. That has happened in Europe but it hasn't happened here yet.

(Remark to reporters, 1935)

At San Francisco they seduced me with fair words. Now, of course, having learned that I was seduced, I am enraged and I am ready to rend my seducers limb from limb.

(Speech at the Annual Convention of the American Federation of Labor announcing withdrawal of the industrial unionists, 1936)

The future of labor is the future of America.

(Labor Day address, September 1936)

Labor, like Israel, has many sorrows. Its women weep for their fallen and they lament for the future of the children of the race.

(Labor Day address, September 1937)

No tin-hat brigade of goose-stepping vigilantes or Bible-babbling mob of blackguarding and corporation-paid scoundrels will prevent the onward march of labor.

(*Time,* 9 September 1937)

You can't dig coal with bayonets.

(Testimony in Washington, 1 March 1956)

Sinclair Lewis (1885–1951): *Writer*

Intellectually I know that America is no better than any other country; emotionally I know she is better than every other country.

(Interview, Berlin, 29 December 1930)

On the whole, with scandalous exceptions, Democracy has given the ordinary worker more dignity than he ever had.

(*It Can't Happen Here*, 1935)

Cure the evils of Democracy with the evils of Fascism! Funny therapeutics! I've heard of their curing syphillis by giving the patient malaria, but I've never heard of their curing malaria by giving the patient syphillis.

(Ibid.)

A. J. Liebling (1904–1963): *Writer*

An Englishman teaching an American about food is like the blind leading the one-eyed.

(Attributed)

Lydia Kamehameha Liliuokalani (1838–1917): *Queen of Hawaii*

Hawaii for the Hawaiians.

(Motto of her reign, 1891)

Oh, honest Americans, as Christians hear me for my downtrodden people! Their form of government is as dear to them as yours is precious to you. Quite as warmly as you love your country, so they love theirs. With all your goodly possessions, . . . do not covet the little vineyard of Naboth's, so far from your shores.

(Appeal to the American people, 1893)

Abraham Lincoln (1809–1865): *Sixteenth president, 1861–1865*

If the good people in their wisdom shall see fit to keep me in the background, I have been too familiar with disappointments to be very much chagrined.

(Speech, Springfield, Illinois, 9 March 1832)

There is no grievance that is a fit object of redress by mob law.

(Speech in Springfield, Illinois, 27 January 1838)

If destruction be our lot we must ourselves be its author and finisher. As a nation of free men we must live through all time, or die by suicide.

(Ibid.)

A universal feeling, whether well or ill founded, cannot be safely disregarded.

(Speech in Peoria, Illinois, 16 October 1854)

No man is good enough to govern another man without that other's consent.

(Ibid.)

I am not a Know-Nothing; that is certain. How could I be? How can anyone who abhors the oppression of Negroes be in favor of degrading classes of white people? Our progress in degeneracy appears to me to be pretty rapid. As a nation we began by declaring that "all men are created equal, except Negroes." When the Know-Nothings get control, it will read "all men are created equal, except Negroes and foreigners and Catholics." When it comes to this, I shall prefer emigrating to some country where they make no pretense of loving liberty—to Russia, for instance, where despotism can be taken pure, and without the base alloy of hypocrisy.

(Letter to Joshua F. Speed, 24 August 1855)

The ballot is stronger than the bullet.

(Speech, 19 May 1856)

Moral principle is a looser bond than pecuniary interest.

(Speech, October 1856)

"A house divided against itself cannot stand." I believe this government cannot endure permanently half slave and half free. I do not expect the Union to be dissolved—I do not expect the house to fall—but I do expect it will cease to be divided. It will become all one thing, or all the other. Either the opponents of slavery will arrest the further spread of it, and place it where the public mind shall rest in the belief that it is in the course of ultimate extinction; or its advocates will push it forward till it shall become alike lawful in all the states, old as well as new, North as well as South.

(Speech in Springfield, Illinois, 16 June 1858)

As I would not be a *slave*, so I would not be a *master*. This expresses my idea of democracy. Whatever differs from this, to the extent of the difference, is no democracy.

(Fragment in his personal papers, 1 August 1858)

You can fool all the people some of the time, and some of the people all the time, but you cannot fool all the people all of the time.

(Speech in Clinton, Illinois, 8 September 1858)

When . . . you have succeeded in dehumanizing the Negro, when you have put him down and made it impossible for him to be but as the beasts in the field . . . are you quite sure that the demon you have roused will not turn and rend you?

(Speech in Edwardsville, Illinois, 11 September 1858)

Familiarize yourself with the chains of bondage and you prepare your own limbs to wear them.

(Ibid.)

That is the issue that will continue in this country when these poor tongues of Judge Douglas and myself shall be silent. It is the eternal struggle between these two principles—right and wrong—throughout the world. They are the two principles that have stood face to face from the beginning of time, and will ever continue to struggle.

(Speech, Alton, Illinois, 15 October 1858)

What is conservatism? Is it not adherence to the old and tried, against the new and untried?

(Speech, New York, 27 February 1860)

Let us have faith that right makes might, and in that faith let us to the end dare to do our duty as we understand it.

(Ibid.)

I am glad to see that a system of labor prevails in New England under which laborers can strike when they want to, where they are not obliged to work under all circumstances and are not tied down and obliged to labor whether you pay them or not.

(Speech in New Haven, Connecticut, 6 March 1860)

If we do not make common cause to save the good old ship of the Union on this voyage, nobody will have a chance to pilot her on another voyage.

(Speech in Cleveland, 15 February 1861)

I take the official oath to-day with no mental reservations, and with no purpose to construe the Constitution or laws by any hyper-critical rules.

(First inaugural address, 4 March 1861)

If by the mere force of numbers a majority should deprive a minority of any clearly written constitutional right, it might, in a moral point of view, justify revolution—certainly would if such a right were a vital one.

(Ibid.)

Why should there not be a patient confidence in the ultimate justice of the people? Is there any better or equal hope in the world?

(Ibid.)

Labor is prior to, and independent of, capital. Capital is only the fruit of labor, and could never have existed if labor had not first existed. Labor is the superior of capital, and deserves much the higher consideration. Capital has its rights, which are as worthy of protection as any other rights.

(First annual message to Congress, 3 December 1861)

I intend no modification of my oft-expressed personal wish that all men everywhere could be free.

(Letter to Horace Greeley, 22 August 1962)

My paramount object in this struggle is to save the Union, and is not either to save or destroy slavery. If I could save the Union without freeing any slave, I would do it; and if I could do it by freeing all the slaves, I would do it; and if I could save it by freeing some and leaving others alone, I would also do that.

(Ibid.)

I think to lose Kentucky is nearly the same as to lose the whole game. Kentucky gone, we cannot hold Missouri, nor, I think, Maryland. These all against us, and the job on our hands is too large for us. We would as well consent to separation at once, including the surrender of this capital.

(Remark in a cabinet meeting, September 1861)

I have just read your dispatch about sore-tongued and fatigued horses. Will you pardon me for asking what the horses of your army have done since the battle of Antietam that fatigues anything.

(Dispatch to General McClellan, 24 October 1862)

A nation may be said to consist of its territory, its people, and its laws. The territory is the only part which is of certain durability.

(Message to Congress, 1 December 1862)

Somewhat like the boy in Kentucky who stubbed his toe while running to see his sweetheart. The boy said he was too big to cry, and far too badly hurt to laugh.

(When asked his reaction to his party's loss of an election in New York, November 1862)

And by virtue of the power, and for the purpose aforesaid I do order and declare that all persons held as slaves within said designated States, and parts of States, are, and henceforward shall be free; and the Executive government of the United States, including the military and naval authorities thereof, will recognize and maintain the freedom of said persons.

(The Emancipation Proclamation, 1 January 1863)

I have heard, in such a way as to believe it, of your recently saying that both the Army and the Government need a Dictator. Of course it is not *for* this, but in spite of it, that I have given you the command. Only those generals who gain successes can set up dictators. What I now ask of you is military success, and I will risk the dictatorship.

(Letter appointing General Joseph Hooker commander of the Army of the Potomac, 26 January 1863)

We had them within our grasp. We had only to stretch forth our hands and they were ours. And nothing I could say or do could make the Army move.

(On the successful retreat of the Confederate Army after the Battle of Gettysburg, July 1863)

The Father of Waters again goes unvexed to the sea.

(On the Union Army's control of the Mississippi River, letter to James
C. Conkling, 26 August 1863)

I have endured a great deal of ridicule without much malice; and
have received a great deal of kindness, not quite free from ridicule.
I am used to it.

(Letter to James H. Hackett, 2 November 1863)

Fourscore and seven years ago our fathers brought forth, on this
continent, a new nation, conceived in Liberty, and dedicated to the
proposition that all men are created equal.

Now we are engaged in a great civil war, testing whether that
nation, or any nation so conceived, and so dedicated, can long endure. We are met on a great battlefield of that war. We have come
to dedicate a portion of that field, as a final resting-place for those
who here gave their lives, that that nation might live . . . that government of the people, by the people, for the people, shall not perish from the earth.

(The Gettysburg Address, 19 November 1863)

As we say out West, if a man can't skin he must hold a leg while
somebody else does.

(Remark after approving General Grant's strategy of moving armies
against all Confederate fronts simultaneously, February 1864)

I claim not to have controlled events, but confess plainly that
events have controlled me.

(Letter to A. G. Hodges, 4 April 1864)

The shepherd drives the wolf from the sheep's throat, for which
the sheep thanks the shepherd as his liberator, while the wolf de-
nounces him for the same act, as the destroyer of liberty, especially
as the sheep was a black one.

(Speech in Baltimore, 18 April 1864)

An old Dutch farmer remarked to a companion once that it was
not best to swap horses in mid-stream.

(Reply to the National Union League on the subject of his renomination for the presidency, 9 June 1864)

Get me the brand, and I'll send a barrel to my other generals.
> (Upon being told that General Grant drank too much whiskey, attributed)

With malice toward none, with charity for all, with firmness in the right as God gives us to see the right, let us finish the work we are in, to bind up the nation's wounds, to care for him who shall have borne the battle, and for his widow and for his orphans, to do all which may achieve and cherish a just and lasting peace among ourselves and with all nations.
> (Second inaugural address, 4 March 1865)

People who like this sort of thing will find this is the sort of thing they like.
> (Criticizing a book, attributed)

Important principles may and must be inflexible.
> (Speech in Washington, 11 April 1865)

Anne Morrow Lindbergh (1906–   ): *Writer*
America, which has the most glamorous present still existing in the world today, hardly stops to enjoy it, in her insatiable appetite for the future.
> (*Gift from the Sea*, 1955)

Charles A. Lindbergh, Jr. (1902–1974): *Celebrated aviator and isolationist leader*
Oriental guns are turning westward. Asia presses towards us on the Russian border.
> (*Readers Digest*, November 1939)

It is our turn to guard our heritage from Mongol, and Persian and Moor, before we become engulfed on a limitless foreign sea.
> (Ibid.)

The greatest danger of Jewish power lies in their ownership and influence in our motion pictures, our press, our radio, and our government.
> (Speech, 1940)

The three most important groups which are pressing this country toward war are the British, the Jewish, and the Roosevelt Administration.

(Speech in Des Moines, 11 September 1941)

Vachel Lindsay (1879–1931): *Poet*

Prairie avenger, mountain lion,
Bryan, Bryan, Bryan, Bryan.
Gigantic troubadour, speaking like a siege gun,
Smashing Plymouth Rock with his boulders from the West.

("Eagle Forgotten," 1914)

Where is Altgeld, brave as the truth,
Whose name the few still say with tears?
Gone to join the ironies with Old John Brown
Whose fame rings loud for a thousand years.

(Ibid.)

Walter Lippmann (1889–1974): *Writer and political adviser*

A pleasant man who, without any important qualifications for the office, would very much like to be President.

(Describing Franklin D. Roosevelt, June 1932)

We are a great country that over-reached itself and is out of breath.

(Interview, *Washington Post*, 23 October 1973)

William Livingston (1723–1790): *Lawyer, revolutionary leader in New York*

We want hands, my Lord, more than heads. The most intimate acquaintance with the classics will not remove our oaks; nor a taste for the *Georgics* cultivate our lands.

(Letter to the bishop of Llandaff, c. 1785)

Henry Demarest Lloyd (1847–1903): *Muckraker and reformer*

Our barbarians come from above. Our great money-makers have sprung in one generation into seats of power kings do not know. The forces and the wealth are new, and have been the opportunity of new men. Without restraints of culture, experience, the pride, or even the inherited caution of class or rank, these men, intoxicated, think they are the wave instead of the float, and that they have created the business which has created them.

They are gluttons of luxury and power, rough, unsocialized, believing that mankind must be kept terrorized.

(*Wealth Against Commonwealth,* 1894)

John Locke (1632–1704): *English philosopher*

In the beginning, all the world was America.

(Second Treatise on Government, 1690)

Henry Cabot Lodge (1850–1924): *Senator from Massachusetts*

New England has a harsh climate, a barren soil, a rough and stormy coast, and yet we love it, even with a love passing that of dwellers in more favored regions.

(Speech, 1884)

Let every man honor and love the land of his birth and the race from which he springs and keep their memory green. It is a pious and honorable duty. But let us have done with British-Americans and Irish-Americans and German-Americans, and so on, and all be Americans. . . . If a man is going to be an American at all let him be so without any qualifying adjectives; and if he is going to be something else, let him drop the word American from his personal description.

(Speech, 1888)

There was no hour down to the end when he would not turn aside from everything else to preach the doctrine of Americanism, of the principles and the faith upon which American government rested, and which all true Americans should wear in their heart of hearts. He was a great patriot, a great man; above all, a great American. His country was the ruling, mastering passion of his life from the beginning even unto the end.

(Eulogy for Theodore Roosevelt before Congress, 9 February 1919)

Henry Cabot Lodge, Jr. (1902–   ): *Senator from Massachusetts*

We live in a welfare state which seeks to put a floor below which no one sinks but builds no ceiling to prevent man from rising.

(Speech, 18 September 1959)

Logan (1725–1780): *Chief of the Mingo Indians*

I appeal to any white man to say, if ever he entered Logan's cabin hungry, and he gave him not meat: if ever he came cold and naked, and he cloathed him not. During the course of the last long and bloody war Logan remained idle in his cabin, an advocate for peace. Such was my love for the whites, that my countrymen pointed as they passed, and said "Logan is the friend of white man." I had even thought to have lived with you, but for the injuries of one man. Colonel Cresap, the last spring, in cold blood, and unprovoked, murdered all the relations of Logan, not even sparing my women and children. There runs not a drop of my blood in the veins of any living creature. This called on me for revenge. I have sought it: I have killed many: I have fully glutted my vengeance: for my country I rejoice at the beams of peace. But do not harbour a thought that mine is the joy of fear. Logan never felt fear. He will not turn on his heel to save his life. Who is there to mourn for Logan?—Not one.

> (Logan's speech to Governor Lord Dunmore of Virginia, 11 November 1774)

Vince Lombardi (1913–1970): *Professional football coach*

Winning isn't everything. It's the only thing.

> (Personal motto, 1960s)

Jack London (1876–1916): *Writer*

I tramped all through the United States, from California to Boston, and up and down, returning to the Pacific Coast by way of Canada, where I got into jail and served a term for vagrancy, and the whole tramping experience made me become a Socialist.

> (*Star Rover*, 1915)

Huey P. Long (1893–1935): *Governor and senator from Louisiana*

Where are the schools that you have waited for your children to have, that have never come? Where are the roads and highways that you sent your money to build, that are no nearer now than ever before? Where are the institutions to care for the sick and disabled? Evangeline wept bitter tears in her disappointment, but it lasted only through one lifetime. Your tears in this country, around this oak, have lasted for generations. Give me the chance to dry the tears of those who still weep here!

(Speech while campaigning for governor of Louisiana, November 1928)

I looked around at the little fishes present, and said, "I'm the Kingfish."

(Attributed upon his inauguration as governor, 1929)

Every man a King.

(Title of book and political slogan, 1931)

As a rule I don't care a damn what any crooked newspaperman says about me, because they're mostly goddamn liars.

(To reporters, 1932)

Soak the Rich.

(Motto of his program)

If Fascism came to America it would be on a program of Americanism.

(Attributed)

Oh, hell, say that I'm *sui generis* and let it go at that.

(Attributed)

Reub Long (?–?): *Cowboy*

If you think all men are equal, you ain't never been afoot and met a man ridin' a *good* horse.

(Quoted in *The Oregon Desert*)

Henry Wadsworth Longfellow (1807–1882): *Poet*

His brow is wet with honest sweat.
He earns whate'er he can,
And looks the whole world in the face,
For he owes not any man.

("The Village Blacksmith," 1839)

This is the forest primeval.

(*Evangeline*, 1847)

Listen, my children, and you shall hear
Of the midnight ride of Paul Revere,
On the eighteenth of April in Seventy-five.
(*Paul Revere's Ride*, 1861)

The fate of a nation was riding that night.
(Ibid.)

Thou, too, sail on, O Ship of State!
Sail on, O Union, strong and great!
Humanity with all its fears,
With all the hopes of future years,
Is hanging breathless on they fate!

Our hearts, our hopes, are all with thee,
Our hearts, our hopes, our prayers, our tears,
Our faith triumphant o'er our fears,
Are all with thee,—are all with thee!
(*The Building of the Ship*, 1849)

Alice Roosevelt Longworth (1884–1980): *Political socialite*

Harding was not a bad man. He was just a slob.
(Attributed, c. 1923)

He looked as if he had been weaned on a pickle.
(Of Calvin Coolidge, in conversation, 1924)

One-third mush and two-thirds Eleanor.
(Of Franklin D. Roosevelt, attributed, 1936)

He has sprung from the grass roots of the country clubs of America.
(Of Wendell Willkie, attributed, 1940)

How can the Republican Party nominate a man who looks like the bridegroom on a wedding cake?
(Of Thomas E. Dewey, attributed, 1944)

You can't make soufflé rise twice.
(On the Republican Party's renomination of Thomas E. Dewey, 1948)

The policeman and the trashman may call me Alice. You cannot.

(To Joseph McCarthy when he addressed her by her first name, attributed, 1950)

John Campbell, Lord Loudun (1705–1782): *British military commander in North America, 1756–1757*

The truth is, Governors here are Cyphers; their Predecessors sold the whole of the Kings Prerogative, to get their Sallaries,—and till you find a Fund, independent of the Province, to pay the Governors, and new model the Government, you can do nothing with the Provinces.

(Letter from New York to the Board of Trade, 22 November 1756)

Louis Philippe (1773–1850): *Duke of Orleans, king of France*

No wonder that the Negroes become lazy. They never benefit from their own work.

(*Diary of My Travels in America,* 1797)

Owen Lovejoy (1811–1864): *Congressman from Illinois*

I hate the British government. I now here publicly avow and record my inextinguishable hatred. . . . I mean to cherish it while I live, and to bequeath it as a legacy to my children when I die. And if I am alive when war with England comes, as sooner or later it must, for we shall never forget this humiliation, and if I can carry a musket in that war, I will carry it.

(Speech in the House of Representatives, upon American capitulation to the British in the seizure of two Confederate diplomats on a British ship, January 1862)

Amy Lowell (1874–1925): *Poet*

This is America,
This vast, confused beauty,
This staring, restless speed of liveliness,
Mighty, overwhelming, crude, of all forms,
Making grandeur out of profusion,
Afraid of no incongruities,
Sublime in its audacity,
Bizarre breaker of moulds.

(*What's O'Clock,* 1925)

James Russell Lowell (1819–1891): *Poet*

I first drew in New England's air, and
    from her hardy breast
Sucked in the tyrant-hating milk that
    will not let me rest;
And if my words seem treason to the
    dullard and the tame,
'Tis but my Bay State dialect—our
    fathers spake the same.

("On the Capture of Fugitive Slaves Near Washington," 1845)

They jest want this Californy
    So's to lug new slave-States
        in
To abuse ye, an' to scorn ye,
    An' to plunder ye like sin.

(*The Biglow Papers,* 1848)

The fault of the free states in the eyes of the South is not one that can be atoned for by any yielding of special points here and there. Their offence is that they are free, and that their habits and prepossessions are those of freedom. Their crime is the census of 1860. Their increases in numbers, wealth and power is a standing aggression. It would not be enough to please the Southern states that we should stop asking them to abolish slavery: what they demand of us is nothing less than we should abolish the spirit of the age. Our very thoughts are a menace.

(*Atlantic Monthly,* February 1861)

The American is nomadic in religion, in ideas, in morals.

(*Fireside Travels,* 1864)

Clare Boothe Luce (1903–1983): *Diplomat*

She is most famous for comforting the afflicted and afflicting the comfortable.

(Introducing Eleanor Roosevelt at a dinner, 1950)

The Democratic Party has a vested interest in depression at home and war abroad. Its leaders are always troubadours of trouble; crooners of catastrophe. Public confusion on vital issues is Democratic weather. A Democratic President is doomed to proceed to his goals like a squid, squirting darkness all about him.

(*New York Times,* 27 February 1959)

Henry R. Luce (1898–1967): *Journalist*

The fundamental trouble with Americans has been, and is, that whereas their nation became in the 20th century the most powerful and the most vital nation in the world, nevertheless Americans were unable to accommodate themselves spiritually and practically to that fact. . . . The cure is this: to accept wholeheartedly our duty and our opportunity as the most powerful and vital nation in the world and in consequence to exert upon the world the full impact of our influence, for such purposes as we see fit and by such means as we see fit.

("The American Century," *Life,* 17 February 1941)

The world of the 20th century, if it is to come to life in any nobility of health and vigor, must be to a significant degree an American century.

(Ibid.)

Seth Luther (1795?–1846): *Labor leader*

We do not believe there can be a *single person* found east of these mountains who ever *thanked God* for *permission* to work in a cotton mill.

(Speech delivered throughout Massachusetts, 1832)

Let us no longer be deceived by the cry of those who produce *nothing* and who enjoy *all,* and who insultingly term us . . . the *lower orders,* and exultingly claim our homage for themselves, as the *higher orders—while the* Declaration of Independence asserts that "All men are created equal."

(Ibid.)

M

Douglas MacArthur (1880–1964): *Army general*

That was a bad-looking mob. It was animated by the essence of revolution.

> (Commenting on his dispersal of the "Bonus Army," World War I veterans demonstrating in Washington on behalf of pensions, July 1932)

I shall return.

> (Message on leaving the Philippines, 11 March 1942)

This is the Voice of Freedom, General MacArthur speaking. People of the Philippines: I have returned. By the grace of Almighty God, our forces stand again on Philippine soil. . . . The hour of your redemption is here. . . . Rally to me.

> (On landing at Leyte Island in the Philippines, 20 October 1944)

We are no longer fearful of their intervention.

> (Report on the Korean War to President Truman, Wake Island, October 1950)

There is no substitute for victory.

> (Message to Congressman Joseph W. Martin, March 1951)

When I joined the army, even before the turn of the century, it was the fulfillment of all my boyish hopes and dreams. . . . Like the old soldier of the ballad, I now close my military career and just fade away.

> (Address to Congress, 19 April 1951)

Only those Americans who are willing to die for their country are fit to live.

> (Attributed)

It is fatal to enter any war without the will to win it.
(Speech, Republican National Convention, 7 July 1952)

Thomas Babington Macaulay (1800–1859): *English historian*
Your Constitution is all sail and no anchor.
(Letter to H. S. Randall, 23 May 1857)

Archibald MacLeish (1892–   ): *Poet*
It was all prices to them: they never looked at it: why should they look at the land? they were Empire Builders: it was all in the bid and the asked and the ink on their books.
("Wildwest," *Collected Poems*, 1952)

Salvador de Madariaga (1886–   ): *Historian*
First the sweetheart of the nation, then the aunt, woman governs America because America is a land of boys who refuse to grow up.
(Attributed)

Lester Maddox (1915–   ): *Segregationist leader and governor of Georgia*
That's part of American greatness, is discrimination. Yes, sir. Inequality, I think, breeds freedom and gives a man opportunity.
(Speech, quoted in the *New York Times*, 6 November 1966)

James Madison (1751–1836): *Fourth president, 1809–1817*
In a democracy the people meet and exercise the government in person; in a republic they assemble and administer it by their representatives and agents. A democracy, consequently, will be confined to a small spot. A republic may be extended over a large region.
(*Federalist Papers*, 1787)

By a faction, understand a number of citizens, whether amounting to a majority or minority of the whole, who are united and actuated by some common impulse of passion, or of interest, adverse to the rights of other citizens, or to the permanent and aggregate interests of the community.
(Ibid.)

I believe there are more instances of the abridgment of the freedom of the people by gradual and silent encroachments of those in power than by violent and sudden usurpations.

(Speech in the Virginia Convention, 16 June 1788)

The Mississippi is to them every thing. It is the Hudson, the Delaware, the Potomac, and all the navigable rivers of the Atlantic States, formed into one stream.

(To Thomas Jefferson on westerners, 1803)

Our commerce has been plundered in every sea, the great staples of our country have been cut off from their legitimate markets, and a destructive blow aimed at our agriculture and maritime interests. . . . Not content with these occasional expedients for laying waste to our neutral trade, the cabinet of Britain resorted at length to the sweeping system of blockades, under the name of orders-in-council, which has been molded and managed as might best suit its political views, its commercial jealousies, or the avidity of British cruisers.

(Message to Congress calling for a declaration of war on Great Britain, 1 June 1812)

Horace Mann (1796–1854): *Educational reformer*

Education then, beyond all other devices of human origin, is a great equalizer of the conditions of men,—the balance wheel of the social machinery.

(Report as secretary of Massachusetts state board of education, 1848)

Without undervaluing any other human agency, it may be safely affirmed that the common school, improved and energized as it can easily be, may become the most effective and benignant of all the forces of civilization.

(Ibid.)

Schoolhouses are the republican line of fortifications.

(Ibid.)

In a republic, ignorance is a crime.

(Ibid.)

Thomas Mann (1875–1955): *German novelist*

Instead of leading the world, America appears to have resolved to buy it.

(Letter, 1947)

Marya Mannes (1904–): *Critic*

An American who can make money, invoke God, and be no better than his neighbor, has nothing to fear but truth itself.

(More in Anger, 1958)

If American men are obsessed with money, American women are obsessed with weight. The men talk of gain, the women talk of loss, and I do not know which talk is the more boring.

(Ibid.)

Michael J. Mansfield (1903–): *Senator from Montana*

A piece of each of us died at that moment.

(Eulogy on President Kennedy, 24 November 1963)

Mao Tse-tung (1893–1976): *Chinese leader*

The atom bomb is a paper tiger which the United States reactionaries use to scare people.

(Interview, August 1946)

William L. Marcy (1786–1857): *Democratic Party politician*

To the victors belong the spoils.

(On the appointment of Martin Van Buren as ambassador to Great Britain, speech in the Senate, January 1832)

Jacques Maritain (1882–1973): *Philosopher*

The great and admirable strength of America consists in this, that America is truly the American people.

(Reflections on America, 1958)

Americans seem sometimes to believe that if you are a thinker you must be a frowning bore, because thinking is so damn serious.

(Ibid.)

Frederick Marryat (1792–1848): *English writer*

It is remarkable how very debased the language has become in a short period in America.

(*A Diary in America*, 1839)

George C. Marshall (1880–1958): *Army general and secretary of state under President Truman*

The truth of the matter is that Europe's requirements for the next 3 or 4 years of foreign food and other essential products—principally from America—are so much greater than her present ability to pay that she must have substantial additional help, or face economic, social, and political deterioration of a very grave character.

The remedy lies in breaking the vicious circle and restoring the confidence of the European people in the economic future of their own countries and of Europe as a whole. The manufacturer and the farmer throughout wide areas must be able and willing to exchange their products for currencies the continuing value of which is not open to question.

(Speech at Harvard University outlining the Marshall Plan, 1947)

Our policy is directed not against any country or doctrine but against hunger, poverty, desperation and chaos.

(Ibid.)

James Marshall (1810–1885): *Carpenter, California pioneer*

Boys, I believe I have found a gold mine.

(To workers at Sutter's sawmill on the American River, California, January 1848)

John Marshall (1755–1835): *Chief justice of the Supreme Court*

So if a law be in opposition to the constitution; if both the law and the constitution apply to a particular case, so that the court must either decide that case conformably to the law, disregarding the constitution, or conformably to the constitution, disregarding the law, the court must determine which of these conflicting rules governs the case. This is of the very essence of judicial duty.

If, then, the courts are to regard the constitution, and the constitution is superior to any ordinary act of the legislature, the constitution, and not such ordinary act, must govern the case to which they both apply.

(*Marbury* v. *Madison*, 1803)

It is emphatically the province and duty of the judicial department to say what the law is. . . . If two laws conflict with each other, the courts must decide on the operation of each. . . . This is of the very essence of judicial duty.

(Ibid.)

An act of the legislature, repugnant to the constitution, is void.

(Ibid.)

If any one proposition could command the universal assent of mankind, we might expect it would be this: that the government of the Union, though limited in its powers, is supreme within its sphere of action. This would seem to result necessarily from its nature. It is the government of all; its powers are delegated by all; it represents all, and acts for all. . . .

(*McCulloch* v. *Maryland*, 1819)

The Government of the Union, then, is emphatically and truly a government of the people. In form and in substance it emanates from them. Its powers are granted by them, and are to be exercised directly on them and for their benefit.

(Ibid.)

The government of the United States, then, though limited in its powers, is supreme; and its laws, when made in pursuance of the constitution, form the supreme law of the land, "any thing in the constitution or laws of any State to the contrary notwithstanding."

(Ibid.)

The power to tax involves the power to destroy.

(Ibid.)

This provision is made in a constitution, intended to endure for ages to come, and consequently, to be adapted to the various crises of human affairs.

(Ibid.)

A constitution is framed for ages to come, and is designed to approach immortality as nearly as human institutions can approach it.
(*Cohens* v. *Virginia,* 1821)

The people made the Constitution, and the people can unmake it. It is the creature of their own will, and lives only by their will.
(Ibid.)

Thomas R. Marshall (1854–1925): *Vice-president under President Wilson*

Once there were two brothers. One ran away to sea, the other was elected Vice-President, and nothing was ever heard of either of them again.
(Attributed)

What this country needs is a good five-cent cigar.
(Attributed)

Frederick T. Martin (1849–1914): *Corporation lawyer and writer*

It matters not one iota what political party is in power, or what president holds the reins of office. We are not politicians or public thinkers; we are the rich; we own America; we got it, God knows how; but we intend to keep it.
(*The Passing of the Idle Rich,* 1911)

Harriet Martineau (1802–1876): *English traveler*

Is it to be understood that the principles of the Declaration of Independence bear no relation to half of the human race?
(*Society in America,* 1837, on the status of women)

George Mason (1725–1792): *Virginia statesman*

That all men are by nature equally free and independent, and have certain inherent rights, of which, when they enter into a state of society, they cannot by any compact deprive or divest their posterity; namely, the enjoyment of life and liberty, with the means of acquiring and possessing property, and pursuing and obtaining happiness and safety.
(Virginia Bill of Rights, 12 June 1776)

The freedom of the press is one of the great bulwarks of liberty, and can never be restrained but by despotic government.

(Ibid.)

Cotton Mather (1663–1728): *Puritan divine*

More than twenty-one have confessed that they . . . engaged in . . . bewitching and ruining our land. . . . The devil has made a dreadful knot of witches in the country.

(Wonders of the Invisible World, 1693)

There are *Two Callings* to be minded by *All Christians*. Every Christian hath a GENERAL CALLING; which is, to Serve the Lord Jesus Christ, and Save his own Soul, in the Services of Religion, that are incumbent on all the Children of men. . . . But then, every Christian hath also a PERSONAL CALLING, or a certain *Particular Employment*, by which his *Usefulness*, in his Neighborhood, is distinguished. . . . We are Beneficial to *Humane Society* by the Works of that Special OCCUPATION, in which we are to be employed, according to the Order of God.

(A Christian at His Calling, 1701)

I write the wonders of the Christian religion, flying from the depravations of Europe, to the American strand: and, assisted by the Holy Author of that religion, I do, with all conscience of truth, required therein by Him, who is the Truth itself, report the wonderful displays of His infinite power, wisdom, goodness, and faithfulness, wherewith his Divine Providence hath irradiated an Indian wilderness.

(Magnalia Christi Americana, 1702)

Increase Mather (1639–1723): *Massachusetts divine*

But our question is concerning *Gynecandrical* Dancing, or that which is commonly called *Mixt* or *Promiscuous Dancing, viz.* of Men and Women (be they elder or younger persons) together: Now this we affirm to be utterly unlawful, and that it cannot be tollerated in such a place as *New-England*, without great Sin.

(An Arrow against Profane and Promiscuous Dancing, 1684)

It were better that Ten Suspected Witches should escape, than that one Innocent Person should be Condemned.

(*Cases of Conscience Concerning Evil Spirits,* 1693)

Theobald Mathew (1790–1856): *Irish priest and temperance crusader*

I promise, while I belong to the Teetotal Abstinence Society, to abstain from all kinds of intoxicating drink, unless used medically.

("The Pledge," sworn to by 500,000 Americans during Father Mathew's tour of the United States, 1849–1851)

Francis P. Matthews (1887–1952): *Secretary of the navy under President Truman*

It would win for us a proud title—we would become the first aggressors for peace.

(Arguing for a preventive war against the Soviet Union, in *Nation,* 9 September 1950)

William G. McAdoo (1863–1941): *Secretary of the treasury under President Wilson and senator from California*

His speeches leave the impression of an army of pompous phrases moving over the landscape in search of an idea. Sometimes these meandering words would actually capture a struggling thought and bear it in triumphantly a prisoner in their midst until it dies of servitude and overwork.

(On President Harding, 1920)

Ward McAllister (1827–1895): *Arbiter of high society*

There are only about four hundred people in New York society.

(Interview in *New York Herald,* 1888)

Anthony C. McAuliffe (1898–1975): *World War II general*

Nuts.

(In response to a German request for his surrender at Bastogne, December 1944)

Eugene J. McCarthy (1916–   ): *Senator from Minnesota and antiwar presidential candidate, 1968*

We've got a wild man in the White House, and we are going to have to treat him as such.

(On Lyndon Baines Johnson, 1967)

Have you ever tried to split sawdust?

(On accusations he was splitting the Democratic Party, May 1968)

Joseph R. McCarthy (1908–1957): *Senator from Wisconsin*

The son of a bitch ought to be impeached.

(Of President Truman upon hearing of his dismissal of General Mac-Arthur, March 1951)

While I cannot take the time to name all of the men in the State Department who have been named as members of the Communist Party and members of a spy ring, I have here in my hand a list of 205 that were known to the Secretary of State as being members of the Communist party and who nevertheless are still working and shaping the policy of the State Department.

(Speech at Wheeling, West Virginia, 9 February 1950)

The issue between the Republicans and Democrats is clearly drawn. It has been deliberately drawn by those who have been in charge of twenty years of treason.

(Campaign speech, 1952)

McCarthyism is Americanism with its sleeves rolled.

(Phrase in various speeches, 1952)

Mary McCarthy (1912–   ): *Writer*

Congress—these, for the most part, illiterate hacks whose fancy vests are spotted with gravy, and whose speeches, hypocritical, unctuous, and slovenly, are spotted also with gravy of political patronage.

(*On the Contrary*, 1961)

An interviewer asked me what book I thought best represented the modern American woman. All I could think of to answer was: *Madame Bovary*.

(Ibid.)

When an American heiress wants to buy a man, she at once crosses the Atlantic. The only really materialistic people I have ever met have been Europeans.

(Ibid.)

It is true that America produces and consumes more cars, soap, and bathtubs than any other nation, but we live among these objects rather than by them.

(Ibid.)

The American character looks always as if it had just had a rather bad haircut, which gives it, in our eyes at any rate, a greater humanity than the European, which even among its beggars has an all too professional air.

(Ibid.)

Who are these advertising men kidding, besides the European tourist? Between the tired, sad gentle faces of the subway riders and the grinning Holy Families of the Ad-Mass, there exists no possibility of even a wishful identification.

(Ibid.)

The immense popularity of American movies abroad demonstrates that Europe is the unfinished negative of which America is the proof.

(Ibid.)

American life, in large cities at any rate, is a perpetual assault on the senses and the nerves; it is out of asceticism, out of unworldliness, precisely, that we bear it.

(Ibid.)

The consumer today is the victim of the manufacturer who launches on him a regiment of products for which he must make room in his soul.

(Ibid.)

The happy ending is our national belief.

(Ibid.)

Life for the European is a career; for the American, it is a hazard.

(Ibid.)

George B. McClellan (1826–1885): *Railroad executive, Civil War general and Democratic Party politician*

All quiet along the Potomac.

(Attributed, 1861)

William McKinley (1843–1901): *Twenty-fifth president*

We want no wars of conquest. We must avoid the temptation of territorial aggression.

(First inaugural address, 4 March 1897)

I speak not of forcible aggression, for that can not be thought of. That, by our code of morality, would be criminal aggression.

(Message to Congress, 6 December 1897)

Not only is the union of the Hawaiian territory to the United States no new scheme, but it is the inevitable consequence of the relation steadfastly maintained with that mid-Pacific domain for three-quarters of a century. Its accomplishment, despite successive denials and postponements, has been merely a question of time.

(Address to Congress, 1898)

When I realized that the Philippines had dropped into our laps I confess I did not know what to do with them. . . . I walked the floor of the White House night after night until midnight; and I am not ashamed to tell you, gentlemen, that I went down on my knees and prayed Almighty God for light and guidance more than one night. And one night it came to me this way—I don't know how it was but it came . . . there was nothing left for us to do but take them all, and to educate the Filipinos, and uplift and civilize and Christianize them, and by God's grace do the very best we could by them, as our fellow-men for whom Christ also died. And then I went to bed, and went to sleep, and slept soundly, and the next morning I sent for the chief engineer of the War Department (our mapmaker), and I told him to put the Philippines on the map of the United States.

(Speech to a delegation of Methodists, Washington, 21 November 1899)

Marshall McLuhan (1911–   ): *Canadian-American social philosopher*

"Real life" often appears, at least, to be an imitation of art. Today, it is poster art.

(*The Mechanical Bride*, 1951)

The car has become an article of dress without which we feel uncertain, unclad, and incomplete.

(*Understanding Media*, 1964)

American youth attributes much more importance to arriving at driver's license age than at voting age.

(Ibid.)

Americans have a peculiar bias. They go outside to be alone and they go home to be social.

(*Sunday Times Magazine*, 26 March 1978)

Robert S. McNamara (1916–   ): *Secretary of defense under Presidents Kennedy and Johnson*

The draft is the largest educational institution in the world.

(Remark to reporters, 1966)

There may be a limit beyond which many Americans and much of the world will not permit the United States to go. The picture of the world's greatest superpower killing or seriously injuring 1,000 noncombatants a week, while trying to pound a tiny backward nation into submission on an issue whose merits are hotly disputed, is not a pretty one. It could conceivably produce a costly distortion in the American national consciousness and in the world image of the United States—especially if the damage to North Vietnam is complete enough to be "successful."

(Memorandum to President Johnson, 19 May 1967)

Andrew W. Mellon (1855–1937): *Secretary of the treasury under Presidents Harding, Coolidge, and Hoover*

A nation is not in danger of financial disaster merely because it owes itself money.

(Attributed, 1933)

Liquidate labor, liquidate stocks, liquidate farmers.
(Advice to President Hoover on the Great Depression, 1931)

H. L. Mencken (1880–1956): *Writer*
The haunting fear that someone, somewhere, may be happy.
(Definition of Puritanism, *A Book of Burlesques*, 1920)

Democracy is the theory that the common people know what they want, and deserve to get it good and hard.
(Ibid.)

The chief business of the nation, as a nation, is the setting up of heroes, mainly bogus.
(*Prejudices: Third Series*, 1922)

The American people, taking one with another, constitute the most timorous, sniveling, poltroonish, ignominious mob of serfs and goose-steppers ever gathered under one flag in Christendom since the end of the Middle Ages.
(Ibid.)

Here the general average of intelligence, of knowledge, of competence, of integrity, of self-respect, of honor is so low that any man who knows his trade, does not fear ghosts, has read fifty good books, and practices the common decencies stands out as brilliantly as a wart on a bald head, and is thrown willy-nilly into a meager and exclusive aristocracy.
(Ibid.)

If experience teaches us anything at all, it teaches us this: that a good politician, under democracy is quite as unthinkable as an honest burglar.
(*Prejudices: Fourth Series*, 1924)

The American, whatever his faults, is at least a less abject and groveling fellow than the Englishman. He may venerate such fifth-rate men as Harding and Coolidge, but he still falls a good deal short of venerating such complete vacuums as King George V. So on lower levels. In his view of the secular magnificoes who come and go—Morgan, the Rockefellers, Andy Carnegie, Andy Mellon, Henry Ford, and so on—there is surely none of the base and menial adulation which in England bathes a lord. To him, more often than not, they are largely comic characters, and in his envy of them there is a sufficient admixture of irony to keep it from becoming quite ignoble. Thus he retains a modicum of dignity, imbecile though he may be. I incline to think that that modicum of dignity is the chief and perhaps the only gift of democracy to mankind. At all events, I don't seem to recall any other.

(Introduction to Cooper's *The American Democrat*, 1931)

He slept more than any other President, whether by day or night. Nero fiddled, but Coolidge only snored. When the crash came at last and Hoover began to smoke and bubble, good Cal was safe in Northampton, and still in the hay.

(*American Mercury*, April 1933)

There were no thrills while he reigned, but neither were there any headaches. He had no ideas but he was not a nuisance.

(Ibid.)

The United States has not only failed to produce a genuine aristocracy; it has also failed to produce an indigenous intelligentsia. The so-called intellectuals of the country are simply weather-vanes blown constantly by foreign winds, usually but not always English.

(*Minority Report*, 1956)

One of the things that makes a Negro unpleasant to white folk is the fact that he suffers from their injustice. He is thus a standing rebuke to them.

(Ibid.)

The urge to save humanity is almost always only a false-face for the urge to rule it.

(Ibid.)

Alice Duer Miller (1874–1942): *Poet*

I am American bred,
I have seen much to hate here—much
    to forgive,
But in a world where England is

> finished and dead,
> I do not wish to live.
> ("The White Cliffs," 1940)

Arthur Miller (1915–   ): *Playwright*

> Because you see the main thing today is—
> shopping. Years ago a person, he was unhappy,
> didn't know what to do with himself—
> he'd go to church, start a revolution—*something*.
> Today you're unhappy? Can't figure it out?
> What is the salvation? Go shopping.
> (*The Price*, 1968)

Henry Miller (1891–   ): *Writer*

It is the American vice, the democratic disease which expresses its tyranny by reducing everything unique to the level of the herd.
> (*The Wisdom of the Heart*, 1941)

It isn't the oceans which cut us off from the world—it's the American way of looking at things.
> (Ibid.)

I have never been able to look upon America as young and vital but rather as prematurely old, as a fruit which rotted before it had a chance to ripen.
> (*The Air-Conditioned Nightmare*, 1945)

The word which gives the key to the national vice is waste.
> (Ibid.)

C. Wright Mills (1916–1962): *Sociologist*

When white-collar people get jobs, they sell not only their time and energy, but their personalities as well. They sell by the week, or month, their smiles and their kindly gestures, and they must practice that prompt repression of resentment and aggression.
> (*White Collar*, 1956)

Jefferson Davis Milton (1861–1947): *Western peace officer, border patrolman*

I never killed a man that didn't need killing; I never shot an animal except for meat.
(*Biography*, 1948)

James M. Minifie (1912–   ): *Canadian writer*

The United States is the glory, jest, and terror of Mankind.
(*The New Romans*, 1968)

Langdon Mitchell (1862–1935): *Playwright*

In America there are no ladies, except salesladies.
(*The New York Idea*, 1907)

William "Billy" Mitchell (1879–1936): *Army general*

As a patriotic American citizen, I can stand by no longer and see these disgusting performances by the navy and war departments, at the expense of the lives of our people, and the delusion of the American public. . . . I considered it my duty to tell what I knew, although it meant sure disciplinary action and probably court-martial.
(Attributed in *Pioneer of Air Power*, 1943)

James Monroe (1758–1831): *Fifth president, 1817–1825*

National honor is national property of the highest value.
(First inaugural address, 4 March 1817)

We owe it, therefore, to candor, and to the amicable relations existing between the United States and those powers, to declare, that we should consider any attempt on their part to extend their system to any portion of this hemisphere, as dangerous to our peace and safety. With the existing colonies or dependencies of any European power, we have not interfered, and shall not interfere. But, with the governments who have declared their independence and maintained it, and whose independence we have, on great consideration, and on just principles, acknowledged, we could not view any interposition for the purpose of oppressing them, or controlling, in any other manner, their destiny, by any European power, in any

other light than as the manifestation of an unfriendly disposition towards the United States.

> (Message to Congress (The Monroe Doctrine), 2 December 1823)

John Pierpont Morgan (1837–1913): *Banker*

If we have done anything wrong, send your man to my man and
they can fix it up.

> (Message to President Roosevelt regarding an antitrust suit against
> Morgan's Northern Securities Company, 1901)

I owe the public nothing.

> (Attributed)

A greater set of perfectly incompetent and apparently crooked
people has never, so far as I know, run, or attempted to run, any
first class country. The Mexicans are far better off, because their
various bosses only murder and rape, but our bosses ruin the country and make life intolerable for a much larger number of people.

> (On the administration of Woodrow Wilson, 1913)

Robin Morgan (1941–   ): *Feminist*

Sisterhood is Powerful.

> (Title of a book and Women's Liberation Movement motto, 1970)

Ted Morgan (Sanche de Gramont) (1932–   ): *Writer*

America's dissidents are not committed to mental hospitals and
sent into exile; they thrive and prosper and buy a house in Nan-
tucket and take flyers in the commodities market.

> (*On Becoming American*, 1978)

Christopher Morley (1890–1957): *Poet*

America is still a government of the naive, for the naive, and by
the naive. He who does not know this, nor relish it, has no inkling of
the nature of his country.

> (*Inward Ho!*, 1923)

George Pope Morris (1802–1864): *Publisher*

The Union of lakes—the union of lands,
The union of States none can sever,

> The union of hearts, the union of hands,
> And the flag of our Union forever.
>> (*The Flag of Our Union*, 1862)

Wright Morris (1910–   ): *Writer*
The man who walks alone is soon trailed by the F.B.I.
>> (*A Bill of Rites*, 1967)

Samuel F. B. Morse (1791–1872): *Inventor and painter*
What hath God wrought?
>> (First message sent by telegraph, 1844)

Wayne Morse (1900–1974): *Senator from Oregon*
We are pursuing neither law nor peace in Southeast Asia. We are not even pursuing freedom.
>> (Speech in the Senate, 1966)

J. Sterling Morton (1832–1902): *Secretary of agriculture under President Cleveland*
The President has a big belly. His brains are not proportioned to it.
>> (Describing President Cleveland, letter to A. J. Sawyer, 1887)

Thomas Morton (?–1647): *Early settler in Massachusetts*
So full of humanity are these infidels before those Christians.
>> (Describing Indians and Plymouth separatists, *New English Canaan*, 1637)

Zero Mostel (1915–1977): *Actor and political activist*
I am a man of a thousand faces, all of them blacklisted.
>> (Remark after failing to cooperate with the House Committee on Un-American Activities, 1947)

Daniel P. Moynihan (1927–   ): *Senator from New York*
The FBI is filled with Fordham graduates keeping tabs on Harvard men in the State Department.
>> (Remark to reporters, October 1971)

Malcolm Muggeridge (1903–): *English pundit*

The pursuit of happiness, which American citizens are obliged to undertake, tends to involve them in trying to perpetuate the moods, tastes and aptitudes of youth.

    (The Most of Malcolm Muggeridge, 1966)

Higher education is booming in the United States; the Gross National Mind is mounting along with the Gross National Product.

    (Ibid.)

American Women: How they mortify the flesh in order to make it appetizing! Their beauty is a vast industry, their enduring allure a discipline which nuns or athletes might find excessive.

    (Ibid.)

William Mulholland (1955–1935): *Engineer, builder of the Los Angeles Aqueduct*

There it is. Take it.

    (Entire text of remarks upon dedicating the Los Angeles Aqueduct, San Fernando, 5 November 1913)

Lewis Mumford (1895–): *Social critic*

Our national flower is the concrete cloverleaf.

    (October 1961)

A. J. Muste (1885–1967): *Pacifist and socialist leader*

We need to get our thinking focused right, and to see the rulers of Jewry and Rome, not Jesus, the Powers, not the Chinese Nationalists, selfish employers or a negligent society, not striking workers, as the cause of disturbance in the social order.

    ("Pacifism and Class War," 1929)

Gunnar Myrdal (1898–): *Swedish social scientist and diplomat*

I think we must save America from the missionary idea that you must get the whole world on to the American way of life. This is really a big world danger.

    (Interview, 1975)

N

Carry Nation (1846–1911): *Prohibitionist*

You have put me in here a cub, but I will come out roaring like a lion, and I will make all hell howl!

(On being jailed in Barber County, Kansas, c. 1901)

Huey P. Newton (1942–   ): *Black youth leader*

There has always existed in the Black colony of Afro-America a fundamental difference over which tactics from the broad spectrum of alternatives Black people should employ in their struggle for national liberation. One side of this difference contends that Black people . . . must employ no tactic that will anger the oppressor whites. This view holds that Black people constitute a hopeless minority and that salvation for Black people lies in developing brotherly relations. . . .

On the other side of the difference, we find that the point of departure is the principle that the oppressor has no rights that the oppressed is bound to respect. Kill the slavemaster, destroy him utterly, move against him with implacable fortitude. Break his oppressive power by any means necessary.

("In Defense of Self-Defense," *The Black Panther*, 3 July 1967)

Richard M. Nixon (1913–   ): *Thirty-seventh president*

Traitors in the high councils of our own government have made sure that the deck is stacked on the Soviet side of the diplomatic tables.

(Remark during Alger Hiss investigation, 1949)

Mr. Truman, Dean Acheson and other administration officials for political reasons covered up this Communist conspiracy and attempted to halt its exposure.

(Campaign speech, September 1952)

Adlai the appeaser carries a Ph.D. from Dean Acheson's cowardly college of Communist containment.

> (Of Democratic presidential nominee, Adlai Stevenson, ibid.)

I should say this—that Pat doesn't have a mink coat. But she does have a respectable Republican cloth coat, and I always tell her that she would look good in anything.

> (Checkers speech, on national television after he was accused of corruption, 23 September 1952)

You won't have Nixon to kick around anymore.

> (Announcing his retirement from public life at a press conference, 7 November 1962)

There is no substitute for victory in South Vietnam.

> (Speech, 1964)

Let us begin by committing ourselves to the truth, to see it like it is and to tell it like it is, to find the truth, to speak the truth and live with the truth. That's what we'll do.

> (Speech accepting Republican presidential nomination, 8 August 1968)

It is time for the great silent majority of Americans to stand up and be counted.

> (Campaign speech, October 1970)

We cannot learn from one another until we stop shouting at one another—until we speak quietly enough so that our words can be heard as well as our voices.

> (First inaugural address, 20 January 1969)

This is the greatest week in the history of the world since the creation.

> (Remark on U.S.S. *Hornet*, four days after the first moon landing, 24 July 1969)

We will not be humiliated. We will not be defeated. If when the chips are down the United States acts like a pitiful helpless giant, the forces of totalitarianism and anarchy will threaten free nations and free institutions throughout the world. It is not our power but our will that is being tested.

> (Speech announcing the invasion of Cambodia, 30 April 1970)

America has never been defeated in the proud 190-year history of this country, and we shall not be defeated in Vietnam.
(Ibid.)

Those who scoff at "balance of power diplomacy" on the world scene should recognize that the only alternative to a balance of power is an imbalance of power—and history shows us that nothing so drastically escalates the danger of war as such an imbalance.
(Press conference, 25 June 1972)

We are all in it together. This is a war. We take a few shots and it will be over. We will give them a few shots and it will be over. Don't worry. I wouldn't want to be on the other side right now. . . . I want the most comprehensive notes on all those who tried to do us in. They didn't have to do it. If we had had a very close election, and they were playing the other side I would understand this. No— they were doing this quite deliberately and they are asking for it and they are going to get it. We have not used the power in this first four years as you know. We have never used it. We have not used the Bureau and we have not used the Justice Department but things are going to change now. And they are either going to do it right or go.
(Tape-recorded telephone conversation with John Dean, 15 September 1972)

There will be no whitewash in the White House.
(Statement on the Watergate affair, 17 April 1973)

The people have got to know whether or not their president is a crook. Well, I'm not a crook.
(Television address, May 1973)

I hereby resign the office of the President of the United States.
(The full text of his letter of resignation to Secretary of State Henry Kissinger, 7 August 1974)

If some of my judgments were wrong, and some were wrong, they were made in what I believed at the time to be the best inter- est of the nation.
(Resignation speech, 8 August 1979)

Something else I'd like you to tell your young people. You know they look at Government, it's a sort of rugged life. They see the mistakes that are made, they get the impression that everybody is here for the purpose of feathering his nest. . . . Not in this Administration: not one single man or woman. And I say this to them. There are many fine careers. The country needs good farmers, good businessmen, good plumbers, good carpenters.

(Farewell speech, 9 August 1974)

When the President does it, that means it is not illegal.

(Television interview, 20 May 1977)

I have a very deep regret . . . [but] if they want me to get down and grovel on the floor, no.

(Ibid.)

Watergate was worse than a crime, it was a blunder.

(Ibid.)

It was not lost on the battlefields. . . . It was lost in the halls of Congress, in the boardrooms of corporations, in the executive suites of foundations, and in the editorial rooms of the great newspapers and television networks.

It was lost in the salons of Georgetown, the drawing rooms of "the beautiful people" in New York and the classrooms of the great universities.

(On the war in Vietnam, *The Real War*, 1980)

People said that my language was bad, but Jesus, you should have heard LBJ!

(Attributed)

If I had my life to live over, I would have liked to have ended up as a sportswriter.

(Attributed)

Frank Norris (1870–1902): *Novelist*

Tell the men of the East to look for the men of the West. The irrepressible Yank is knocking at the doors of their temples and he will want to sell 'em carpet sweepers for their harems and electric light plants for their temple shrines.

(*The Octopus*, 1901)

George W. Norris (1861–1944): *Senator from Nebraska*

We are going into the war upon the command of gold. We are going to run the risk of sacrificing millions of our countrymen's lives in order that other countrymen may coin their lifeblood into money.

(Speech during the war debate, 4 April 1917)

I know that I am powerless to stop it. I know that this war madness has taken possession of the financial and political powers of our country. I know that nothing I can say will stay the blow that is soon to fall. I feel that we are committing a sin against our humanity and our countrymen. . . . I feel that we are about to put the dollar sign upon the American flag.

(Ibid.)

O

Dion O'Bannion (1892–1924): *Chicago gangster*

We're businessmen without high hats.

(On his bootleg liquor syndicate, attributed, c. 1923)

Adolph S. Ochs (1858–1935): *Newspaper publisher*

All the news that's fit to print.

(Motto of the *New York Times* after 1896)

Carl Oglesby (1935–   ): *New Left leader*

They are not moral monsters. They are all honorable men. They are all liberals.

(On the leadership of the Vietnam War effort, speech in Washington, 27 October 1965)

Richard Olney (1835–1917): *Attorney-general and secretary of state under President Cleveland*

[The Interstate Commerce Commission] can be made of great

use to the railroads. It satisfies the popular clamor for a government supervision of railroads, at the same time that such supervision is almost entirely nominal. The part of wisdom is not to destroy the Commission, but to utilize it.

(On the passage of the Interstate Commerce Act, 1888)

Today the United States is practically sovereign on this continent, and its fiat is law upon the subjects to which it confines its interposition.

(Note to the British Foreign Office on the occasion of the Venezuela-British Guiana boundary dispute, July 1895)

Eugene O'Neill (1888–1953): *Playwright*

We talk about the American Dream, and want to tell the world about the American Dream, but what is that Dream, in most cases, but the dream of material things? I sometimes think that the United States for this reason is the greatest failure the world has ever seen.

(Attributed)

J. Robert Oppenheimer (1904–1967): *Nuclear scientist*

Now I am become death, the destroyer of worlds.

(Quoting a Hindu scripture to himself while witnessing the explosion of the first atomic bomb, Los Alamos, New Mexico, 16 July 1945)

The physicists have known sin; and this is a knowledge which they cannot lose.

(Lecture, 25 November 1947)

John L. O'Sullivan (1813–1895): *Democratic Party journalist*

Our manifest destiny to overspread the continent allotted by Providence for the free development of our yearly multiplying millions.

(*Democratic Review,* July 1845)

Texas has been absorbed into the Union in this inevitable fulfillment of the general law which is rolling our population westward; the connexion of which with that ratio of growth in population which is destined within a hundred years to swell our numbers to the enormous population of two hundred and fifty million (if not more), is too evident to leave us in doubt of the manifest design of Providence in regard to the occupation of this continent.

(Ibid.)

James Otis (1725–1783): *Revolutionary agitator*

Taxation without representation is tyranny.

(In a trial before the Admiralty Court, February 1761)

An act against the Constitution is void; an act against natural equity is void.

(Ibid.)

There is no foundation for the distinction some make in England between an internal and an external tax on the colonies.

(Attributed)

P

William Tyler Page (1868–1942): *Writer*

I believe in the United States of America as a Government of the people, by the people, for the people; whose just powers are derived from the consent of the governed; a democracy in a republic; a sovereign Nation of many sovereign States; a perfect Union one and inseparable; established upon those principles of freedom, equality, justice and humanity for which American patriots sacrificed their lives and fortunes. I therefore believe it is my duty to my country to love it, to support its Constitution, to obey its laws, to respect its flag, and to defend it against all enemies.

(*The American's Creed*, 1918)

Thomas Paine (1737–1809): *American revolutionary agitator and writer*

> From the east to the west blow the
>   trumpet to arms!
> Through the land let the sound of it
>   flee;
> Let the far and the near all unite, with
>   a cheer,
> In defense of our Liberty Tree.
>
> *(The Liberty Tree,* July 1775)

A long habit of not thinking a thing wrong, gives it a superficial appearance of being right, and raises at first a formidable outcry in defense of custom.

> *(Common Sense,* 1776)

A French bastard landing with an armed banditti and establishing himself King of England against the consent of the natives is, in plain terms, a very paltry rascally original. . . . The plain truth is that the antiquity of English monarchy will not bear looking into.

> (Ibid.)

O! ye that love mankind! Ye that dare oppose not only the tyranny but the tyrant, stand forth! Every spot of the Old World is overrun with oppression. Freedom hath been hunted round the globe. Asia and Africa have long expelled her. Europe regards her as a stranger and England hath given her warning to depart. O! receive the fugitive and prepare in time an asylum for mankind.

> (Ibid.)

Society in every state is a blessing, but government, even in its best state, is but a necessary evil; in its worst state an intolerable one.

> (Ibid.)

No nation ought to be without a debt. A national debt is a national bond; and when it bears no interest, is in no case a grievance.

> (Ibid.)

When we are planning for posterity, we ought to remember that virtue is not hereditary.

> (Ibid.)

Not a place upon earth might be so happy as America. Her situation is remote from all the wrangling world, and she has nothing to do but to trade with them.

(*The American Crisis*, 23 December 1776)

We fight not to enslave, but to set a country free, and to make room upon the earth for honest men to live in.

(Ibid.)

These are the times that try men's souls. The summer soldier and the sunshine patriot, will, in this crisis, shrink from the service of his country; but he that stands it *now* deserves the love and thanks of man and woman. Tyranny, like hell, is not easily conquered; yet we have this consolation with us, that the harder the conflict, the more glorious the triumph.

(Ibid.)

The guilt of a government is the crime of a whole country.

(Ibid.)

The nearer any disease approaches to a crisis, the nearer it is to a cure. (Danger and deliverance make their advances together; and it is only in the last push that one or the other takes the lead.)

(Ibid.)

A thing moderately good is not so good as it ought to be. Moderation in temper is always a virtue; but moderation in principle is always a vice.

(Ibid.)

It is the object only of war that makes it honorable. And if there was ever a *just* war since the world began, it is this in which America is now engaged.

(*The American Crisis*, 21 March 1778)

The world is my country, all mankind are my brethren, and to do good is my religion. I believe in one God and no more.

(*The Rights of Man*, 1791)

Every age and generation must be as free to act for itself in all cases as the ages and generations which preceded it. The vanity and

presumption of governing beyond the grave is the most ridiculous and insolent of all tyrannies.
(Ibid.)

Dorothy Parker (1893–1967): *Writer, wit*

How can they tell?
(Upon being told Calvin Coolidge had died, 1933)

John Parker (1729–1775): *Commander of minutemen at Lexington*

Stand your ground. Don't fire unless fired upon, but if they mean to have a war let it begin here!
(To his men at Lexington, 19 April 1775)

Theodore Parker (1810–1860): *Reformer and abolitionist*

We consider slavery your calamity, not your crime.
(To slaveowners, said commonly in speeches)

To know what is right I need not ask what is the current practice, what say the Revised Statutes, what said holy men of old, but what says conscience? What God?
(Attributed)

A democracy, that is, a government of all the people, by all the people, for all the people; of course, a government after the principles of eternal justice, the unchanging law of God; for shortness' sake, I will call it the idea of freedom.
(Speech at the New England Anti-Slavery Convention, Boston, 29 May 1850)

Larry Parks (1914–1975): *Actor*

Don't present me with this choice of either being in contempt of this committee and going to jail or forcing me to really crawl through the mud to be an informer. For what purpose?
(Testimony before the House Committee on Un-American Activities, 1951)

Rosa Parks (1913–): *Civil rights worker*

My only concern was to get home after a hard day's work.

> (On her refusal to yield a seat on a bus that launched the civil rights movement, in 1955, *Time*, 15 December 1975)

George S. Patton (1885–1945): *World War II general*

The quickest way to get it over with is to go get the bastards. . . . There's one thing you'll be able to say when you do go home. When you're sitting around your fireside with your brat on your knee, and he asks you what you did in the great World War II, you won't have to say you shoveled shit in Louisiana.

> (Speech to the troops of the Third Army, July 1944)

We won't just shoot the sonsabitches—we're going to cut out their living guts and use them to grease the treads of our tanks.

> (Ibid.)

I peed in the Rhine.

> (Marginal note on operations report, March 1945)

I do like to see the arms and legs fly.

> (Attributed)

Old Blood and Guts.

> (His nickname for himself)

William Penn (1644–1718): *English Quaker and founder of Pennsylvania*

No Cross, No Crown.

> (Title of pamphlet, 1669)

I have led the greatest colony into America that ever any man did upon a private credit, and the most prosperous beginnings that were ever in it are to be found among us.

> (Report on foundation of Pennsylvania, 1684)

[There is] no law in Pennsylvania against riding on broomsticks.

> (In dismissing charges of witchcraft, 1689)

Let the people think they govern and they will be governed.
(*Some Fruits of Solitude*, 1693)

Oliver Hazard Perry (1785–1819): *Naval commander*

We have met the enemy and they are ours—two ships, two brigs, one schooner and one sloop.
(Message to General William Henry Harrison announcing the American victory at the Battle of Lake Erie, 10 September 1813)

John J. Pershing (1860–1948): *World War I general*

I hope that here on the soil of France and in the school of French heroes, our American soldiers may learn to battle and vanquish for the liberty of the world.
(Address at Lafayette's tomb, 4 July 1917)

Laurence J. Peter (1919–   ): *Writer*

America is a country that doesn't know where it is going but is determined to set a speed record getting there.
(*The Peter Principle*, 1969)

Peter G. Peterson (1926–   ): *Secretary of Commerce under Nixon*

The era of low-cost energy is almost dead. Popeye is running out of spinach.
(Testifying at confirmation hearings, 1972)

John W. Philip (1840–1900): *Naval captain*

Don't cheer, men. The poor devils are dying.
(To sailors on the U.S.S. *Texas* at the Battle of Santiago, 3 July 1898)

David Graham Phillips (1867–1911): *Muckraking journalist*

A scurvy lot they are, are they not, with their smirking and cringing and voluble palaver about God and patriotism and their eager offerings of endowments for hospitals and colleges whenever the American people so much as looks hard in their direction.
(Of U.S. senators, *Cosmopolitan*, April 1906)

Wendell Phillips (1811–1884): *Abolitionist leader*

Revolutions are not made; they come. A revolution is as natural a growth as an oak. It comes out of the past. Its foundations are laid far back.

> (Speech, 8 January 1852)

We live under a government of men and morning newspapers. . . . Let me make the newspapers, and I care not what is preached in the pulpit or what is enacted in Congress.

> (Speech, 28 January 1852)

What the Puritans gave the world was not thought, but action.

> (Speech, 21 December 1855)

One on God's side is a majority.

> (Speech in Brooklyn, 1 November 1859)

You can always get the truth from an American statesman after he has turned seventy, or given up all hope of the Presidency.

> (Speech, 7 November 1860)

Governments exist to protect the rights of minorities. The loved and the rich need no protection: they have many friends and few enemies.

> (Speech in Boston, 21 December 1860)

Eternal vigilance is the price of liberty.

> (Attributed)

What is fanaticism today is the fashionable creed tomorrow, and trite as the multiplication table a week later.

> (Ibid.)

George E. Pickett (1825–1875): *Confederate infantry commander*

Up, men, and to your posts! Don't forget today that you are from Old Virginia.

> (To his men before Pickett's Charge at the Battle of Gettysburg, the "high-water mark of the Confederacy," 3 July 1863)

James A. Pike (1913–1969): *Episcopalian bishop and philosopher*

The eleven o'clock hour on Sunday is the most segregated hour in American life.

(Interview in *U.S. News & World Report,* 16 May 1960)

Gifford Pinchot (1865–1946): *Conservationist, chief forester*

The outgrowth of conservation, the inevitable result, is national efficiency. In the great commercial struggle between nations which is eventually to determine the welfare of all, national efficiency will be the deciding factor.

(The Fight for Conservation, 1910)

Charles Cotesworth Pinckney (1746–1825): *Federalist politician and diplomat*

Millions for defense but not one cent for tribute.

(Attributed to him upon being solicited for a bribe by Talleyrand as a prerequisite to negotiating a treaty, 1797. In fact, Pinckney insisted, he actually said, "Not a sixpence.")

William Pitt, Lord Chatham (1708–1788): *British prime minister*

I rejoice that America has resisted. Three millions of people, so dead to all the feelings of liberty, as voluntarily to submit to be slaves, would have been fit instruments to make slaves of the rest.

(Speech in the House of Commons, 14 January 1766)

I love the Americans because they love liberty, and I love them for the noble efforts they made in the last war.

(Speech in the House of Lords, 2 March 1770)

The spirit which now resists your taxation in America is the same which formerly opposed loans, benevolences and ship-money in England; the same spirit which called all England on its legs, and by the Bill of Rights vindicated the English constitution; the same spirit which established the great fundamental, essential maxim of your liberties—that no subject of England shall be taxed but by his own consent. This glorious spirit of Whiggism animates three millions in America, who prefer poverty with liberty to gilded chains and sordid affluence; and who will die in defence of their rights as men, as freemen.

(Speech in the House of Lords, 20 January 1775)

As an American, I would recognize to England her supreme right of regulating commerce and navigation; as an Englishman by birth and principle, I recognize to the Americans their supreme unalienable right to their property—right which they are justified in the defence of to the last extremity. To maintain this principle is the common cause of the Whigs on the other side of the Atlantic and on this. . . . In this great cause they are immovably allied; it is the alliance of God and nature—immutable, eternal, fixed as the firmament of heaven.

(Ibid.)

If I were an American, as I am an Englishman, while a foreign troop was landed in my country, I never would lay down my arms,—never—never—never—! You cannot conquer America.

(Speech in the House of Lords, 18 November 1777)

George Washington Plunkitt (1842–1924): *Machine politician and philosopher*

There's an honest graft, and I'm an example of how it works. I might sum up the whole thing by sayin': "I seen my opportunities and I took 'em."

Just let me explain by examples. My party's in power in the city, and it's goin' to undertake a lot of public improvements. Well, I'm tipped off, say, that they're going to lay out a new park at a certain place.

I see my opportunity and I take it. I go to that place and I buy up all the land I can in the neighborhood. Then the board of this or that makes its plan public, and there is a rush to get my land, which nobody cared particular for before.

Ain't it perfectly honest to charge a good price and make a profit on my investment and foresight? Of course, it is. Well, that's honest graft.

(Very Plain Talks on Practical Politics, 1905)

I want to say that I don't own a dishonest dollar. If my worst enemy was given the job of writin' my epitaph when I'm gone, he couldn't do more than write: "George W. Plunkitt. He Seen His Opportunities, and He Took 'Em."

(Ibid.)

Edgar Allan Poe (1809–1849): *Poet*

The Romans worshipped their standard; and the Roman standard happened to be an eagle. Our standard is only one tenth of an eagle—a dollar—but we make all even by adoring it with tenfold devotion.

(Attributed)

James K. Polk (1795–1849): *Eleventh president*

The people of this continent alone have the right to decide their own destiny.

(Message to Congress, 2 December 1845)

But now, after reiterated menaces, Mexico has passed the boundary of the United States, has invaded our territory, and shed American blood upon the American soil. She has proclaimed that hostilities have commenced, and that the two nations are now at war.

As war exists, and, notwithstanding all our efforts to avoid it, exists by the act of Mexico herself, we are called upon by every consideration of duty and patriotism to vindicate with decision the honor, the rights, and the interests of our country.

(Message to Congress, May 1846)

Horace Porter (1837–1921): *Railroad executive, diplomat*

A mugwump is a person educated beyond his intellect.

(Attributed, 1884)

Henry C. Potter (1835–1908): *Episcopalian bishop*

We have exchanged the Washingtonian dignity for the Jeffersonian simplicity, which in due time came to be only another name for the Jacksonian vulgarity.

(Speech in Washington, 30 April 1889)

Paul Potter (1940–): *New Left leader*

The incredible war in Vietnam has provided the razor, the terrifying sharp cutting edge that has finally severed the last vestiges of illusion that morality and democracy are the guiding principles of American foreign policy.

(Speech in Washington, 17 April 1965)

Adam Clayton Powell (1908–1972): *Baptist preacher and congressman from New York*

We have produced a world of contented bodies and discontented minds.

(*Keep the Faith, Baby!*, 1967)

A man's respect for law and order exists in precise relationship to the size of his paycheck.

(Ibid.)

Beware of Greeks bearing gifts, colored men looking for loans, and whites who understand the Negro.

(Ibid.)

The black man continues on his way. He plods wearily no longer—he is striding freedom road with the knowledge that if he hasn't got the world in a jug, at least he has the stopper in his hand.

(Ibid.)

George D. Prentice (1802–1870): *Journalist*

In New York City, the common bats fly only at twilight. Brickbats fly at all hours.

(*Prenticeana*, 1860)

William Prescott (1726–1795): *Revolutionary War officer*

Don't fire till you see the whites of their eyes.

(To his men at the Battle of Bunker Hill, 1775. Also attributed to Israel Putnam)

J. B. Priestley (1894–): *English writer*

California, that advance post of our civilisation, with its huge aircraft factories, TV and film studios, automobile way of life . . . its flavourless cosmopolitanism, its charlatan philosophies and religions, its lack of anything old and well-tried, rooted in tradition and character.

(*Thought in the Wilderness*, 1957)

Israel Putnam (1718–1790): *Revolutionary War general*

Men, you are all marksmen—don't one of you fire until you see the whites of their eyes.

(Bunker Hill, 1775, also attributed to William Prescott)

Q

Matthew S. Quay (1833–1904): *Republican Party "boss"*

If you have a weak candidate and a weak platform, wrap yourself up in the American flag and talk about the Constitution.

(Attributed, 1886)

Josiah Quincy the elder (1744–1775): *Revolutionary War leader*

Blandishments will not fascinate us, nor will threats of a "halter" intimidate. For, under God, we are determined that wheresoever, whensoever, or howsoever we shall be called to make our exit, we will die free men.

(*Observations on the Boston Port Bill*, 1774)

Josiah Quincy the younger (1772–1864): *Federalist politician*

If this bill passes it is my deliberate opinion that it is virtually a dissolution of this Union; that it will free the states from their moral obligation; and, as it will be the right of all, so it will be the duty of some, definitely to prepare for a separation—amicably if they can, violently if they must.

(Speech in Congress on the bill to admit Orleans Territory as a state, 14 January 1811)

R

Milton Rakove (1918–   ): *Political scientist*
The amount of effort put into a campaign by a worker expands in proportion to the personal benefits that he will derive from his party's victory.
(The Virginia Quarterly Review, Summer 1965)

A. Philip Randolph (1889–1979): *Labor and civil rights leader*
The essential value of an all-Negro movement such as the March on Washington is that it helps to create faith by Negroes in Negroes. It develops a sense of self-reliance with Negroes depending on Negroes in vital matters. It helps to break down the slave psychology and inferiority-complex in Negroes which comes and is nourished with Negroes relying on white people for direction and support. This inevitably happens in mixed organizations that are supposed to be in the interest of the Negro.
(Speech to March on Washington Committee, September 1942)

Jeannette Rankin (1880–1973): *Congresswoman from Montana*
As a woman I can't go to war, and I refuse to send anyone else.
(On casting the single vote in Congress against the declaration of war on Japan, 8 December 1941)

John J. Raskob (1879–1950): *Industrialist and politician*
Everybody Ought To Be Rich.
(Title of a magazine article in the *Ladies' Home Journal,* October 1929)

Ronald Reagan (1911–   ): *Governor of California and fortieth president*

Once you've seen one redwood tree, you've seen them all.

(Alleged remark at a press conference, 1966, later denied)

I am very proud to be called a pig. It stands for pride, integrity, and guts.

(At a press conference, 1970)

This would be a good time for a botulism epidemic.

(Remark when kidnappers of Patricia Hearst demanded free canned goods be distributed to the poor, May 1974)

We are told that détente is our best hope for a lasting peace. Hope it may offer, but only so long as we have no illusions about it. . . . When the stakes are war and peace, we can bargain successfully only if we are strong militarily and only if we are willing to defend ourselves if necessary. We must also have a sense of unity and a national purpose in our foreign policy.

(Speech at Phillips Exeter Academy, 10 February 1974)

Double—no triple—our troubles and we'd still be better off than any other people on earth.

It is time that we recognized that ours was, in truth, a noble cause.

(On the Vietnam War, speech in Boston, August 1980)

We are threatened with an economic calamity of tremendous proportions, and the old business-as-usual treatment can't save us.

(Speech in Washington, 5 January 1981)

I hope you're all Republicans.

(Remark to physicians when he was wounded in an assassination attempt by the son of an oil man, 1981)

They came home without a victory not because they had been defeated but because they had been denied permission to win.

(On Vietnam speech in Washington, 24 February 1981)

I could see where you could have the exchange of tactical [nuclear] weapons against troops in the field without it bringing either of the major powers to pushing the button.

(Interview, 16 October 1981)

Let us be aware that while they preach the supremacy of the state and predict its eventual domination of all peoples on earth, they are the focus of evil in the modern world. Let us pray for the salvation of all those who live in that totalitarian darkness—pray they will discover the joy of knowing God. But until they do, let us be aware they are the focus of evil in the world.

(Speech on Communists to North American Evangelical Association, Orlando, Florida, March 1983)

Red Jacket (1758?–1808): *Seneca Indian chief*

Brother, our seats were once large, and yours were very small; you have now become a great people, and we have scarcely left a place to spread our blankets; you have got our country, but are not satisfied; you want to force your religion upon us.

(Speech to missionaries, Buffalo, 1805)

Thomas B. Reed (1839–1902): *Speaker of the House of Representatives from Maine*

Isn't this a billion-dollar country?

(When the Congress he headed was called the "billion-dollar Congress" for its huge appropriations, May 1891)

Ten million Malays at two dollars a head.

(On the payment of $20 million to Spain as compensation for annexing the Philippine Islands, which he opposed, February 1899)

A statesman is a successful politician who is dead.

(Attributed)

The right of the minority is to draw its salaries and its function is to make a quorum.

(Attributed)

James Reston (1909–   ): *Newspaper columnist*

This is the devilish thing about foreign affairs: they are foreign and will not always conform to our whim.

(*New York Times*, 16 December 1964)

America started the sixties thinking it could save the world and ended them wondering whether it could save face.

(*New York Times*, 30 December 1969)

Walter P. Reuther (1907–1970): *Labor leader*

Mr. John Foster Dulles—the world's longest-range misguided missile.

(July 1956)

Paul Revere (1735–1818): *Silversmith and Revolutionary War agitator*

The British are coming.

(Warning to the farmers around Boston, 18 April 1775)

Charles H. Revson (1906–1975): *Businessman*

I don't meet my competition, I crush it.

(At a business meeting)

Grantland Rice (1880–1954): *Sports journalist*

For when the one Great Scorer comes
To write against your name,
He marks—not that you won or lost—
But how you played the game.

(*Alumnus Football,* 1925)

Donald Richberg (1881–1960): *Adviser to Franklin D. Roosevelt*

In the first months of N.R.A. it seemed as though a great part of the business world has "got religion."

(*The Rainbow,* 1936)

Robert Leroy Ripley (1893–1949): *Journalist*

Believe it or not.

(Title of a newspaper feature, mid-twentieth century)

John D. Rockefeller (1839–1937): *Industrial entrepreneur and philanthropist*

This movement was the origin of the whole system of modern economic administration. It has revolutionized the way of doing business all over the world. The time was ripe for it. It had to come, though all we saw at the moment was the need to save ourselves from wasteful conditions. . . . The day of combination is here to stay. Individualism has gone, never to return.

(On his monopolization of the petroleum refining industry, 1895)

I ascribe the success of the Standard Oil Company to its consistent policy of making the volume of its business large enough through the merit and cheapness of its products.

(Ibid.)

God gave it to me.

(When asked about his fortune, attributed)

John D. Rockefeller, Jr. (1874–1960): *Industrialist and philanthropist*

I believe that every right implies a responsibility; every opportunity, an obligation; every possession, a duty.

(Attributed)

The growth of a large business is merely the survival of the fittest. The American Beauty Rose can be produced in the splendor and fragrance which bring cheer to its beholder only by sacrificing the early buds which grow up around it. This is not an evil tendency in business. It is merely the working out of a law of nature and a law of God.

(Sunday school lesson, attributed)

George Lincoln Rockwell (1918–1967): *American Nazi leader*

Goose pimples rose all over me, my hair stood on end, my eyes filled with tears of love and gratitude for this greatest of all conquerors of human misery and shame, and my breath came in little gasps. If I had not known that the leader would have scorned such adulation I might have fallen to my knees in unashamed worship, but instead I drew myself to attention, raised my arms in the eternal salute of the ancient Roman Legions and repeated the holy words, "Heil Hitler!"

(Speech to party members, 1965)

Roy Rogers (1912–   ): *"Singing Cowboy" movie actor*

They'll have to shoot me first to take my gun.

(Interview on California gun control law, 1982)

Will Rogers (1879–1935): *Humorist*

All I know is just what I read in the papers.
(Catch phrase in his lectures)

They got him in the morning editions, but the afternoon ones let him get away.
(On General Pershing's pursuit of Pancho Villa, 1916)

The more you read and observe about this Politics thing, you got to admit that each party is worse than the other. The one that's out always looks the best.
(*The Illiterate Digest*, 1924)

More men have been elected between Sundown and Sunup than ever were elected between Sunup and Sundown.
(Ibid.)

The Income Tax has made more Liars out of the American people than golf has.
(Ibid.)

We'll hold the distinction of being the only nation in the history of the world that ever went to the poorhouse in an automobile.
(Remark, 1932)

I tell you, Folks, all Politics is Apple Sauce.
(Ibid.)

A Country can get more real joy out of just Hollering for their Freedom than they can if they get it.
(*Autobiography*, 1927)

If you can build a business up big enough, it's respectable.
(Ibid.)

A Congressman is never any better than his roads, and sometimes worse.
(Ibid.)

Communism is like Prohibition, it's a good idea but it won't work.
(Ibid.)

Let Wall Street have a nightmare and the whole country has to help get them back in bed again.

(Ibid.)

One of the evils of democracy is, you have to put up with the man you elect whether you want him or not.

(Ibid.)

The United States never lost a war or won a conference.

(Ibid.)

If we ever pass out as a great nation we ought to put on our tombstone "America died from a delusion that she had moral leadership."

(Ibid.)

I don't make jokes—I just watch the government and report the facts.

(Ibid.)

It's not politics that is worrying this Country; it's the Second Payment.

(Ibid.)

Coolidge is a better example of evolution than either Bryan or Darrow, for he knows when not to talk, which is the biggest asset the monkey possesses over the human.

(Ibid.)

Any nation is heathen that ain't strong enough to punch you in the jaw. . . . Missionaries teach em not only to serve the Lord but run a Ford car . . . then the American agent sells em one. . . . You take religion backed up by Commerce and it's awful hard for a heathen to overcome.

(Ibid.)

The way to judge a good Comedy is by how long it will last and how people talk about it. Now Congress has turned out some that have lived for years and people are still laughing about them.

(Ibid.)

Eleanor Roosevelt (1884–1962): *Wife of Franklin D. Roosevelt, reformer*

I think if the people of this country can be reached with the truth, their judgment will be in favor of the many, as against the privileged few.

(Ladies' Home Journal, May 1942)

Many of the Asiatic people have a profound distrust of white people. This is understandable since the white people they have known intimately in the past have been the colonial nations and in the case of the United States our businessmen.

(Report to President Truman, 1950)

We cannot exist as a little island of well-being in a world where two-thirds of the people go to bed hungry every night.

(Speech at a Democratic Party dinner, 8 December 1959)

Franklin Delano Roosevelt (1882–1945): *Thirty-second president*

Hoover certainly is a wonder, and I wish we could make him President of the United States. There could not be a better one.

(On Herbert Hoover, 1919)

The facts are that I wrote Haiti's constitution myself, and, if I do say it, I think it is a pretty good constitution.

(Campaign speech, 1920)

The forgotten man at the bottom of the economic pyramid.

(Radio speech, 7 April 1932)

I pledge you—I pledge myself—to a new deal for the American people.

(Speech accepting Democratic nomination for the presidency, Chicago, 2 July 1932)

The country needs and, unless I mistake its temper, the country demands bold, persistent experimentation. It is common sense to take a method and try it. If it fails, admit it frankly and try another. But above all, try something.

(Speech, Atlanta, Georgia, 1932)

It is the purpose of the government to see that not only the legitimate interests of the few are protected but that the welfare and rights of the many are conserved.

(Speech, Portland, Oregon, 21 September 1932)

Knowledge—that is, education in its true sense—is our best protection against unreasoning prejudice and panic-making fear, whether engendered by special interest, illiberal minorities, or panic-stricken leaders.

(Speech, Boston, 31 October 1932)

The fate of America cannot depend on any one man. The greatness of America is grounded in principles and not on any single personality.

(Speech, New York City, 5 November 1932)

The only thing we have to fear is fear itself.

(First inaugural address, 4 March 1933)

In the field of world policy I would dedicate this nation to the policy of the good neighbor.

(Ibid.)

There is no group in America that can withstand the force of an aroused public opinion.

(Statement on signing the National Industrial Recovery Act, 16 June 1933)

I sometimes think that the saving grace of America lies in the fact that the overwhelming majority of Americans are possessed of two great qualities—a sense of humor and a sense of proportion.

(Speech, Savannah, Georgia, 18 November 1933)

Self-help and self-control are the essence of the American tradition.

(State of the Union Message, 3 January 1934)

The time is ripe for an alliance of all forces bent upon the business of recovery. In such an alliance will be found business and banking, agriculture and industry, and labor and capital. What an All-American team that would be!

(Address to American Bankers Association, October 1934)

If Great Britain is even suspected of preferring to play with Japan to playing with us, I shall be compelled, in the interest of American security, to approach public sentiment in Canada, Australia, New Zealand and South Africa in a definite effort to make these Dominions clearly understand that their future security is linked with us in the United States.

(Memorandum to Norman Davis, 1934)

Nationwide thinking, nationwide planning and nationwide action are the three great essentials to prevent nationwide crises for future generations to struggle through.

(Speech, New York City, 25 April 1936)

Governments can err. Presidents do make mistakes, but the immortal Dante tells us that divine justice weighs the sins of the cold-blooded and the sins of the warm-hearted in different scales. Better the occasional faults of a Government that lives in a spirit of charity than the consistent omissions of a Government frozen in the ice of its own indifference.

(Speech accepting renomination, Philadelphia, 27 June 1936)

This generation of Americans has a rendezvous with destiny.

(Ibid.)

I hate war. I have passed unnumbered hours, I shall pass unnumbered hours, thinking and planning how war may be kept from this nation.

(Radio address, August 1936)

If I came out for the anti-lynching bill now, they [southern congressmen] will block every bill I ask Congress to pass to keep America from collapsing. I just can't take that risk.

(To leaders of the National Association for the Advancement of Colored People, 1936)

Labor Day symbolizes our determination to achieve an economic freedom for the average man which will give his political freedom reality.

(Radio speech, 6 September 1936)

Inside the polling booth every American man and woman stands as the equal of every other American man and woman. There they have no superiors. There they have no masters save their own minds and consciences.

(Speech, Worcester, Massachusetts, 21 October 1936)

Taxes, after all, are the dues that we pay for the privileges of membership in an organized society.

(Ibid.)

I see one-third of a nation ill-housed, ill-clad, ill-nourished.

(Second inaugural address, 20 January 1937)

The nation that destroys its soil destroys itself.

(Letter to the governors urging uniform soil conservation laws, 26 February 1937)

It is the duty of the President to propose and it is the privilege of the Congress to dispose.

(Press conference, 23 July 1937)

Quarantine the aggressors.

(Speech, Chicago, 5 October 1937)

America hates war. America hopes for peace. Therefore, America actively engages in the search for peace.

(Ibid.)

No democracy can long survive which does not accept as fundamental to its very existence the recognition of the rights of minorities.

(Letter to the National Association for the Advancement of Colored People, 25 June 1938)

Our national debt after all is an internal debt owed not only *by* the nation but *to* the nation. If our children have to pay interest on it they will pay that interest to *themselves*.

(Speech before the American Retail Foundation, Washington, D.C., 22 May 1939)

When peace has been broken anywhere, the peace of all countries everywhere is in danger.

(Radio broadcast, 3 September 1939)

A conservative is a man with two perfectly good legs who, however, has never learned to walk forwards. . . . A reactionary is a somnambulist walking backwards. . . . A radical is a man with both feet firmly planted in the air. . . . A Liberal is a man who uses his legs and his hands at the behest—at the command—of his head.

(Radio speech, 26 October 1939)

I have told you once and I will tell you again—your boys will not be sent into any foreign wars.

(Campaign speech, 1940)

On this tenth day of June 1940, the hand that held the dagger has struck it into the back of its neighbor. . . . Neither those who sprang from that ancient stock nor those who have come hither in later years can be indifferent to the destruction of freedom in their ancestral lands across the seas.

(On Mussolini's invasion of France, speech, Charlottesville, Virginia, 10 June 1940)

No man can tame a tiger into a kitten by stroking it. There can be no appeasement with ruthlessness. There can be no reasoning with an incendiary bomb.

(Radio speech, 29 December 1940)

It is one of the characteristics of a free and democratic modern nation that it have free and independent labor unions.

(Address before the Teamsters' Union convention, Washington, D.C., 11 September 1940)

We must be the great arsenal of democracy.

(Ibid.)

The best immediate defense of the United States is the success of Great Britain defending itself.

(Press conference, 17 December 1940)

We look forward to a world founded upon four essential human freedoms. The first is freedom of speech and expression—everywhere in the world. The second is freedom of every person to worship God in his own way—everywhere in the world. The third is freedom from want . . . everywhere in the world. The fourth is freedom from fear . . . anywhere in the world.

(Speech to Congress, 6 January 1941)

Yesterday, December 7, 1941—a date which will live in infamy—the United States of America was suddenly and deliberately attacked by naval and air forces of the Empire of Japan.

(Speech to Congress, 8 December 1941)

Defeat of Germany means the defeat of Japan, probably without firing a shot or losing a life.

(Message to Winston Churchill, 1942)

We all know that books burn—yet we have the greater knowledge that books cannot be killed by fire. People die, but books never die. No man and no force can abolish memory. . . . In this war, we know, books are weapons.

(Message to American Booksellers Association, 23 April 1942)

It is fun to be in the same decade with you.

(Cable to Winston Churchill, responding to congratulations on his sixtieth birthday, 1942)

Stalin hates the guts of all your top people. He thinks he likes me better and I hope he will continue to do so.

(In conversation with Churchill, attributed)

True individual freedom cannot exist without economic security and independence. People who are hungry and out of a job are the stuff of which dictatorships are made.

(Message to Congress, 11 January 1944)

You sometimes find something good in the lunatic fringe. In fact, we have got as part of our social and economic government today a whole lot of things which in my boyhood were considered lunatic fringe, and yet they are now part of everyday life.

(Press conference, 30 May 1944)

More than an end to war, we want an end to the beginnings of all wars.

(Speech written to be broadcast, 13 April 1945, the day after his death)

Theodore Roosevelt (1858–1919): *Twenty-sixth president*

I don't go so far as to think that the only good Indians are dead Indians, but I believe nine out of every ten are, and I shouldn't inquire too closely into the cause of the tenth. The most vicious cowboy has more moral principle than the average Indian.

(Letter to Owen Wister, 1885)

I like to see a mob handled by the regulars, or by good State-Guards, not over-scrupulous about bloodshed.

(On President Cleveland's use of federal troops in the American Railway Union's Pullman car boycott, 1894)

As much backbone as a chocolate éclair.

(On his predecessor in the presidency, William McKinley, attributed, 1898)

Let the fight come if it must. I rather hope that the fight will come soon. The clamor of the peace faction has convinced me that this country needs a war.

(Letter to John Hay, 1898)

I wish to preach, not the doctrine of ignoble ease, but the doctrine of the strenuous life.

(Speech, Chicago, 10 April 1899)

It is a dreadful thing to come into the presidency in this way; but it would be a far worse thing to be morbid about it.

(On McKinley's assassination and his own inauguration as president, September 1901)

How I wish I wasn't a reformer, oh, Senator! But I suppose I must live up to my part, like the Negro minstrel who blacked himself all over.

(To Chauncey Depew, president of the New York Central Railroad, 1901)

There is a homely adage which runs, "Speak softly and carry a big stick; you will go far." If the American nation will speak softly and yet build and keep at a pitch of the highest training a thoroughly efficient navy, the Monroe Doctrine will go far.
(Speech in Minnesota, 2 September 1901)

The first requisite of a good citizen in this Republic of ours is that he shall be able and willing to pull his weight.
(Speech, New York City, 11 November 1902)

From the very beginning our people have markedly combined practical capacity for affairs with power of devotion to an ideal. The lack of either quality would have rendered the other of small value.
(Speech, Philadelphia, 22 November 1902)

Damn the law! I want the canal built.
(Attributed, 1903)

A man who is good enough to shed his blood for the country is good enough to be given a square deal afterwards. More than that no man is entitled to, and less than that no man shall have.
(Speech at Springfield, Illinois, 4 June 1903)

Perdicaris alive or Raisuli dead.
(Cable to Morocco referring to the kidnapping of an American citizen (Perdicaris) by a Moroccan bandit (Raisuli), 1904)

A wise custom which limits the President to two terms regards the substance and not the form, and under no circumstances will I be a candidate for or accept another nomination.
(Statement after his election, November 1904)

In the Western hemisphere the adherence of the United States to the Monroe Doctrine may force the United States, however reluctantly, in flagrant cases of wrongdoing or impotence, to the exercise of an international police power.
(Message to Congress, 6 December 1904)

I never take a step in foreign policy unless I am assured that I shall be able eventually to carry out my will by force.
(Remark, 1905)

The men with the muckrakes are often indispensable to well-being of society; but only if they know when to stop raking the muck.

(Speech in Washington, D.C., 14 April 1906)

The great virtue of my radicalism lies in the fact that I am perfectly ready, if necessary, to be radical on the conservative side.

(Letter to William Howard Taft, 4 September 1906)

I do not like the social conditions at present. The dull, pure-blind folly of the very rich men, their greed and arrogance . . . have tended to produce a very unhealthy condition of excitement in the popular mind, which shows itself in part in the enormous increase in the socialist propaganda.

(Letter to William Howard Taft, 1906)

A really great people, proud and high-spirited, would face all the disasters of war rather than purchase that base prosperity which is bought at the price of national honor.

(Speech at Harvard University, 23 February 1907)

Malefactors of great wealth. . . .

(Speech, Provincetown, Massachusetts, 20 August 1907)

A man who has never gone to school may steal from a freight car; but if he has a university education, he may steal the whole railroad.

(Ibid.)

Personally I believe in woman's suffrage, but I am not an enthusiastic advocate of it, because I do not regard it as a very important matter. I am unable to see that there has been any special improvement in the position of women in those states in the West that have adopted woman's suffrage, as compared with those states adjoining them that have not adopted it. I do not think that giving the women suffrage will produce any marked improvement in the condition of women. I do not believe that it will produce any of the evils feared, and I am very certain that when women as a whole take any special interest in the matter they will have suffrage if they desire it.

(Letter, 1908)

The White House is a bully pulpit!

(Attributed)

Every man holds his property subject to the general right of the community to regulate its use to whatever degree the public welfare may require it.

(Speech at Osawatomie, Kansas, July 1910)

I am interested in the Panama Canal because I started it. If I had followed traditional, conservative methods I would have presented a dignified state paper of 200 pages to Congress and the debates on it would have been going on yet; but I took the Canal Zone and let Congress debate; and while the debate goes on the Canal does also.

(Speech in Berkeley, California, 1911)

My hat's in the ring! The fight is on and I am stripped to the buff!

(Declaring his candidacy for president, February 1912)

We fight in honorable fashion for the good of mankind; fearless of the future, unheeding of our individual fates, with unflinching hearts and undimmed eyes; we stand at Armageddon, and we battle for the Lord.

(On the eve of the Republican Party convention, 1912)

I am as strong as a bull moose and you can use me to the limit.

(Speech to Progressive Party rally, 14 October 1912)

We stand for the Constitution, but we will not consent to make of the Constitution a fetish for the protection of fossilized wrong.

(Final campaign speech, 1912)

Do not hit at all if it can be avoided, but never hit softly.

(*Autobiography*, 1913)

It is vitally necessary to move forward and to shake off the dead hand, often a fossilized dead hand, of the reactionaries; and yet we have to face the fact that there is apt to be a lunatic fringe among the votaries of any forward movement.

(Ibid.)

We demand that big business give the people a square deal; in return we must insist that when anyone engaged in big business honestly endeavors to do right he shall himself be given a square deal.

(*Autobiography,* 1913)

Don't flinch, don't foul, and hit the line hard.

(Address to Boys Progressive League, 1913)

There is no room in this country for hyphenated Americanism.

(Speech, New York City, 12 October 1915)

There can be no fifty-fifty Americanism in this country. There is room here for only hundred percent Americanism, only for those who are Americans and nothing else.

(Speech, Saratoga, New York, 19 July 1918)

The hyphenated American always hoists the American flag undermost.

(Ibid.)

We have room in this country for but one flag, the Stars and Stripes. . . . We have room for but one loyalty, loyalty to the United States. . . . We have room for but one language, the English language.

(Final speech before the American Defense Society, 3 January 1919)

The most successful politician is he who says what everybody is thinking most often and in the loudest voice.

(Attributed)

Elihu Root (1845–1937): *Secretary of state*

What a disgusting, dishonest fakir Bryan is! When I see so many Americans running after him, I feel very much as I do when a really lovely woman falls in love with a cad.

(Letter to William M. Laffa, 31 October 1900)

You have made a very good start in life, and your friends have great hopes for you when you grow up.

(To Theodore Roosevelt on his forty-sixth birthday, 1904)

George F. Root (1820–1895): *Songwriter*

> Yes, we'll rally round the flag, boys, we'll rally
>   once again,
>   Shouting the battle-cry of Freedom.
> We will rally from the hill-side, we'll gather from
>   the plain,
>   Shouting the battle-cry of Freedom.

("Battle Cry of Freedom," 1863)

Julius Rosenberg (1918–1953): *Convicted spy*

We are innocent. That is the whole truth. To forsake this truth is to pay too high a price even for the priceless gift of life. For life thus purchased we could not live out in dignity.

(Final petition for clemency to President Eisenhower, June 1953)

Edward A. Ross (1866–1951): *Sociologist*

One man one vote does not make Sambo equal to Socrates in the state.

(*Changing America*, 1912)

Observe immigrants. . . . You are struck by the fact that from ten to twenty percent are hirsute, low-browed, big-faced persons of obviously low mentality. . . . They clearly belong in skins, in wattled huts at the close of the Great Ice Age. These oxlike men are descendants of those who always stayed behind.

(Ibid.)

Harold Ross (1892–1951): *Editor and publisher*

Not for the little old lady in Dubuque.

(Prospectus for the *New Yorker* magazine, 1925)

Theodore Roszak (1933–   ): *Historian*

Nothing less is required than the subversion of the scientific world view with its intrenched commitment to an egocentric and cerebral mode of consciousness. In its place there must be a new culture in which the non-intellective capacities of personality—those capacities that take fire from visionary splendor and the experiences of human communion—become the arbiters of the true, the good and the beautiful.

(*The Making of a Counter-Culture*, 1968)

Philip Roth (1933–): *Novelist*

In America everything goes and nothing matters. While in Europe nothing goes and everything matters.

(Interview, *Time*, November 1983)

Henry V. Rothschild (1834–1911): *Manufacturer*

I say the legislature has no right to encroach upon me as to whether I shall employ men eight hours, or ten, or fifteen hours. It is a matter of mutual agreement, and the legislature has no right, according to the principles of the Declaration of Independence, to impose upon me what hours of labor I shall have between myself and my employees.

(Testimony to select committee of the House of Representatives, 1879)

Carl Rowan (1925–): *Newspaper columnist*

My advice to any diplomat who wants to have a good press is to have two or three kids and a dog.

(*New Yorker*, 7 December 1963)

Jerry Rubin (1940–): *Youth-movement leader and stockbroker*

Screw work. We want to know ourselves.

(*Do It!*, 1970)

When in doubt, burn. Fire is the revolutionary's god. Fire is instant theater. No words can match fire.

Politicians only notice poverty when the ghettos burn.

The burning of the first draft card caused earth tremors under the Pentagon.

Burn the flag. Burn churches.

Burn, burn, burn. . . .

(Ibid.)

I'm famous. That's my job.

(*Growing Up at 37*, 1976)

Mark Rudd (1947–): *Collegiate revolutionary leader*

If we win, we will take control of your world, your corporations, your university, and attempt to mold a world in which we and other people can live as human beings.

(Speech at Columbia University, April 1968)

Stanley Rudin (1929–   ): *Writer*

Frustrate a Frenchman, he will drink himself to death; an Irishman, he will die of angry hypertension; a Dane, he will shoot himself; an American, he will get drunk, shoot you, then establish a million-dollar aid program for your relatives. Then he will die of an ulcer.

(*New York Times,* 22 August 1963)

Dean Rusk (1909–   ): *Secretary of state under Presidents Kennedy and Johnson*

I wouldn't make the slightest concession for moral leadership. It's much over-rated.

(Remark, 1962)

We're eyeball to eyeball, and the other fellow just blinked.

(Remark to reporters during the Cuban missile crisis, October 1962)

I saw my first movie in Atlanta, Georgia, during World War I. It was a William S. Hart western and was shown in a small neighborhood theatre with player piano and a ten-cent admission. . . . As for lasting influence of the William S. Hart westerns and the serialized thrillers of those early days, I am not especially aware of one, unless it be that the "Good-uns" somehow managed to overcome the "Bad-uns."

(Interview in *Show,* April 1963)

The pace of events is moving so fast that unless we can find some way to keep our sights on tomorrow, we cannot expect to be in touch with today.

(Interview in *Time,* 6 December 1963)

While we are sleeping, two-thirds of the world is plotting to do us in.

(Attributed)

We tried to do in cold blood perhaps what can only be done in hot blood, when sacrifices of this order are involved.

(Reminiscing on the Vietnam War, 1980)

Richard Russell (1897–1971): *Senator from Georgia*
If we have to start over again with another Adam and Eve, I want them to be Americans, not Russians.
(Speech on defense, 1968)

George Herman "Babe" Ruth (1894–1948): *Baseball player*
I had a better year than he did.
(When told that Herbert Hoover made less than the $80,000 annual salary Ruth demanded, attributed, 1931)

S

Nicola Sacco (1891–1927): *Italian-born anarchist*
If it had not been for these things I might live out my life talking at street corners to scorning men. I might have died unmarked, a failure, unknown. Now we are not a failure. This is our career and our triumph. Never in our full life could we hope to do such work for tolerance, for justice and for man's understanding of man.
(Final statement before his execution, 1927)

Mort Sahl (1927–   ): *Canadian-born comedian*
Would you buy a used car from this man?
(Of Richard M. Nixon, catch phrase in his routine, 1960)

Carl Sandburg (1878–1967): *Poet*
Hog Butcher for the World,
Tool Maker, Stacker of Wheat,
Player with Railroads and the
Nation's Freight
Handler. . . .
(*Chicago*, 1916)

Sometime they'll give a war and nobody will come.

(*The People, Yes,* 1936)

Slang is a language that rolls up its sleeves, spits on its hands and goes to work.

(*New York Times,* 13 February 1959)

Margaret Sanger (1883–1966): *Birth-control pioneer*

No woman can call herself free who does not own and control her body. No woman can call herself free until she can choose consciously whether she will or will not be a mother.

(*Motherhood in Bondage,* 1928)

Awaken the womanhood of America to free the motherhood of the world!

(*My Fight for Birth Control,* 1931)

George Santayana (1863–1952): *Philosopher*

It is right to prefer our own country to all others, because we are children and citizens before we can be travellers or philosophers.

(*The Life of Reason,* 1905)

America is the greatest of opportunities and the worst of influences.

(*The Last Puritan,* 1935)

American life is a powerful solvent. It seems to neutralize every intellectual element, however tough and alien it may be, and to fuse it in the native goodwill, complacency, thoughtlessness, and optimism.

All his life [the American] jumps into the train after it has started and jumps out before it has stopped; and he never once gets left behind, or breaks a leg.

(*Character and Opinion in the United States,* 1920)

Mario Savio (1942–): *Student-movement leader*

There is a time when the operation of the machine becomes so odious, makes you so sick at heart that you can't take part; you can't even tacitly take part, and you've got to put your bodies upon the levers, upon all that apparatus and you've got to make it stop. And you've got to indicate to the people who run it, to the people who own it, that unless you're free the machine will be prevented from working at all.

(Speech to rebellious students, Berkeley, California, 2 December 1964)

Gloria Schaffer (1930–): *Connecticut politician*

Women's place is in the House and in the Senate.

(Remark, 1976)

Thomas D. Schall (1877–1935): *Senator from Minnesota*

To hell with Europe!

(Speech in Congress, May 1953)

Arthur M. Schlesinger, Jr. (1917–): *Historian*

Corruption appears to visit the White House in 50-year cycles. This suggests that exposure and retribution inoculate the Presidency against its latent criminal impulses for about half a century. Around the year 2023 the American people would be well advised to go on the alert and start nailing down everything in sight.

(*The Imperial Presidency*, 1973)

Charles M. Schulz (1922–): *Cartoonist*

The way I see it, it doesn't matter what you believe just so you're sincere.

(*Go Fly a Kite, Charlie Brown*, 1963)

How can we lose when we're so sincere?

(*Peanuts*, 1968)

Carl Schurz (1829–1906): *German revolutionary of 1848, later senator from Missouri*

Our country, right or wrong. When right, to be kept right; when wrong, to be put right.

(Speech, Chicago, 1899)

Cordial international understanding rests upon a very simple, natural and solid basis. We rejoice with the nations of the Old

World in all their successes, all their prosperity, and all their happiness, and we profoundly and earnestly sympathize with them whenever a misfortune overtakes them. But one thing we shall never think of doing, and that is, interfering in their affairs.
(Ibid.)

Winfield Scott (1786–1866): *Army commander*
The enemy say that Americans are good at a long shot, but cannot stand the cold iron. I call upon you instantly to give a lie to the slander. Charge!
(To the 11th Infantry, Chippewa, Canada, 5 June 1814)

Say to the seceded States, "Wayward sisters, depart in peace."
(Letter to William H. Seward, 3 March 1861)

I am amazed that any man of judgment should hope for the success of any cause in which Jefferson Davis is a leader. There is contamination in his touch. If secession was "the holiest cause that tongue or sword of mortal ever lost or gained," he would ruin it! He will bear a great amount of watching. . . . He is not a cheap Judas. I do not think he would have sold the Saviour for thirty shillings; but for the successorship to Pontius Pilate he would have betrayed Christ and the apostles and the whole Christian Church.
(On the Confederacy, 1861)

Robert Service (1874–1958): *Popular poet*
This is the Law of the Yukon, that only the strong shall thrive;
That surely the weak shall perish, and only the Fit survive.
(*The Law of the Yukon*, 1907)

Cynthia Propper Seton (1926–   ): *Writer*
In America, to look a couple of years younger than you actually are is not only an achievement for which you are to be congratulated, it is patriotic.
(*A Special and Curious Blessing*, 1968)

William H. Seward (1801–1872): *Republican Party politician and secretary of state under Presidents Lincoln and Johnson*
There is a higher law than the Constitution.
(Speech in the Senate attacking Fugitive Slave Law, 11 March 1850)

Shall I tell you what this collision means? They who think it is accidental, unnecessary, the work of interested or fanatical agitators, and therefore ephemeral, mistake the case altogether. It is an irrepressible conflict between opposing and enduring forces, and it means that the United States must and will, sooner or later, become either entirely a slave-holding nation, or entirely a free-labour nation.

(On the conflict between pro- and antislavery forces, speech, Rochester, New York, 25 October 1858)

I would demand explanations from Spain and France, categorically, at once. I would seek explanations from Great Britain and Russia. . . . And if satisfactory explanations are not received, would convene Congress and declare war against them.

(Memorandum to Lincoln, 1 April 1961, suggested as a means to halt the secession movement in the South)

Anna Howard Shaw (1847–1919): *English-born suffragist*

No other country has subjected its women to the humiliating position to which the women of this nation have been subjected by men. . . . In Germany, German women are governed by German men; in France, French women are governed by Frenchmen; and in Great Britain, British women are governed by British men; but in this country, American women are governed by every kind of a man under the light of the sun. There is no race, there is no color, there is no nationality of men who are not the sovereign rulers of American women. . . .

(Presidential address to the National American Women's Suffrage Association, 1914)

George Bernard Shaw (1856–1950): *British playwright and social critic*

The haughty American nation . . . makes the Negro clean its boots and then proves the moral and physical inferiority of the Negro by the fact that he is a bootblack.

(Attributed)

Henry Wheeler Shaw (Josh Billings) (1818–1885): *Humorist*

Put an Englishman into the Garden of Eden, and he would find fault with the whole blarsted consarn: put a Yankee in, and he would see where he could alter it to advantage; put an Irishman in, and he would want tew boss the thing; put a Dutchman in, and he would proceed tew plant it.

(*Affurisms*, 1865)

John Holroyd, Lord Sheffield (1735–1831): *English politician*

The only use of the American colonies is the monopoly of their consumption and the carriage of their produce.

(Speech in Parliament, 1774)

Philip H. Sheridan (1831–1888): *Civil War and Indian Wars Army general*

If I owned Texas and Hell, I would rent out Texas and live in Hell.

(Alleged remark as a junior officer, Fort Clark, Texas, 1855)

A crow could not fly over it without carrying his rations with him.

(On his campaign of destruction in the Shenandoah Valley, October 1864)

The only good Indian is a dead Indian.

(Replying to Tochaway, a Comanche chief who introduced himself, "Me good Indian," Fort Cobb, Indian Territory, January 1869)

John Sherman (1823–1900): *Senator from Ohio and secretary of the treasury*

Every contract, combination in the form of trust or otherwise, or conspiracy in restraint of trade or commerce among the several States, or with foreign nations, is hereby declared to be illegal.

(Sherman Anti-Trust Act, passed 2 July 1890, and probably drafted by Senator George F. Hoar)

Sidney Sherman (1805–1873): *Texan army officer*

Remember the Alamo!

(Battle cry uttered at the Battle of San Jacinto, 21 April 1836)

William Tecumseh Sherman (1820–1891): *Civil War general*

You will please inform him that Upper California is now American territory.

(Message to be relayed to Pio Pico, the Mexican governor of Alta California, July 1846)

Vox populi, vox humbug.

(Letter to his wife, 2 June 1863)

Hold the fort. I am coming.

(Flag signal to beleaguered General John M. Corse, Kenesaw Mountain, Georgia, 1864)

We have devoured the land and our animals eat up the wheat and corn fields close. All the people retire before us and desolation is behind. To realize what war is one should follow our tracks.

(On the campaign around Atlanta, 26 June 1864)

We have now provided reservations for all, off the great roads. All who cling to their old hunting grounds are hostile and will remain so till killed off. We will have a sort of predatory war for years . . . but the country is so large and the advantage of the Indians so great, that we cannot make a single war end it.

(On the settlement of the Plains Indians on reservations, 1868)

You can make an Injun of a white man but you can never make a white man of an Injun.

(Attributed, 1868)

War is cruelty, and you cannot refine it.

(*Memoirs*, 1875)

I am tired and sick of war. Its glory is all moonshine. It is only those who have neither fired a shot nor heard the shrieks and groans of the wounded who cry aloud for blood, more vengeance, more desolation. War is hell.

(Speech at Michigan Military Academy, 19 June 1879)

There is many a boy here to-day who looks on war as all glory, but, boys, it is all hell. You can bear this warning voice to generations yet to come. I look upon war with horror.

(Speech, Columbus, Ohio, 11 August 1880)

I will not accept if nominated and will not serve if elected.

(Telegram to Republican Convention, June 1884)

David M. Shoup (1904–   ): *Marine corps commandant and critic of the Vietnam War*

I want to tell you, I don't think the whole of Southeast Asia, as related to the present and future safety and freedom of the people of this country, is worth the life or limb of a single American.

(Speech at Los Angeles, 14 May 1966)

Louis Simpson (1923–   ): *Poet*

It's complicated, being an American,
Having the money and the bad conscience, both at the
    same time.

("On the Lawn at the Villa," *Selected Poems*, 1965)

Upton Sinclair (1878–1968): *Muckraking writer*

There was never the least attention paid to what was cut up for sausage; there would come all the way back from Europe old sausage that had been rejected, and that was mouldy and white—it would be closed with borax and glycerine, and dumped into the hoppers, and made over again for home consumption. There would be meat that had tumbled out on the floor, in the dirt and sawdust, where the workers had tramped and spit uncounted billions of germs. There would be meat stored in great piles in rooms; and the water from leaky roofs would drip over it, and thousands of rats would race about on it. It was too dark in these storage places to see well, but a man could run his hand over these piles of meat and sweep off handfuls of the dried dung of rats. These rats were nuisances, and the packers would put poisoned bread out for them; they would die, and then rats, bread, and meat would go into the hoppers together.

(*The Jungle*, 1906)

Sirhan Sirhan (1944–   ): *Jordanian-born assassin of Robert F. Kennedy*

They can gas me, but I am famous. I have achieved in one day what it took Robert Kennedy all his life to do.

(Shortly after shooting Kennedy, June 1968)

Sitting Bull (1831?–1890): *Hunkpapa Sioux chief and entertainer*

I wish all to know that I do not propose to sell any part of my country, nor will I have the whites cutting our timber along the rivers, more especially the oak. I am particularly fond of the little groves of oak trees. I love to look at them, because they endure the wintry storm and the summer's heat and—not unlike ourselves—seem to flourish by them.

(To army officers, 1875)

There is no use in talking to these Americans. They are all liars. You cannot believe anything they say.

(To James MacLeod, Royal Canadian Mounted Police commissioner, when the U. S. government requested Sitting Bull's return from Canada, Fort Walsh, Saskatchewan, September 1877)

When I was a boy the Sioux owned the world; the sun rose and set on their land; they sent ten thousand men to battle. Where are the warriors today? Who slew them? Where are our lands? Who owns them? What white man can say I ever stole his land or a penny of his money? Yet, they say I am a thief. What white woman, however lonely, was ever captive or insulted by me? Yet they say I am a bad Indian. What white man has ever seen me drunk? Who has ever come to me hungry and unfed? Who has ever seen me beat my wives or abuse my children? What law have I broken? Is it wrong for me to love my own? Is it wicked for me because my skin is red? Because I am a Sioux; because I was born where my father lived; because I would die for my people and my country?

(On returning to the U. S. from Canada, 1881)

The white man knows how to make everything, but he does not know how to distribute it.

(In conversation with Annie Oakley, when, touring with *Buffalo Bill's Wild West Show*, he saw the slums of American cities, 1885)

Eric Sloane (1910–   ): *Artist and author*

Capitalism equals love of money in my view, and we didn't start out that way. We started out with a love of individual enterprise.

(*The Spirits of '76*, 1973)

Adam Smith (1723–1790): *English economist*

England purchased for some of her subjects, who found themselves uneasy at home, a great estate in a distant country.

(*Wealth of Nations*, 1776)

Alfred E. Smith (1873–1944): *Governor of New York and Democratic Party presidential nominee, 1928*

I know nothing whatsoever about papal bulls and encyclicals.

(Response to an argument in the *Atlantic Monthly* that he, as a Roman Catholic, could not take the presidential oath of allegiance, May 1927)

I recognize no power in the institutions of my church to interfere with the operations of the Constitution of the United States or the enforcement of the law of the land.

(Ibid.)

All the ills of democracy can be cured by more democracy.

(Campaign speech, October 1928)

No matter how thin you slice it, it's still baloney.

(Speech, 1936)

John Smith (1579–1631): *English colonizer*

You must obey this, now, for a law—that "he that will not work shall not eat."

(Orders to settlers at Jamestown, 1608, *General Historie of Virginia*, 1624)

Samuel Francis Smith (1808–1895): *Baptist minister*

My country, 'tis of thee,
Sweet land of liberty,
    Of thee I sing:
Land where my fathers died,
Land of the pilgrims' pride,
From every mountain side
    Let freedom ring.

("America" [sung to the tune of "God Save the King"], 4 July 1831)

Sydney Smith (1771–1845): *English divine and wit*

In the four quarters of the globe, who reads an American book? or goes to an American play? or looks at an American picture or statue? What does the world yet owe to American physicians or surgeons? What new substances have their chemists discovered? or what old ones have they analyzed? What new constellations have been discovered by the telescopes of Americans?—what have they done in the mathematics? Who drinks out of American glasses? or eats from American plates? or wears American coats or gowns? or sleeps in American blankets?—Finally, under which of the old tyrannical governments of Europe is every sixth man a slave, whom his fellow-creatures may buy and sell and torture?

(Edinburgh Review, 1820)

John Babson Soule (1815–1891): *Journalist*

Go west, young man.

(Terre Haute, Indiana Express, 1851, usually attributed to Horace Greeley)

Benjamin M. Spock (1903–   ): *Pediatrician and antinuclear arms agitator*

To win in Vietnam, we will have to exterminate a nation.

(Dr. Spock on Vietnam, 1968)

Charles E. Stanton (1859–1933): *World War I colonel*

America has joined forces with the Allied Powers, and what we have of blood and treasure are yours. Therefore it is with loving pride we drape the colors in tribute of respect to this citizen of your great republic. And here and now in the presence of the illustrious dead we pledge our hearts and our honor in carrying this war to a successful issue. Lafayette, we are here.

(Speech at Lafayette's tomb, Paris, 4 July 1917)

Edwin M. Stanton (1814–1869): *Secretary of war under Presidents Lincoln and Johnson*

Now he belongs to the ages.

(On the death of Abraham Lincoln, 15 April 1865)

Elizabeth Cady Stanton (1815–1902): *Feminist*

We hold these truths to be self-evident: that all men and women are created equal.

(*Declaration of Sentiments*, 1848)

The history of mankind is a history of repeated injuries and usurpations on the part of man toward woman, having in direct object the establishment of an absolute tyranny over her. To prove this, let facts be submitted to a candid world.

He has never permitted her to exercise her inalienable right to the elective franchise. . . .

He has withheld from her rights which are given to the most ignorant and degraded men—both natives and foreigners. . . .

He has made her, morally, an irresponsible being, as she can commit many crimes with impunity, provided they be done in the presence of her husband. . . .

He has usurped the prerogative of Jehovah himself, claiming it as his right to assign for her a sphere of action, when that belongs to her conscience and her God.

(Ibid.)

Abraham Lincoln immortalized himself by the emancipation of four million Southern slaves. Speaking for my suffrage coadjutors, we now desire that you, Mr. President, who are already celebrated for so many noble deeds and honourable utterances, immortalize yourself by bringing about the complete emancipation of thirty-six million women.

(Message from her deathbed to President Theodore Roosevelt, 1901)

John Stark (1728–1822): *Revolutionary War general*

There, my boys, are your enemies, redcoats and Tories. You must beat them—or Molly Stark is a widow tonight.

(Charge to his troops, Battle of Bennington, Vermont, 16 August 1777)

Ronald Steele (1952–   ): *University student demonstrator*

My God! My God! They're killing us!

(On gunfire by the Ohio National Guard, Kent State University, May 1970)

Lincoln Steffens (1866–1936): *Muckraking journalist*

The Shame of the Cities

> (Title of a series of articles exposing political corruption, 1902)

I have seen the future and it works.

> (After traveling in the Soviet Union, 1920)

Gertrude Stein (1874–1946): *Exile literateuse*

In the United States there is more space where nobody is than where anybody is. This is what makes America what it is.

> (*The Geographical History of America*, 1936)

When you get there, there isn't any there there.

> (Of Oakland, California, her birthplace, ibid.)

John Steinbeck (1902–1968): *Writer*

Okie use' to mean you was from Oklahoma. Now it means you're scum. Don't mean nothing itself, it's the way they say it.

> (*The Grapes of Wrath*, 1939)

A red is any son of a bitch who wants thirty cents when we're paying twenty five.

> (Ibid.)

Alexander H. Stephens (1812–1883): *Vice-president of the Confederacy*

The people run mad. They are wild with passion and frenzy, doing they know not what.

> (On the secession movement in Georgia, 3 December 1860)

Our new government's foundations are laid, its cornerstone rests, upon the great truth that the Negro is not equal to the white man, that slavery—subordination to the superior race—is his natural and normal condition.

> (On the Confederate constitution, speech at Montgomery, 21 March 1861)

John L. Stevens (1820–1895): *Ambassador to Hawaii*

The Hawaiian pear is now fully ripe and this is the golden hour for the United States to pluck it.

(Communiqué to Washington, 1893)

Thaddeus Stevens (1792–1868): *Radical Republican leader*

I wish I were the owner of every Southern slave, that I might cast off the shackles from their limbs, and witness the rapture which would excite them in the first dance of their freedom.

(Speech in Congress, 1850)

There is no such person running as James Buchanan. He is dead of lockjaw. Nothing remains but a platform and a bloated mass of political putridity.

(Speech, 1856)

The future condition of the conquered power depends on the will of the conqueror.

(Speech in Congress, 18 December 1865)

You will remember that in Egypt He sent frogs, locusts, murrain, lice, and finally demanded the first-born of everyone of the oppressors. Almost all of these have been taken from us. We have been oppressed with taxes and debts, and He has sent us worse than lice, and has afflicted us with Andrew Johnson.

(Speech in Congress, August 1866)

I am for negro suffrage in every rebel state. If it be just, it should not be denied; if it be necessary, it should be adopted; if it be a punishment to traitors, they deserve it.

(Speech in Congress, 3 January 1867)

This is not a "white man's government." To say so is political blasphemy, for it violates the fundamental principles of our gospel of liberty. This is man's government, the government of all men alike.

(Ibid.)

I repose in this quiet and secluded spot, not from any natural preference for solitude, but finding other cemeteries limited as to race, by charter rules, I have chosen this that I might illustrate in my death the principles which I advocated through a long life, equality of man before his Creator.

(Epitaph, written for his burial in a Negro cemetery, 1868)

Adlai E. Stevenson (1900–1965): *Governor of Illinois and Democratic Party presidential nominee, 1952 and 1956*

Communism is the corruption of a dream of justice.

(Speech, Urbana, Illinois, 1951)

Let's talk sense to the American people. Let's tell them the truth, that there are no gains without pains.

(Speech accepting Democratic presidential nomination, Chicago, 21 July 1952)

Self-criticism is the secret weapon of democracy, and candor and confession are good for the political soul.

(Ibid.)

A man doesn't save a century, or a civilization, but a militant party wedded to a principle can.

(Ibid.)

The sound of tireless voices is the price we pay for the right to hear the music of our opinions.

(Speech, New York City, 28 August 1952)

You know how it is in an election year. They pick a president and then for four years they pick on him.

(Ibid.)

Your public servants serve you right.

(Speech in Los Angeles, 11 September 1952)

Man has wrested from nature the power to make the world a desert or to make the deserts bloom. There is no evil in the atom; only in men's souls.

(Speech, Hartford, Connecticut, 18 September 1952)

When political ammunition runs low, inevitably the rusty artillery of abuse is always wheeled into action.

(Speech, New York City, 22 September 1952)

Nature is indifferent to the survival of the human species, including Americans.

(Television speech, 29 September 1952)

My definition of a free society is a society where it is safe to be unpopular.

(Speech in Detroit, October 1952)

If we value the pursuit of knowledge, we must be free to follow wherever that search may lead us. The free mind is no barking dog, to be tethered on a ten-foot chain.

(Speech, University of Wisconsin, 8 October 1952)

Someone asked . . . how I felt and I was reminded of a story that a fellow townsman of ours used to tell—Abraham Lincoln. They asked him how he felt once after an unsuccessful election. He said he felt like a little boy who has stubbed his toe in the dark. He said that he was too old to cry, but it hurt too much to laugh.

(On his defeat for the presidency the preceding day, 5 November 1952)

The idea that you can merchandise candidates for high office like breakfast cereal—that you can gather votes like box tops—is I think, the ultimate indignity to the democratic process.

(Speech accepting Democratic presidential nomination, 18 August 1956)

We have confused the free with the free and easy.

(*Putting First Things First,* 1960)

With the supermarket as our temple and the singing commercial as our litany, are we likely to fire the world with an irresistible vision of America's exalted purpose and inspiring way of life?

(Interview, *Wall Street Journal,* 1 June 1960)

She would rather light candles than curse the darkness, and her glow has warmed the world.

(On Eleanor Roosevelt, 11 November 1962)

The patriots are those who love America enough to see her as a model to mankind.

(*Harper's Magazine,* July 1963)

As long as the peoples of that area are determined to preserve their independence and ask for our help in preserving it, we will extend it.

(Statement on South Vietnam in the United Nations, 21 May 1964)

The elephant has a thick skin, a head full of ivory, and as everyone who has seen a circus parade knows, proceeds best by grasping the tail of his predecessor.

(Attributed)

Joseph W. "Vinegar Joe" Stilwell (1883–1946): *Army general*

Chiang K'ai-shek is confronted with an idea, and that defeats him. He is bewildered by the spread of Communist influence. He can't see that the mass of Chinese people welcome the Reds as being the only visible hope of relief from crushing taxation, the abuses of the Army and Tai Li's Gestapo. Under Chiang K'ai-shek they now begin to see what they may expect. Greed, corruption, favoritism, more taxes, a ruined currency, terrible waste of life, callous disregard of all the rights of men.

(Journal, 1944, published in *The Stilwell Papers*, 1948)

The cure for China's trouble is the elimination of Chiang K'ai-shek. The only thing that keeps the country split is his fear of losing control. He hates the Reds and will not take any chances on giving them a toehold in the government. The result is that each side watches the other and neither gives a damn about the war. If this condition persists, China will have civil war immediately after Japan is out.

(Ibid.)

Henry L. Stimson (1867–1950): *Secretary of state under President Hoover, secretary of war under President Roosevelt*

It was like sitting in a bath of ink.

(On conferring with President Hoover, attributed)

The bombs dropped on Hiroshima and Nagasaki ended a war. They also made it wholly clear that we must never have another war.

(Speech, 1947)

I. F. Stone (1907–   ): *Journalist*

The Truman era was the era of the moocher. The place was full of Wimpys who could be had for a hamburger.

(*The Truman Era*, 1943)

Lucy Stone (1818–1893): *Feminist*

"We, the people of the United States." Which "We, the people"? The women were not included.

(Speech in New York, April 1853)

J. B. Stoner (1924–   ): *Ku Klux Klan leader*

You cannot have law and order and niggers too.

(Common conceit in speeches)

Emery Storrs (1835–1885): *Republican orator from Illinois*

The Democratic Party is like a mule, without pride of ancestry or hope of posterity.

(Attributed)

William Stoughton (1631–1701): *Colonial official and judge*

God hath sifted a Nation that he might send Choice Grain into this Wilderness.

(On Massachusetts, 1669)

Harriet Beecher Stowe (1811–1896): *Abolitionist writer*

The Man Who Was a Thing.

(Original subtitle for *Uncle Tom's Cabin*)

"Do you know who made you?" "Nobody, as I knows on," said the child, with a short laugh . . . "I 'spect I grow'd."

(*Uncle Tom's Cabin*, 1852)

"Who was your mother?" "Never had none," said the child, with another grin. "Never had any mother? What do you mean? Where were you born?" "Never was born," persisted Topsy; "Never had no father, nor mother, nor nothin'. I was raised by a speculator."

(Ibid.)

Adolph Strasser (1871–1910): *Trade union leader*

We have no ultimate ends. We are going on from day to day. We are fighting only for immediate objects.

(Testimony before a Senate committee, 21 August 1883)

Charles Sumner (1811–1874): *Senator from Massachusetts*

There is the national flag. He must be cold, indeed, who can look upon its folds rippling in the breeze without pride of country. If in a foreign land, the flag is companionship, and country itself with all its endearments. . . . White is for purity; red for valor; blue, for justice. And altogether, bunting, stripes, stars, and colors, blazing in the sky, make the flag of our country, to be cherished by all our hearts, to be upheld by all our hands.

(Speech, 19 November 1867)

We must see that the freedmen are established on the soil. The great plantations, which have been so many nurseries of the rebellion, must be broken up, and the freedmen must have the pieces.

(Speech in the Senate, 1866)

William Graham Sumner (1840–1910): *Philosopher*

At bottom there are two chief things with which government has to deal. They are the property of men and the honor of women. These it has to defend against crime.

(*What the Social Classes Owe to each other*, 1883)

You need not think it necessary to have Washington exercise a political providence over the country. God has done that a good deal better by the laws of political economy.

(Ibid.)

My patriotism is of the kind which is outraged by the notion that the United States never was a great nation until in a petty three months' campaign it knocked to pieces a poor, decrepit, bankrupt old state like Spain. To hold such an opinion as that is to abandon all American standards, to put shame and scorn on all that our ancestors tried to build up here, and to go over to the standards of which Spain is a representative.

(On the Spanish-American War, speech, Yale University, January 1899)

The most important thing which we shall inherit from the Spaniards could be the task of suppressing rebellions.

(Ibid.)

Billy Sunday (1862–1935): *Baseball player and revivalist preacher*

Hit the sawdust trail.

(His term for accepting grace at revival meetings)

Oh Lord, smite the hungry, wolfish Hun whose fangs drip with blood, and we will forever raise our voice in praise.

(Prayer, April 1917, after the U.S. declared war on Germany)

Good-bye John. You were God's worst enemy. You were Hell's best friend.

(Sermon on the beginning of prohibition—"John" was John Barleycorn—Norfolk, Virginia, 16 July 1920)

That old bastard theory of evolution. Jackass nonsense.

(Sermon on the Scopes "Monkey Trial," 1925)

Our country is filled with a socialistic, IWW, communistic, radical, lawless, anti-American, anti-Church, anti-God, anti-marriage gang and they are laying the eggs of rebellion and unrest in labour and capital and home; and we have some of them in the universities. I can take you back through the universities and pick out a lot of black-hearted communistic fellows who are teaching that to the boys and sending them out to undermine America. If this radical bunch could have their way, my friends, the laws of nature would be repealed, or they would reverse them. Oil and water would mix, the turtle dove would marry the turkey buzzard, the sun would rise in the west and set in the east, chickens would give milk and cows would lay eggs, the pigs would crow and the roosters would squeal, cats would bark and dogs would mew, the least would be the greatest, a part would be greater than the whole, yesterday would be today if that crowd were in control.

(Sermon in Nashville, 1925)

William H. Sylvis (1828–1869): *Labor leader*

We must adopt a system which will divide the profits of labor among those who produce them.

(To the National Labor Union, August 1866)

T════════════════════════════

Robert A. Taft (1889–1953): *Senator from Ohio*

You really have to get to know Dewey to dislike him.

(Attributed, 1944)

William Howard Taft (1857–1930): *Twenty-seventh president and chief justice of the Supreme Court*

Constitutions are checks upon the hasty action of the majority. They are the self-imposed restraints of a whole people upon a majority of them to secure sober action and a respect for the rights of the minority.

(Veto of Arizona Enabling Act, 22 August 1911)

I think I might as well give up so far as being a candidate is concerned. There are so many people in the country who don't like me.

(On his campaign for reelection, July 1912)

Politics makes me sick.

(Common phrase in his correspondence)

Charles M. de Talleyrand (1754–1838): *French statesman*

What would you give for the whole of Louisiana?

(To American legates in Paris attempting to secure the right of deposit in New Orleans, 1803)

The United States has thirty-two religions but only one dish.
(Attributed)

Roger B. Taney (1777–1864): *Chief justice of the Supreme Court*

The question before us is, whether the class of persons described in the plea in abatement compose a portion of this people, and are constituent members of this sovereignty. We think they are not. . . . They were at that time considered as a subordinate and inferior class of beings. . . . They had no rights which the white man was bound to respect.
(*Dred Scott* v. *Sanford*, 1857)

James "Corporal" Tanner (1844–1927): *Head of veterans' organization and commissioner of pensions*

God help the surplus.
(Regarding his plans to pay pensions to Union veterans, 1889)

Harold Taylor (1914–   ): *Canadian-born educator*

I know of no time in our history when the gap between the generations has been wider or more potentially dangerous.
(Commencement address, June 1968)

Zachary Taylor (1784–1850): *General and twelfth president*

Tell him to go to hell.
(Replying to General Santa Anna's demand he surrender his outnumbered army on the eve of the Battle of Buena Vista, 22 February 1847)

A little more grape, Captain Bragg.
(At the battle, 23 February 1847)

Hurrah for Old Kentuck! That's the way to do it. Give them hell, damn them.
(To the 2nd Kentucky Regiment, ibid.)

I will not say I would not serve if the good people were imprudent enough to elect me.
(Accepting Whig nomination for the presidency, July 1848)

Tecumseh (1768?–1813): *Shawnee Indian chief*

The way, and the only way, to check and stop this evil, is for all the Redmen to unite in claiming a common and equal right in the land, as it was and should be yet; for it was never divided, but belongs to all for the use of each. That no part has a right to sell, even to each other, much less to strangers—those who want all and will not do with less.

(Speech at Vincennes, Indiana, 12 August 1810)

My heart is a stone: heavy with sadness for my people; cold with the knowledge that no treaty will keep the whites out of our lands; hard with the determination to resist as long as I live and breathe. Now we are weak and many of our people are afraid. But hear me: a single twig breaks, but the bundle of twigs is strong. Someday I will embrace our brother tribes and draw them into a bundle and together we will win our country back from the whites.

(Ibid.)

Where today are the Pequot? Where are the Narragansett, the Mohican, the Pakanoket, and many other once powerful tribes of our people? They have vanished before the avarice and the oppression of the White Man, as snow before a summer sun.

Will we let ourselves be destroyed in our turn without a struggle, give up our homes, our country bequeathed to us by the Great Spirit, the graves of our dead and everything that is dear and sacred to us? I know you will cry with me "Never! Never!"

(Speech before the Battle of the Thames, 5 October 1813)

Sell the country? Why not sell the air, the clouds, the great sea?

(Attributed)

Edward Teller (1908–   ): *Hungarian-born nuclear scientist*

A night-time atomic explosion high over Tokyo, in full sight of Emperor Hirohito and his Cabinet, would have been just as terrifying as Hiroshima. And it would have frightened the right people.

(*The Legacy of Hiroshima*, 1962)

Henry M. Teller (1830–1914): *Senator from Colorado*

That the United States hereby disclaims any disposition or intention to exercise sovereignty, jurisdiction, or control over said

Island except for the pacification thereof, and asserts its determination, when that is accomplished, to leave the government in control of the Island to its people.

(Amendment to the declaration of war against Spain, 1898)

Ernest Lawrence Thayer (1863–1940): *Journalist*

But there is no joy in Mudville, mighty Casey has struck out.

(Casey at the Bat, 1888)

Webster Thayer (1856–1933): *Massachusetts judge*

This man, although he may not actually have committed the crime attributed to him, is nevertheless morally culpable, because he is the enemy of our existing institutions.

(Of Nicola Sacco, accused of armed robbery, charge to the jury, 1920)

Did you see what I did to those anarchistic bastards?

(Overheard at a Dartmouth College football game, October 1922)

William M. Thayer (1820–1898): *Writer*

From Log Cabin to White House

(Title of biography of James A. Garfield, 1881)

Gabriel Thomas (?–?): *English Quaker colonial promoter*

Of Lawyers and Physicians I shall say nothing, because this Countrey is very Peaceable and Healthy; long may it so continue and never have occasion for the Tongue of the one, nor the Pen of the other, both equally destructive to Mens Estates and Lives; besides forsooth, they, Hang-Man like, have a License to Murder and make Mischief.

(An Account of Pennsylvania, 1698)

Norman Thomas (1884–1968): *Socialist leader*

Mr. Roosevelt did not carry out the Socialist platform, unless he carried it out on a stretcher.

(Attributed)

Henry David Thoreau (1817–1862): *Writer*

The authority of government . . . must have the sanction and consent of the governed. It can have no pure right over my person

and property but what I concede to it. The progress from an absolute to a limited monarchy, from a limited monarchy to a democracy, is a progress toward a true respect for the individual. Is a
democracy, such as we know it, the last improvement possible in
government? Is it not possible to take a step further towards recog-
nizing and organizing the rights of man?

("Essay on Civil Disobedience," 1846)

How does it become a man to behave toward this American government to-day? I answer that he cannot without disgrace be associated with it. I cannot for an instant recognize that political
organization as my government which is the slave's government
also.

(Ibid.)

I heartily accept the motto—"That government is best which
governs least"; and I should like to see it acted up to more rapidly
and systematically. Carried out, it finally amounts to this, which also
I believe,—"That government is best which governs not at all"; and
when men are prepared for it, that will be the kind of government
which they will have.

(Ibid.)

When a sixth of the population of a nation which has undertaken
to be the refuge of liberty are slaves, and a whole country is unjustly
overrun and conquered by a foreign army, and subjected to military
law, I think that it is not too soon for honest men to rebel and
revolutionize. What makes this duty the more urgent is the fact that
the country so overrun is not our own, but ours is the invading
army.

(Ibid.)

Under a government which imprisons any unjustly, the true
place for a just man is also a prison.

(Ibid.)

Any man more right than his neighbors constitutes a majority of
one.

(Ibid.)

I went to the woods because I wanted to live deliberately, to confront only the essential facts of life, and see if I could not learn what it had to teach, and not, when I came to die, discover that I had not lived.

    (Walden, 1854)

If anything ail a man, so that he does not perform his functions, if he have a pain in his bowels even,—for that is the seat of sympathy,—he forthwith sets about reforming the world.

    (Ibid.)

The mass of men lead lives of quiet desperation.

    (Ibid.)

There are a thousand hacking at the branches of evil to one who is striking at the root.

    (Ibid.)

If a man does not keep pace with his companions, perhaps it is because he hears a different drummer. Let him step to the music he hears, however measured or far away.

    (Ibid.)

Benjamin "Pitchfork Ben" Tillman (1847–1918): *Senator from South Carolina*

We have done our level best. We have scratched our heads to find out how we could eliminate every last one of them. We stuffed ballot boxes. We shot them. We are not ashamed of it.

    (Speech in the Senate on the disenfranchisement of Negroes, November 1900)

Henry Timrod (1828–1867): *"Poet laureate" of the Confederacy*

            At last, we are
      A nation among nations; and the world
      Shall soon behold in many a distant port
         Another flag unfurled!
      Now, come what may, whose favor need we court?
      And, under God, whose thunder need we fear?

    (On the occasion of the founding of the Confederacy, 8 March 1861)

Alexis de Tocqueville (1805–1859): *French politician and philosopher*

The aspect of American society is animated, because men and things are always changing; but it is monotonous, because all these changes are alike.

(*Democracy in America*, 1835–1839)

Democratic institutions generally give men a lofty notion of their country and themselves.

(Ibid.)

The first and most intense passion which is engendered by the equality of conditions is, I need hardly say, the love of that same equality.

(Ibid.)

Americans are so enamored of equality that they would rather be equal in slavery than unequal in freedom.

(Ibid.)

In the United States the more opulent citizens take great care not to stand aloof from the people; on the contrary, they constantly keep on easy terms with the lower classes: they listen to them, they speak to them every day. They know that the rich in democracies always stand in need of the poor; and that in democratic ages you attach a poor man to you more by your manner than by benefits conferred.

(Ibid.)

The principle of equality does not destroy the imagination, but lowers its flight to the level of the earth.

(Ibid.)

I know no country in which there is so little true independence of mind and freedom of discussion as in America.

(Ibid.)

The hatred which men bear to privilege increases in proportion as privileges become more scarce and less considerable, so that democratic passions would seem to burn most fiercely at the very time when they have least fuel.

(Ibid.)

Whatever may be the general endeavor of a community to render its members equal and alike, the personal pride of individuals will always seek to rise above the line, and to form somewhere an inequality to their own advantage.

(Ibid.)

Men living in democratic times have many passions, but most of their passions either end in the love of riches, or proceed from it.

(Ibid.)

In democracies, nothing is more great or more brilliant than commerce: it attracts the attention of the public, and fills the imagination of the multitude; all energetic passions are directed towards it.

(Ibid.)

I know of no country, indeed, where the love of money has taken stronger hold on the affections of men and where a profounder contempt is expressed for the theory of the permanent equality of property.

(Ibid.)

If an American were condemned to confine his activity to his own affairs, he would be robbed of one half of his existence.

(Ibid.)

I never met in America with any citizen so poor as not to cast a glance of hope and envy on the enjoyments of the rich, or whose imagination did not possess itself by anticipation of those good things which fate still obstinately with-held from him.

On the other hand, I never perceived amongst the wealthier inhabitants of the United States that proud contempt of physical gratifications which is sometimes to be met with even in the most opulent and dissolute aristocracies. Most of these wealthy persons were once poor: they have felt the sting of want; they were long a prey to adverse fortunes; and now that the victory is won, the passions which accompanied the contest have survived it; their minds are, as it were, intoxicated by the small enjoyments which they have pursued for forty years.

(Ibid.)

In America . . . everyone finds facilities, unknown elsewhere, for making or increasing his fortune. The spirit of gain is always on the stretch, and the human mind, constantly diverted from the pleasures of imagination and the labours of the intellect, is there swayed by no impulse but the pursuit of wealth. Not only are manufacturing and commercial classes to be found in the United States, as they are in all other countries; but, what never occurred elsewhere, the whole community is simultaneously engaged in productive industry and commerce.

(Ibid.)

A native of the United States clings to this world's goods as if he were certain never to die; and he is so hasty in grasping at all within his reach, that one would suppose he was constantly afraid of not living long enough to enjoy them. He clutches everything, he holds nothing fast, but soon loosens his grasp to pursue fresh gratifications.

(Ibid.)

In America I saw the freest and most enlightened men, placed in the happiest circumstances which the world affords: it seemed to me as if a cloud habitually hung upon their brow, and I thought them serious and almost sad even in their pleasures . . . , forever brooding over advantages they do not possess.

(Ibid.)

An American, instead of going in a leisure hour to dance merrily at some place of public resort, as the fellows of his calling continue to do throughout the greater part of Europe, shuts himself up at home to drink. He thus enjoys two pleasures; he can go on thinking of his business, and he can get drunk decently by his own fireside.

(Ibid.)

In America the passion for physical well-being is not always exclusive, but it is general; and if all do not feel it in the same manner, yet it is felt by all. Carefully to satisfy all, even the least wants of the body, and to provide the little conveniences of life, is uppermost in every mind.

(Ibid.)

America is a land of wonders, in which everything is in constant motion and every change seems an improvement. The idea of novelty is there indissolubly connected with the idea of amelioration. No natural boundary seems to be set to the efforts of man; and in his eyes what is not yet done is only what he has not yet attempted to do.

(Ibid.)

If I were asked . . . to what the singular prosperity and growing strength of that people ought mainly to be attributed, I should reply: To the superiority of their women.

(Ibid.)

In America the independence of woman is irrecoverably lost in the bonds of matrimony: if an unmarried woman is less constrained there than elsewhere, a wife is subjected to stricter obligations. The former makes her father's house an abode of freedom and of pleasure; the latter lives in the home of her husband as if it were a cloister.

(Ibid.)

I have often remarked in the United States that it is not easy to make a man understand that his presence may be dispensed with; hints will not always suffice to shake him off. I contradict an American at every word he says, or show him that his conversation bores me; he instantly labours with fresh pertinacity to convince me: I preserve a dogged silence, and he thinks I am meditating deeply on the truths he is uttering: at last I rush from his company, and he supposes that some urgent business hurries me elsewhere. This man will never understand that he wearies me to extinction unless I tell him so: and the only way to get rid of him is to make him my enemy for life.

(Ibid.)

Thus not only does democracy make every man forget his ancestors, but it hides his descendants, and separates his contemporaries from him; it throws him back for ever upon himself alone, and threatens in the end to confine him entirely within the solitude of his own heart.

(Ibid.)

Nothing is so petty, so insipid, so crowded with paltry interests, in one word, so anti-poetic, as the life of man in the United States.
(Ibid.)

Robert Toombs (1810–1885): *Southern politician*

I do not hesitate to a vow before this house and the country that if by your legislation you seek to drive us from the territories of California and New Mexico and to abolish slavery in this District of Columbia, I am for disunion.
(Speech in the House of Representatives, January 1850)

Johnny Torrio (1882–1957): *Gangster*

It's all yours, Al. Me, I'm quitting. It's Europe for me.
(In Chicago to Al Capone, upon Torrio's retirement, 1925)

Arnold Toynbee (1889–1975): *English historian*

America is a large, friendly dog in a very small room. Every time it wags its tail, it knocks over a chair.
(*News summaries,* 14 July 1954)

John Trevelyan (1903–   ): *British writer*

The Americans are nice people but right now they're behaving like small boys who've just discovered what sex is.
(Remark, 1970)

Frances Trollope (1780–1863): *Writer*

Let no one who wishes to receive agreeable impressions of American manners, commence their travels in a Mississippi steamboat.
(*Domestic Manners of the Americans,* 1832)

Leon Trotsky (1879–1940): *Russian revolutionary*

In the third year of Soviet rule in America you will no longer chew gum!
("If America Should Go Communist," *Liberty,* 23 March 1935)

Harry S Truman (1884–1972): *Thirty-third president*

If we see that Germany is winning, we ought to help Russia, and if we see Russia is winning, we ought to help Germany, and that way let them kill as many as possible.

(Attributed, July 1941)

I don't know whether you fellows ever had a load of hay or a bull fall on you. But last night the moon, the stars and all the planets fell on me. If you fellows ever pray, pray for me.

(To newspapermen after his inauguration as president, 13 April 1945)

The responsibility of great states is to serve and not to dominate the world.

(Message to Congress, 16 April 1945)

Carry out your agreements and you won't get talked to like that.

(Reply to V. M. Molotov who protested the belligerency of the president by saying, "I have never been talked to like that in my life," 23 April 1945)

General, there is nothing that you may want that I won't try to help you get. That definitely includes the presidency in 1948.

(Remark to General Eisenhower at Potsdam, July 1945)

Sixteen hours ago an American plane dropped one bomb on Hiroshima, an important Japanese army base. That bomb had more power than 20,000 tons of TNT.

(Radio speech, 6 August 1945)

Having found the bomb we have used it. We have used it against those who attacked us without warning at Pearl Harbor, against those who have starved and beaten and executed American prisoners of war, against those who have abandoned the pretense of obeying international laws of warfare. We have used it in order to shorten the agony of war, in order to save the lives of thousands and thousands of young Americans.

We shall continue to use it until we completely destroy Japan's power to make war. Only a Japanese surrender will stop us.

(Ibid.)

Every segment of our population, and every individual, has a right to expect from his government a Fair Deal.

(Speech to Congress, 6 September 1945)

I believe that it must be the policy of the United States to support free peoples who are resisting subjugation by armed minorities or by outside pressures.

(Message to Congress, 12 March 1947)

I'm going to fight hard. I'm going to give them hell.

(Remark to Alben Barkley on the presidential campaign, August 1948)

The President spends most of his time kissing people on the cheek in order to get them to do what they ought to do without getting kissed.

(Newspaper interview, February 1949)

. . . we must embark on a bold new program for making the benefits of our scientific advances and industrial progress available for the improvement and growth of underdeveloped areas. More than half the people of the world are living in conditions approaching misery. Their food is inadequate. They are victims of disease. Their economic life is primitive and stagnant. Their poverty is a handicap and a threat both to them and to more prosperous areas.

(The Point IV Program, 1949)

The attack upon Korea makes it plain beyond all doubt that Communism has passed beyond the use of subversion to conquer independent nations and will now use armed invasion and war.

(Radio speech, 27 June 1950)

Slander, lies, character assassination—these things are a threat to every single citizen everywhere in this country. When even one American—who has done nothing wrong—is forced by fear to shut his mind and close his mouth, then all Americans are in peril. It is the job of all of us—of every American who loves his country and his freedom—to rise up and put a stop to this terrible business.

(Speech on McCarthyism to the American Legion, 1950)

He'll sit here and he'll say, "Do this! Do that!" And nothing will happen! Poor Ike.

(Of President-elect Eisenhower, attributed, December 1952)

It's a nice prison, but a prison nonetheless. No man in his right mind would want to come here of his own accord.

(On the White House, attributed)

The buck stops here.
> (Notice on his desk at the White House in reference to the saying, "Passing the buck.")

He's a good man. The only trouble was, he had a lot of damn fool Republicans around him.
> (Comment to newspaper reporters about President Eisenhower, December 1953)

I never allowed myself to forget that the final authority was mine. I would ask the Cabinet to share their counsel with me, even encouraging disagreement and argument to sharpen up the different points of view. On major issues I would frequently ask them to vote, and I expected the Cabinet officers to be frank and candid in expressing their opinions to me. At the same time, I insisted that they keep me informed of the major activities of their departments in order to make certain that they supported the policy once I had made a decision.
> (*Memoirs*, 1955)

Being a President is like riding a tiger. A man has to keep on riding or be swallowed.
> (Ibid.)

A politician is a man who understands government, and it takes a politician to run a government. A statesman is a politician who's been dead ten or fifteen years.
> (Interview, *New York World Telegram*, 12 April 1958)

It's a recession when your neighbor loses his job; it's a depression when you lose your own.
> (Ibid.)

The President is the representative of the whole nation and he's the only lobbyist that all the 160 million people in this country have.
> (Lecture, Columbia University, 27 April 1959)

Whenever you have an efficient government you have a dictatorship.
> (Lecture, Columbia University, 28 April 1959)

He never told the truth in his life.
> (Of Richard M. Nixon, attributed, 1960)

I fired MacArthur because he wouldn't respect the authority of the President. I didn't fire him because he was a dumb son of a bitch, although he was.
> (Attributed, 1961)

There was something about that other fellow that people just never did trust. He had a mustache, for one thing, and since those days, during the war, people were aware of Hitler, that mustache didn't do him any good.
> (Of Thomas E. Dewey, interview with Merle Miller, *Plain Speaking*, 1974)

If you can't stand the heat, stay out of the kitchen.
> (On holding high office, favorite saying)

Harriet Tubman (1820?–1913): *Abolitionist*
Dere's two things I've got a right to, and dese are, Death or Liberty—one or t'other I mean to have.
> (*Scenes in the Life of Harriet Tubman*, 1869)

I have heard their groans and sighs, and seen their tears, and I would give every drop of blood in my veins to free them.
> (Ibid.)

Frederick Jackson Turner (1861–1932): *Historian*
Up to our own day American history has been in a large degree the history of the colonization of the Great West. The existence of an area of free land, its continuous recession, and the advance of American settlement westward, explain American development.
> ("The Significance of the Frontier in American History," 1894)

To the frontier the American intellect owes its striking characteristics. That coarseness and strength combined with acuteness and inquisitiveness; that practical, inventive turn of mind, quick to find expedients; that masterful grasp of material things, lacking in the artistic but powerful to effect great ends; that restless, nervous energy; that dominant individualism, working for good and for evil,

and withal that buoyancy and exuberance which comes with freedom—these are traits of the frontier, or traits called out elsewhere
because of the existence of the frontier.

(Ibid.)

Nat Turner (1800–1831): *Rebel slave*

On the 12th of May, 1828, I heard a loud noise in the heavens,
and the Spirit instantly appeared to me and said the Serpent was
loosened, and Christ had laid down the yoke he had borne for the
sins of men, and that I should take it on and fight against the Serpent, for the time was fast approaching when the first should be last
and the last should be first. . . . And on the appearance of the sign I
should arise and prepare myself, and slay my enemies with their
own weapons.

(The Confessions of Nat Turner, 1831)

Mark Twain (Samuel Langhorne Clemens) (1835–1910): *Writer*

All Kings is mostly rapscallions.

(The Adventures of Huckleberry Finn, 1884)

In Boston they ask, How much does he know? In New York,
How much is he worth? In Philadelphia, Who were his parents?

(North American Review, January 1895)

There isn't a single human characteristic that can be safely la-
beled as "American."

(Ibid.)

It is by the goodness of God that in our country we have those
three unspeakably precious things: freedom of speech, freedom of
conscience, and the prudence never to practice either of them.

(Following the Equator, 1897)

It could probably be shown by facts and figures that there is no
distinctly native American criminal class except Congress.

(Ibid.)

We are the lavishest and showiest and most luxury-loving people on the earth; and at our masthead we fly one true and honest symbol, the gaudiest flag the world has ever seen.

("Diplomatic Pay and Clothes," 1899)

Shall we go on conferring our Civilization upon the peoples that sit in darkness, or shall we give those poor things a rest?

("To the Person Sitting in the Darkness," 1901)

To forget pain is to be painless; to forget care is to be rid of it; to go abroad is to accomplish both.

(*Autobiography,* 1924)

We Americans worship the almighty dollar! Well, it is a worthier god than Heredity Privilege.

(Notebook, published posthumously, 1935)

Irreverence is the champion of liberty and its only sure defense.

(Ibid.)

At bottom he was probably fond of them, but he was always able to conceal it.

(Of Thomas Carlyle and Americans, Ibid.)

Guides cannot master the subtleties of the American joke.

(*Innocents Abroad,* 1869)

William Marcy "Boss" Tweed (1823–1878): *Democratic Party political boss*

As long as I count the votes what are you going to do about it? Say.

(Reply to a reporter who accused him of corruption, 1870)

I don't care a straw for your newspaper articles, my constituents don't know how to read, but they can't help seeing them damned pictures.

(On cartoonist Thomas Nast's cartoon criticisms of Tweed's peculation, in conversation, 1871)

U

Stewart L. Udall (1920–   ): *Secretary of the interior under President Kennedy*
We have, I fear, confused power with greatness.
(Commencement address, Dartmouth College, 13 June 1965)

Jesse Unruh (1922–   ): *California politician*
Money is the mother's milk of politics.
(Attributed)

Ecology has become the political substitute for the word "mother."
(Ibid.)

John Updike (1932–   ): *Writer*
What is it that distinguishes the American Man from his counterparts in other climes; what *is* it that makes him so special? He is quietly affirmative. He is trustworthy, loyal, helpful, friendly, courteous, kind, obedient, cheerful, thrifty, brave, clean and reverent.
(*Assorted Prose*, 1965)

V

Jack Valenti (1921–   ): *Presidential aide*
I sleep each night a little better, a little more confidently because Lyndon Johnson is my President. For I know he lives and
thinks and works to make sure that for all America and indeed, the
growing body of the free world, the morning shall always come.
(Attributed, 1964)

Mariano G. Vallejo (1808–1890): *California politician*
The Yankees are a wonderful people. If they emigrated to hell
itself they would somehow manage to change the climate.
(Attributed, c. 1855)

Martin Van Buren (1782–1862): *Eighth president*
The second, sober thought of the people is seldom wrong, and
always efficient.
(Letter, 1829)

Arthur Vandenberg (1884–1951): *Senator from Indiana*
I had the feeling, as the result of the ballot was announced, that
I was witnessing the suicide of the Republic.
(After passage of Lend Lease, 1940)

We Republicans can cooperate with only one secretary of state at
a time.
(Cable to President Truman from Paris, September 1946)

Cornelius Vanderbilt (1794–1877): *Railroad entrepreneur*
Gentlemen: You have undertaken to cheat me. I won't sue you,
for law is too slow. I will ruin you.
(Letter to Nicaragua Transit Company, a competitor, 1853)

Law! What do I care about the law? Hain't I got the power?
(Attributed)

I'll never give up trust in Jesus. How could I let that go?
(Attributed)

Can't I do what I want with my own?
(Attributed)

William H. Vanderbilt (1821–1885): *Railroad owner*

Yes, they are very shrewd men. I don't believe that by any legislative enactment or anything else, through any of the States or all of the States, you can keep such men down. You can't do it! They will be on top all the time. You see if they are not.

(On the directors of the Standard Oil Company, testimony before a congressional committee, 1879)

The railroads are not run for the benefit of the dear public. That cry is all nonsense! They are built for men who invest their money and expect to get a fair percentage on the same.

(*New York Times,* 1882)

The public be damned! I'm working for my stockholders.

(Reply to a newspaper reporter who asked him if the proposed withdrawal of an unprofitable express train was against the public interest, Chicago, 1883)

I have had no real gratification or enjoyment of any sort more than my neighbor on the next block who is worth only half a million.

(On his deathbed, 1885)

Willard D. Vandiver (1854–1932): *Senator from Missouri*

I come from a state that raises corn and cotton and cockleburs and Democrats, and frothy eloquence neither convinces nor satisfies me. I'm from Missouri; you've got to show me.

(Speech in the Senate, 1912)

Henry Van Dyke (1852–1933): *Clergyman, diplomat*

Oh, it's home again, and home again,
America for me!

I want a ship that's westward bound
    to plough the rolling sea,
To the blessed land of Room Enough
    beyond the ocean bars,
Where the air is full of sunlight
    and the flag is full of stars.

    (Out of Doors in the Holy Land, 1908)

Bartolomeo Vanzetti (1888–1927): *Italian-born anarchist martyr*

I am suffering because I am a radical and indeed I am a radical; I have suffered because I was an Italian, and indeed I am an Italian; I have suffered more for my family and for my beloved than for myself; but I am so convinced to be right that if you could execute me two times, and if I could be reborn two other times, I would live again to do what I have done already.

    (Last statement in court, 9 April 1927)

Gore Vidal (1925–   ): *Writer*

American writers want to be not good but great; and so are neither.

    (Myra Breckinridge, 1968)

The astronauts! . . . Rotarians in outer space.

    (Ibid.)

W

Davis Hanson Waite (1825–1901): *Populist governor of Colorado*

It is better, infinitely better, that blood should flow to the horses' bridles, rather than our national liberties should be destroyed.

    (Speech to Colorado State Silver League Convention, 1893)

David Walker (1785–1830): *Abolitionist*

Treat us like men, and there is no danger but we will all live in peace and happiness together. For we are not like you, hard-hearted, unmerciful, and unforgiving. What a happy country this will be, if the whites will listen.

(*Appeal*, 28 September 1829)

Francis A. Walker (1840–1897): *Civil War officer, commissioner of Indian affairs*

Every year's advance of our frontier takes in a territory as large as some of the kingdoms of Europe. We are richer by hundreds of millions, the Indian is poorer by a large part of the little that he has. This growth is bringing imperial greatness to the nation; to the Indian it brings wretchedness, destitution, beggary.

(*Report*, 1870)

When dealing with savage men, as with savage beasts, no question of national honor can arise. Whether to fight, to run away, or to employ a ruse, is solely a question of expediency.

(Message to subordinates in the Bureau of Indian Affairs, 1871)

James J. Walker (1881–1946): *Playboy mayor of New York*

There are three things a man must do alone—be born, die, and testify.

(On the investigation of corruption in his administration, 1927)

A reformer is a guy who rides through a sewer in a glass-bottomed boat.

(Speech in New York City, 1928)

There comes a time in politics when a man must rise above principle.

(Attributed)

George C. Wallace (1919–   ): *Governor of Alabama*

I'll never be out-niggered again.

(Attributed after losing an election to a racist politician, 1958)

I stand here today, as Governor of this sovereign state, and refuse to willingly submit to illegal usurpation of power by the Central Government. I claim today for all the people of the State of Alabama those rights reserved to them under the Constitution of the United States. Among those powers so reserved and claimed is the right of state authority in the operation of the public schools, colleges, and universities.

> (Statement when he attempted to block the registration of a Negro student at the University of Alabama, September 1963)

Henry A. Wallace (1888–1965): *Vice-president and cabinet member*

I doubt if even China can equal our record of soil destruction.

> (Quoted in A. M. Schlesinger, Jr., *The Coming of the New Deal*, 1959)

The century on which we are entering can be and must be the century of the common man.

> (Speech, 8 May 1942)

The object of this war is to make sure that everybody in the world has the privilege of drinking a quart of milk a day.

> (Speech, 1942)

We should recognize that we have no more business in the political affairs of Eastern Europe than Russia has in the political affairs of Latin America, Western Europe and the United States. We may not like what Russia does in Eastern Europe. Her type of land reform, industrial expropriation, and suppression of basic liberties offends the great majority of the people of the United States. But whether we like it or not the Russians will try to socialize their sphere of influence just as we try to democratize our sphere of influence.

> (Speech in New York, 12 September 1946)

Under friendly peaceful competition the Russian world and the American world will gradually become more alike. The Russians will be forced to grant more and more of the personal freedoms; and we shall become more and more absorbed with the problems of social-economic justice.

> (Ibid.)

Horace Walpole (1717–1797): *British writer*

The next Augustan age will dawn on the other side of the Atlantic. There will, perhaps, be a Thucydides at Boston, a Xenophon at

New York, and, in time, a Virgil at Mexico, and a Newton at Peru. At last, some curious traveler from Lima will visit England and give a description of the ruins of St. Paul's like the editions of Balbec and Palmyra.

(Letter to Horace Mann, 24 November 1774)

Artemus Ward (Charles Farrar Browne) (1834–1867): *Newspaper columnist*

My pollertics, like my religion, being of an exceedin' accommodatin' character.

(*Artemus Ward His Book*, 1861)

The prevailin' weakness of most public men is to Slop over. G. Washington . . . never slopt over!

(Ibid.)

Did you ever have the measels, and if so, how many?

(On "The Census," 1860)

We are decendid from the Puritans, who nobly fled from a land of despitism to a land of freedim, where they could not only enjoy their own religion, but prevent everybody else from enjoyin' *his*.

(*Artemus Ward in London*, 1872)

I'm not a politician and my other habits are good.

("Fourth of July Oration," 1882)

Eugene Ware (1841–1911): *Military officer and writer*

Oh dewy was the morning
Upon the first of May,
And Dewey was the admiral
Down in Manila Bay.
And dewy were the Regent's eyes,
The orbs of royal blue,
And dew we feel discouraged,
I dew not think we dew.

(On the Battle of Manila Bay, *Topeka Capital*, 10 May 1893)

Andy Warhol (1928–   ): *Artist and filmmaker*

The day will come when everyone will be famous for fifteen minutes.

(Remark on a television show, 1969)

Jack L. Warner (1892–1978): *Film producer*

No, No! Jimmy Stewart for governor—Reagan for best friend

(On hearing that Ronald Reagan was a candidate for governor of California, 1966)

Earl Warren (1891–1974): *Chief justice of the Supreme Court*

Segregation of white and colored children in public schools has a detrimental effect upon the colored children. The impact is greater when it has the sanction of the law; for the policy of separating the races is usually interpreted as denoting the inferiority of the Negro group. A sense of inferiority affects the motivation of a child to learn.

(Unanimous opinion, *Brown* v. *School Board of Topeka et al.*, 1954)

We come then to the question presented: Does segregation of children in public schools solely on the basis of race, even though the physical facilities and other "tangible" factors may be equal, deprive the children of the minority group of equal educational opportunities? We believe that it does.

(Ibid.)

We conclude that in the field of public education the doctrine of "separate but equal" has no place. Separate educational facilities are inherently unequal.

(Ibid.)

The Commission has found no evidence that either Lee Harvey Oswald or Jack Ruby was part of any conspiracy, domestic or foreign, to assassinate President Kennedy.

(*Report of the President's Commission on the Assassination of President Kennedy*, 1964)

Booker T. Washington (1856–1915): *Educator and Negro leader*

One-third of the population of the South is of the Negro race. No enterprise seeking the material, civil, or moral welfare of this section can disregard this element of our population and reach the highest success.

(Speech in Atlanta, 18 September 1895)

Our greatest danger is that in the great leap from slavery to freedom we may overlook the fact that the masses of us are to live by the productions of our hands, and fail to keep in mind that we shall prosper in proportion as we learn to dignify and glorify common labour and put brains and skill into the common occupations of life; shall prosper in proportion as we learn to draw the line between the superficial and the substantial, the ornamental gewgaws of life and the useful. No race can prosper till it learns that there is as much dignity in tilling a field as in writing a poem. It is at the bottom of life we must begin, and not at the top. Nor should we permit our grievances to overshadow our opportunities.

Whatever other sins the South may be called to bear, when it comes to business, pure and simple, it is in the South that the Negro is given a man's chance in the commercial world.

(Ibid.)

To those of my race who depend on bettering their condition in a foreign land or who underestimate the importance of cultivating friendly relations with the Southern white man, who is their next-door neighbour, I would say: "Cast down your bucket where you are"—cast it down in making friends in every manly way of the people of all races by whom we are surrounded.

(Ibid.)

In all things that are purely social we can be as separate as the fingers, yet one as the hand in all things essential to mutual progress.

(Ibid.)

The life of Frederick Douglass is the history of American slavery epitomized in a single human experience. He saw it all, lived it all, and overcame it all.

(*Frederick Douglass*, 1907)

George Washington (1732–1799): *Revolutionary war commander and first president*

I heard the bullets whistle; and believe me, there is something charming in the sound.

(Letter to his mother during French and Indian War, 1754)

Discipline is the soul of an army. It makes small numbers formidable; procures success to the weak, and esteem to all.

(Letter of instructions to the Virginia regiments, 29 July 1759)

Let us therefore animate and encourage each other, and show the whole world that a Freeman, contending for liberty on his own ground, is superior to any slavish mercenary on earth.

(General orders, New York, 2 July 1776)

The time is now near at hand which must probably determine whether Americans are to be freemen or slaves; whether they are to have any property they can call their own; whether their houses and farms are to be pillaged and destroyed, and themselves consigned to a state of wretchedness from which no human efforts will deliver them. The fate of unborn millions will now depend, under God, on the courage and conduct of this army. Our cruel and unrelenting enemy leaves us only the choice of brave resistance, or the most abject submission. We have, therefore, to resolve to conquer or die.

(Address to the Continental Army before the Battle of Long Island, 27 August 1776)

Let us raise a standard to which the wise and honest can repair; the event is in the hands of God.

(Ibid.)

You will therefore send me none but natives.

(Orders regarding his bodyguard, after an attempt to poison him, 30 April 1777. It is often quoted as, "Put none but Americans on guard tonight.")

We are fast verging to anarchy and confusion.

(Remark on hearing the news of Shays' Rebellion, 1787)

The eyes of Argus are upon me, and no slip will pass unnoticed.

(Remark on assuming the presidency, 1789)

To be prepared for war is one of the most effectual means of preserving peace.

(First annual address to Congress, 8 January 1790)

The basis of our political system is the right of the people to make and to alter their constitutions of government.

(Farewell address, 17 September 1796)

Let me now . . . warn you in the most solemn manner against the baneful effects of the spirit of party.

(Ibid.)

Europe has a set of primary interests which to us have none or a very remote relation. Hence she must be engaged in frequent controversies, the causes of which are essentially foreign to our concerns. Hence, therefore, it must be unwise of us to implicate ourselves by artificial ties in the ordinary vicissitudes of her politics or the ordinary combinations or collisions of her friendships or enmities.

(Farewell address, 17 September 1796)

It is our true policy to steer clear of permanent alliance with any portion of the foreign world.

(Ibid.)

I have always given it as my decided opinion that no nation had a right to intermeddle in the internal concerns of another; that everyone had a right to form and adopt whatever government they liked best to live under themselves.

(Attributed)

Thomas Watson (1856–1922): *Southern journalist and politician*

To the emasculated individual who cries "Negro supremacy!" there is little to be said. His cowardice shows him to be a degeneration from the race which has never yet feared any other race.

("The Negro Question," *The Arena*, October 1892)

You are kept apart that you may be separately fleeced of your earnings. You are made to hate each other because upon that hatred

is rested the keystone of the arch of financial despotism which en-
slaves you both. You are deceived and blinded that you may not see
how his race antagonism perpetuates a monetary system which beggars both.

(Ibid.)

The blare of the bugle drowned the voice of the reformer.

(On the Spanish-American War, 1900)

In the South, we have to lynch him occasionally, and flog him,
now and then, to keep him from blaspheming the Almighty, by his
conduct, on account of his smell and his color.

(On Negroes, 4 January 1917)

Henry Watterson (1840–1921): *Editor and politician*

Things have come to a helluva pass
When a man can't cudgel his own jackass.

(Catch phrase)

John Wayne (1907–1979): *Popular film actor*

I don't feel we did wrong in taking this great country away from
them. There were great numbers of people who needed new land,
and the Indians were selfishly trying to keep it for themselves.

(Reflecting on his "western" films, interview, 1975)

Daniel Webster (1782–1852): *Senator from Massachusetts and orator*

There is always room at the top.

(Remark upon being advised not to become a lawyer as the profession
was overcrowded, attributed)

It is, sir, as I have said, a small college, and yet there are those
who love it.

(Before the Supreme Court in the Dartmouth College Case, 1818)

Whatever makes men good Christians, makes them good citizens.

(Speech, Plymouth, 22 December 1820)

Let our object be our country, our whole country and nothing but our country.

(Speech, Bunker Hill, 17 June 1825)

Sink or swim, live or die, survive or perish, I give my hand and heart to this vote.

(Discourse in commemoration of Adams and Jefferson, Boston, 1826)

It is my living sentiment, and by the blessing of God it shall be my dying sentiment,—Independence now and Independence forever.

(Ibid.)

The people's government, made for the people, made by the people, and answerable to the people.

(Ibid.)

He smote the rock of the national resources, and abundant streams of revenue gushed forth. He touched the dead corpse of the Public Credit, and it sprang upon its feet.

(Of Alexander Hamilton, speech, New York, 10 March 1831)

One country, one constitution, one destiny.

(Speech in the Senate, 15 March 1837)

There are persons who constantly clamor. They complain of oppression, speculation, and pernicious influence of wealth. They cry out loudly against all banks and corporations, and a means by which small capitalists become united in order to produce important and beneficial results. They carry on mad hostility against all established institutions. They would choke the fountain of industry and dry all streams.

(Speech in the Senate, 12 March 1838)

When tillage begins, other arts follow. The farmers therefore are the founders of human civilization.

(Speech in the Senate, 13 January 1840)

America has furnished to the world the character of Washington. And if our American institutions had done nothing else, that alone would have entitled them to the respect of mankind.

(Speech on the completion of Bunker Hill monument, 17 June 1843)

Thank God! I—I also—am an American!
(Ibid.)

Liberty exists in proportion to wholesome restraint.
(Speech in Charlestown, Mass., 10 May 1847)

I have read their platform, and though I think there are some
unsound places in it, I can stand upon it pretty well. But I see
nothing in it both new and valuable. "What is valuable is not new,
and what is new is not valuable."
(Speech at Marshfield, Massachusetts, on the Whig platform, 1 September 1848)

When my eyes shall be turned to behold, for the last time, the
sun in heaven, may I not see him shining on the broken and dishonored fragments of a once glorious Union; on States dis-severed, dis-
cordant, belligerent, in a land rent with civil feuds, or drenched, it
may be, in fraternal blood.
(Speech in the Senate, 17 July 1850)

Let their last feeble and lingering glance . . . behold the gorgeous
ensign of the republic . . . bearing for its motto . . . in characters of
living light, blazing on all its ample folds, as they float over the sea
and over the land, and in every wind under the whole heavens, that
other sentiment, dear to every true American heart, "Liberty and
Union, now and forever, one and inseparable!"
(Ibid.)

I was born an American; I will live an American; I shall die an
American.
(Ibid.)

What do we want with this worthless area, this region of savages
and wild beasts, of shifting sands and whirlwinds of dust, of cactus
and prairie dogs? To what use could we ever hope to put these great
deserts and these endless mountain ranges?
(Speech on the territorial acquisition from Mexico, 1852)

Men hang out their signs indicative of their respective trades:
shoemakers hang out a gigantic shoe; jewelers, a monster watch; and
the dentist hangs out a gold tooth; but up in the mountains of New

Hampshire, God Almighty has hung out a sign to show that there He makes men.

(Of the Old Man of the Mountain, attributed)

Noah Webster (1758–1834): *Lexicographer*

In fifty years from this time, the American-English will be spoken by more people than all the other dialects of the language.

(Preface, *Compendious Dictionary of the English Language,* 1806)

Mason L. "Parson" Weems (1759–1825): *Clergyman and biographer of Washington*

"George," said his father, "do you know who killed that beautiful little cherry tree yonder in the garden?"

. . . Looking at his father with the sweet face of youth brightened with the inexpressible charm of all-conquering truth, he bravely cried out, "I can't tell a lie. I did cut it with my hatchet."

(*The Life of George Washington: With Curious Anecdotes, Equally Honorable to Himself and Exemplary to His Young Countrymen,* 1800)

Robert Welch (1899–   ): *Manufacturer and anti-Communist crusader*

He has been sympathetic to ultimate Communist aims, realistically and even mercilessly willing to help them achieve their goals, knowingly receiving and abiding by Communist orders, and consciously serving the Communist conspiracy, for all his adult life.

(Of President Eisenhower, *The Politician,* 1963)

The whole country is one vast insane asylum and they're letting the worst patients run the place.

(Attributed)

Charles E. Weller (1840–1925): *Educator*

Now is the time for all good men to come to the aid of their party.

(Speed test sentence for typists, late-nineteenth century)

Nathanael West (1902–1940): *Writer*

Americans have dissipated their radical energy in an orgy of stone breaking. In their few years they have broken more stones than did centuries of Egyptians. And they have done their work hysterically, desperately, almost as if they knew that the stones would some day break them.

(*Miss Lonelyhearts*, 1933)

The Church is our only hope, the First Church of Christ Dentist, where He is worshipped as Preventer of Decay.

(Ibid.)

William C. Westmoreland (1914–   ): *Vietnam War commander*

Had President Johnson provided reinforcements, and had he authorized the operations I had planned in Laos and Cambodia and north of the DMZ, along with intensified bombing and the mining of Haiphong Harbor, the North Vietnamese would have broken. But that was not to be. Press and television had created an aura not of victory but of defeat, and timid officials in Washington listened more to the media than to their own representatives on the scene.

(*A Soldier Reports*, 1976)

Thomas Whately (?–1772): *British member of Parliament*

The Fact is, that the Inhabitants of the Colonies are represented in Parliament: they do not indeed chuse the Members of that Assembly; neither are Nine Tenths of the People of Britain Electors; for the Right of Election is annexed to certain Species of Property, to peculiar Franchises, and to Inhabitancy in some particular Places; but these Descriptions comprehend only a very small Part of the Land, the Property, and the People of this Island. . . .

The Colonies are in exactly the same Situation: All British Subjects are really in the same; none are actually, all are virtually represented in Parliament; for every Member of Parliament sits in the House, not as Representative of his own Constituents, but as one of that august Assembly by which all the Commons of Great Britain are represented.

(*The Regulations Lately Made*, 1765)

E. B. White (1899–   ): *Editor, writer*

Everything in life is somewhere else, and you get there in a car.

(*One Man's Meat,* 1944)

The trouble with the profit system has always been that it was highly unprofitable to most people.

(Ibid.)

Whatever else an American believes or disbelieves about himself, he is absolutely sure he has a sense of humor.

(*The Second Tree from the Corner,* 1954)

George H. White (1852–1918): *Congressman from North Carolina*

It is rather hard to be accused of shiftlessness and idleness when the accuser closes the avenue of labor and industrial pursuits to us. It is hardly fair to accuse us of ignorance when it was made a crime under the former order of things to learn enough about letters to even read the Word of God.

(Farewell speech in Congress, 23 February 1900. White was the last Negro congressman to survive politically in the period of black disenfranchisement)

Theodore H. White (1915–   ): *Political writer*

Politics in America is the binding secular religion.

(*Breach of Faith,* 1975)

William Allen White (1868–1944): *Writer and presidential adviser*

That's the stuff! Give the prosperous man the dickens! Legislate the thriftless man into ease, whack the stuffing out of the creditors and tell the debtors who borrowed the money five years ago when money "per capita" was greater than it is now, that the contraction of currency gives him a right to repudiate.

Whoop it up for the ragged trousers; put the lazy, greasy, fizzle, who can't pay his debts, on the altar, and bow down and worship him. Let the state ideal be high. What we need is not the respect of our fellow men, but the chance to get something for nothing.

("What's the Matter with Kansas?" *Emporia Gazette,* 15 August 1896)

This is a middle-class country, and the middle class will have its will and say. For the middle class is the real owner of American industry.

    (Autobiography, 1946)

Roosevelt bit me and I went mad.

    (Ibid.)

All dressed up, with nowhere to go.

    (On the Progressive Party after Theodore Roosevelt refused to be its candidate in 1916, ibid.)

He has lived and will die, no matter where fate send him, Cal Coolidge, of Northampton, of Ludlow and of Plymouth, the small-town American who is more typical of America than our cosmopolitan boulevardier. No boulevardier—Calvin Coolidge. One flag, one country, one conscience, one wife, and never more than three words will do him all his life.

    (Puritan in Babylon, 1938)

Walt Whitman (1819–1892): *Poet*

The United States themselves are essentially the greatest poem. . . . Here at last is something in the doings of man that corresponds with the broadcast doings of the day and night. . . . The proof of a poet is that his country absorbs him as affectionately as he has absorbed it.

    (Preface, *Leaves of Grass*, 1855)

The genius of the United States is not best or most in its executives or legislatures, nor in its ambassadors or authors or colleges or churches or parlors, nor even in its newspapers or inventors . . . but always most in the common people.

    (Ibid.)

If anything is sacred the human body is sacred.

    (*I Sing the Body Electric*, 1855)

I hear it was charged against me that I sought to destroy institutions, But really I am neither for nor against institutions.

    (*I Hear It Was Charged Against Me*, 1860)

He leaves for America's history and biography, so far, not only its most dramatic reminiscence—he leaves, in my opinion, the greatest, best, most characteristic, artistic, moral personality.

(On Abraham Lincoln, *Notes and Fragments*, 16 April 1865)

Shift and turn the combinations of the statement as we may, the problem of the future of America is in certain respects as dark as it is vast. Pride, competition, segregation, vicious wilfulness, and license beyond example brood already upon us. Unwieldy and immense, who shall hold in behemoth? who bridle leviathan? Flaunt it as we choose, athwart and over the roads of our progress loom huge uncertainty, and dreadful thickening gloom. It is useless to deny it: Democracy grows rankly up the thickest, noxious, deadliest plants and fruits of all—brings worse and worse invaders—needs newer larger, stronger, keener compensations and compellers.

(*Democratic Vistas*, 1871)

In nothing is there more evolution than the American mind.

(*Notes Left Over*, 1881)

Richard Whitney (1886–1974): *Banker*

I claim that this country has been built by speculation, and further progress must be made in that line.

(Attributed)

John Greenleaf Whittier (1807–1892): *Poet*

> "Shoot, if you must, this old gray head,
> But spare your country's flag," she said.

("Barbara Freitchie," 1863)

No fetters in the Bay State—no slave upon our land!

("Massachusetts to Virginia," 1843)

> From those great eyes
> The soul has fled:
> When faith is lost, when honor dies,
> The man is dead!

(Of Daniel Webster, "Ichabod," 1850)

We cross the prairie as of old
  The pilgrims crossed the sea,
To make the West, as they the East
  The homestead of the free!
("The Kansas Emigrants," 1855)

Norbert Wiener (1894–   ): *Philosopher, theologian*

It is possible to believe in progress as a fact without believing in progress as an ethical principle; but in the catechism of many Americans, the one goes with the other.
(*The Human Use of Human Beings*, 1954)

Oscar Wilde (1854–1900): *Anglo-Irish writer and wit*

In America the President reigns for four years, and Journalism governs for ever and ever.
(*The Soul of Man Under Socialism*, 1891)

The youth of America is their oldest tradition.
(*A Woman of No Importance*, 1893)

When I went to America I had two secretaries, one for autographs, the other for locks of hair. Within six months the one had died of writer's cramp, the other was completely bald.
(Attributed)

Thornton Wilder (1897–1975): *Writer*

It is difficult to be an American because there is as yet no code, grammar, decalogue by which to orient oneself. Americans are still engaged in inventing what it is to be an American. That is at once an exhilarating and a painful occupation. All about us we see the lives that have been shattered by it—not least the lives that have tried to resolve the problem by the European standards.
("Towards an American Language," 1952)

Alexander Wiley (1884–1967): *Senator from Wisconsin*

The Jews and Arabs should settle their dispute in the true spirit of Christian charity.
(Attributed)

Frances E. Willard (1839–1898): *Temperance reformer*

> I promise not to buy, sell or give
> Alcoholic liquors while I live;
> From all tobacco I'll abstain
> And never take God's name in vain.

(Pledge for the Loyal Temperance Union, 1883)

Roger Williams (1603–1683): *Puritan divine, founder of Rhode Island*

Nature knows no difference between European and American in blood, birth, bodies, etc., God having of one blood made all mankind.

(Sermon in Plymouth, 1633)

Boast not proud English of thy birth and blood. Thy brother Indian is by birth as good. Of one blood God made him, and thee and all, as wise, as fair, as strong, as personal.

(Ibid.)

We have not our land by patent from the King, but that the natives are the true owners of it, and that we ought to repent of such a receiving it by patent.

(Sermon, 1634)

All lawful magistrates in the world . . . have, and can have no more power, than fundamentally lies in the bodies of fountains themselves, which power, might, or authority, is not religious, Christian, etc., but natural, human, and civil.

(*The Bloody Tenent*, 1644)

It is unnecessary, unlawful, dishonorable, ungodly, unchristian in most cases in the world [to persecute people for their faith], for there is a possibility of keeping sweet peace in most cases, and if it be possible, it is the express command of God that peace be kept.

(Ibid.)

This conscience is found in all mankind, more or less, in Jews, Turks, Papists, Protestants, pagans, etc.

(*Bloody Tenent Yet More Bloody*, 1652)

Tennessee Williams (1911–1983): *Playwright*

That Europe is nothin' on earth but a great big auction.
(Cat on a Hot Tin Roof, 1955)

William Appleman Williams (1921–   ): *Historian*

Men who began by defining the United States and the world in economic terms, and explaining its operation by the principles of capitalism and a frontier thesis of historical development, came finally to define the United States in military terms as an embattled outpost in a hostile world. When a majority of the leaders of America's corporate society reached that conclusion, the nation went to war—at first covertly, then overtly.
(The Tragedy of American Diplomacy, 1959)

René de Visme Williamson (1908–   ): *Educator*

If the American dream is for Americans only, it will remain our dream and never be our destiny.
(Christianity Today, 19 June 1961)

Wendell Willkie (1892–1944): *Republican Party presidential nominee, 1940*

The constitution does not provide for first and second class citizens.
(An American Programme, 1940)

One World
(Title of a book, 1943)

There exists in the world today a gigantic reservoir of good will toward us, the American people.
(One World, 1943)

Freedom is an indivisible word. If we want to enjoy it, and fight for it, we must be prepared to extend it to everyone, whether they are rich or poor, whether they agree with us or not, no matter what their race or the color of their skin.
(Ibid.)

David Wilmot (1815–1868): *Congressman from Pennsylvania*

Neither slavery nor involuntary servitude shall ever exist in any part [of the territory taken from Mexico] except for crime, whereof the party shall first be duly convicted.

> ("Wilmot Proviso," 8 August 1846, unsuccessfully appended to a bill appropriating money to negotiate a peace treaty with Mexico)

Charles E. Wilson (1890–1961): *Secretary of defense under President Eisenhower, formerly chairman of the board, General Motors*

For many years I thought what was good for the country was good for General Motors and vice versa.

> (Testimony before a congressional committee, 23 January 1953)

Edmund Wilson (1895–1972): *Writer*

The American ideology is not to have any ideology.

> (Letter to William Faulkner, 1956)

Woodrow Wilson (1856–1924): *Twenty-eighth president*

I would never read a book if it were possible to talk half an hour with the man who wrote it.

> (Advice to his students at Princeton, 1900)

Nothing has spread socialistic feeling more than the use of the automobile . . . a picture of the arrogance of wealth.

> (Magazine article, 1906)

Would that we could do something, at once dignified and effective, to knock Mr. Bryan once and for all into a cocked hat.

> (Letter, 1907)

The President is at liberty, both in law and conscience, to be as big a man as he can. His capacity will set the limit; and if Congress be overborne by him, it will be no fault of the Constitution.

> (Magazine article, 1908)

No man can sit down and withhold his hands from the warfare against wrong and get peace from his acquiescence.

> (Address, Denver, 7 May 1911)

We have a great ardor for gain; but we have a deep passion for the rights of man.

(Speech, New York City, 6 December 1911)

America was established not to create wealth but to realize a vision, to realize an ideal—to discover and maintain liberty among men.

(Speech, Chicago, 12 February 1912)

Big business is not dangerous because it is big, but because its bigness is an unwholesome inflation created by privileges and exemptions which it ought not to enjoy.

(Acceptance speech, Democratic National Convention, 7 July 1912)

The history of liberty is a history of limitation of government power, not the increase of it.

(Address, New York City, 9 September 1912)

The masters of the government of the United States are the combined capitalists and manufacturers of the United States.

(Ibid.)

You cannot tear up ancient rootages and safely plant the tree of liberty in soil that is not native to it.

(Speech, 25 September 1912)

I am President of the United States and not of a small group of American investors with vested interests in Mexico.

(On a flare-up in the Mexican Revolution, February 1913)

We can afford to exercise the self-restraint of a really great nation which realizes its own strength and scorns to misuse it.

(Message to Congress, 27 August 1913)

Human rights, national integrity, and opportunity as against material interests—that . . . is the issue which we now have to face. I want to take this occasion to say that the United States will never again seek one additional foot of territory by conquest.

(Speech at Mobile, Alabama, 27 October 1913)

Liberty does not consist in mere general declarations of the rights of men. It consists in the translation of those declarations into definite action.

(Speech, Philadelphia, 4 July 1914)

The people of the United States are drawn from many nations, and chiefly from the nations now at war. . . . Some will wish one nation, others another, to succeed in this momentous struggle. . . . I venture . . . to speak a solemn word of warning. . . . The United States must be neutral in fact as well as in name during these days that are to try men's souls. We must be impartial in thought as well as in action.

(Message to the Senate, 19 August 1914)

Our whole duty for the present, at any rate, is summed up in the motto "America First: Let us think of America before we think of Europe."

(Speech in Washington, D.C., April 1915)

There is such a thing as a man being too proud to fight. There is such a thing as a nation being so right that it does not need to convince others by force that it is right.

(Speech in Philadelphia, 10 May 1915)

It is like writing history with lightning.

(On D. W. Griffiths' film about Reconstruction, *Birth of a Nation*, 1915)

England is fighting our fight.

(In conversation, 1915)

Just what is it that America stands for? If she stands for one thing more than another it is for the sovereignty of self-governing people.

(Speech, Pittsburgh, 29 January 1916)

America cannot be an ostrich with its head in the sand.

(Speech, Washington, D.C., 1 February 1916)

For my own part, I cannot consent to any abridgment of the rights of American citizens in any respect. . . . Once accept a single abatement of a right, and many other humiliations would certainly follow, and the whole fine fabric of international law might crumble under our hands piece by piece.

(Letter to Senate Committee on Foreign Relations, February 1916)

I can't keep the country out of war. Any little German lieutenant can put us into war at any time by some calculated outrage.

(In conversation, October 1916)

Once lead this people into war, and they'll forget there ever was such a thing as tolerance. To fight you must be ruthless and brutal, and the spirit of ruthless brutality will enter into the very fiber of our national life, infecting Congress, the courts, the policeman on the beat, the man on the street.

(In conversation with a newspaper reporter, April 1917)

Armed neutrality.

(Message to Congress, 26 February 1917)

The world must be made safe for democracy. Its peace must be planted upon the tested foundations of political liberty. We have no selfish ends to serve. We desire no conquest, no dominion. We seek no indemnities for ourselves, no material compensation for the sacrifices we shall freely make. We are but one of the champions of the rights of mankind. We shall be satisfied when those rights have been made as secure as the faith and the freedom of nations can make them.

It is a fearful thing to lead this great peaceful people into war, into the most terrible and disastrous of all wars, civilization itself seeming to be in the balance. But the right is more precious than peace, and we shall fight for the things which we have always carried nearest our hearts—for democracy, for the right of those who submit to authority to have a voice in their own governments, for the rights and liberties of small nations, for a universal dominion of right by such a concert of free peoples as shall bring peace and safety to all nations and make the world itself at last free.

(War message to Congress, 2 April 1917)

To such a task we dedicate our lives and our fortunes, everything that we are and everything that we have, with the pride of those who know that the day has come when America is privileged to spend her blood and her might for the principles that gave her birth and peace which she has treasured. God helping her, she can do no other.

(Ibid.)

A little group of willful men, representing no opinion but their own, have rendered the great Government of the United States helpless and contemptible.

(Remark on antiwar congressmen, April 1917)

It is not an army that we must train for war: it is a nation.

(Speech, Washington, D.C., 12 May 1917)

The mob spirit is displaying itself here and there in this country.

(During a cabinet meeting, fall 1917)

What we demand in this war is nothing peculiar to ourselves. It is that the world be made fit and safe to live in. . . . The programme of the world's peace, therefore, is our programme; and that programme, the only possible programme, as we see it is this: I. Open covenants of peace, openly arrived at, after which there shall be no private international understandings of any kind but diplomacy shall proceed always frankly and in the public view. . . . XIV. A general association of nations must be formed under specific covenants for the purpose of affording mutual guarantees of political independence and territorial integrity to great and small states alike.

(Speech to Congress, "The Fourteen Points," 8 January 1918)

There shall be no annexations, no contributions, no punitive damages. . . . Peoples and provinces must not be bartered about from sovereignty to sovereignty as if they were chattels or pawns in a game. Self-determination is not a mere phrase. It is an imperative principle which statesmen will henceforth ignore at their peril.

(Message to Congress, 11 February 1918)

To conquer with arms is to make only a temporary conquest; to conquer the world by earning its esteem is to make a permanent conquest.

(Address to Congress, 1 November 1918)

Sometimes people call me an idealist. Well, that is the way I know I am an American. America is the only idealistic nation in the world.

(Speech, Sioux Falls, South Dakota, 8 September 1919)

I will never consent to the pardon of this man.

> (Marginal note on Attorney-General A. Mitchell Palmer's request that
> he pardon Socialist leader Eugene V. Debs, 22 February 1921)

Edward, Duke of Windsor (1894–1972): *Abdicated British king*

The thing that impresses me most about America is the way parents obey their children.

> *(Look*, 5 March 1957)

John Winthrop (1588–1649): *English Puritan governor of the Massachusetts Bay Colony*

For we must consider that we shall be a citty upon a hill. The eyes of all people are upon us, so that if we shall deal falseley with our God in this work we have undertaken, and so cause Him to withdraw His present help from us, we shall be made a story and a byword through the world.

> ("A Model of Christian Charity," a sermon delivered on board the
> *Arabella*, 1630)

God Almightie in his most holy and wise providence hath soe disposed of the Condicion of mankinde, as in all times some must be rich some poore, some highe and eminent in power and dignitie; others meane and in subieccion.

> (Ibid.)

From hence wee may frame these Conclusions.
1. first all true Christians are of one body in Christ 1. Cor. 12: 12-13. 17. (27) Ye are the body of Christ and members of (your?) parte.
2ly. The ligamentes of this body which knitt together are loue.
3ly. Noe body can be perfect which wants its propper ligamentes.
4ly. All the partes of this body being thus vnited are made soe contiguous in a speciall relacion as they must needes partake of each others strength and infirmity, ioy, and sorrowe, weale and woe. 1. Cor. 12:26. If one member suffers all suffer with it, if one be in honour, all reioyce with it.
5ly. This sensiblenes and Sympathy of each others Condicions will necessarily infuse into each parte a natiue desire and endeavour, to strengthen defend preserue and comfort the other.

> (Ibid.)

I prayse God, we have many occasions of comfort heer, and doe hope, that our dayes of Afflication will soon haue an ende, and that the Lord will doe vs more goode in the ende, then we could haue expected, that will abundantly recompence for all the trouble we haue endured. yet we may not looke at great thinges heer, it is enough that we shall haue heaven, though we should passe through hell to it. we heer enjoye God and Jesus Christ, is not this enough? What would we haue more? I thanke God, I like so well to be heer, as I doe not repent my comminge. . . . I neuer fared better in my life, neuer slept better, neuer had more contente of minde, which comes meerly of the Lordes good hande, for we haue not the like meanes of these comforts heer which we had in England, but the Lord is all sufficient, blessed be his holy name, if he please, he can still vphold vs in this estate, but if he shall see good to make vs partakers with others in more Affliction, his will be doone, he is our God, and may dispose of vs as he sees good.

(Letter to His Wife, 1630)

Mrs. Hutchinson, the sentence of the court you hear is that you are banished from out of our jurisdiction as being a woman not fit for our society, and are to be imprisoned till the court shall send you away.

(Examination of Mrs. Ann Hutchinson, Boston, November 1637)

Owen Wister (1860–1938): *Writer*

When you call me that, smile!

(*The Virginian*, 1902)

P. G. Wodehouse (1881–1975): *English writer*

As a rule, from what I've observed, the American captain of industry doesn't do anything out of business hours. When he has put the cat out and locked up the office for the night, he just relapses into a state of coma from which he emerges only to start being a captain of industry again.

(*My Man Jeeves*, 1919)

Like so many substantial Americans, he had married young and kept on marrying, springing from blonde to blonde like the chamois of the Alps leaping from crag to crag.

(Ibid.)

James Wolfe (1727–1759): *British commander in North America*

The formidable sea and land armament, which the people of Canada now behold in the heart of their country, is intended by the King, my master, to check the insolence of France, to revenge the insults offered to the British colonies, and totally to deprive the French of their most valued settlement in North America.

> (Proclamation to the people of Quebec from Wolfe's headquarters at Laurent, 28 June 1759)

What, do they run already? Then I die happy.

> (Last words, Battle of Quebec, 13 September 1759)

Thomas Wolfe (1900–1938): *Novelist*

Making the world safe for hypocrisy.

> (*Look Homeward, Angel*, 1929)

Victoria Woodhull (1838–1927): *Reformer*

I have an inalienable constitutional and natural right to love whom I may, to love as long or as short a period as I can, to change that love every day if I please.

> (*Woodhull and Claflin's Weekly*, 20 November 1871)

John Woolman (1720–1772): *Early abolitionist agitator*

Men having Power too often misapplied it; that though we made Slaves of the Negroes, and the Turks made Slaves of the Christians, I believed that Liberty was the natural Right of all Men equally.

> (Sermon in Maryland, 1757)

Henry Clay Work (1832–1884): *Songwriter*

Bring the good old bugle, boys! We'll sing another song! Sing it with a spirit that will start the world along; Sing it as we used to sing it—fifty thousand strong, As we were marching through Georgia.

> ("Marching Through Georgia," 1864)

Wovoka (1856?–1932): *Paiute religious leader of the Ghost Dance religion*

All Indians must dance, everywhere, keep on dancing. Pretty soon in next spring Great Spirit comes. He bring back all game of every kind. The game be thick everywhere. All dead Indians come back and live again. They all be strong just like young men, be young again. Old blind Indian see again and get young and have fine time. When Great Spirit comes this way then all Indians go to mountains, high up away from whites. Whites can't hurt Indians then. Then while Indians way up high, big flood comes like water and all white people die, get drowned. After that, water go away and then nobody but Indians everywhere and game all kinds thick. Then medicine man tell Indians to send word to all Indians to keep up dancing and the good time will come. Indians who don't dance, who don't believe in this word, will grow little, just about a foot high, and stay that way. Some of them will be turned into wood and be burned in fire.

(Sermon, 1889)

Philip Wylie (1902–1971): *Writer*

A few suits of clothes, some money in the bank, and a new kind of fear constitute the main differences between the average American today and the hairy men with clubs who accompanied Attila to the city of Rome.

(*Generation of Vipers*, 1942)

The chaos of our society is the product of the dishevelment of our idea.

(Ibid.)

Malcolm X (Malcolm Little) (1925–1965): *Black separatist leader*

Chickens come home to roost. Being an old farmboy myself, chickens coming home to roost never did make me feel sad; they've always made me feel glad.

(Commenting on the assassination of President Kennedy, 1 December 1963)

Be peaceful, be courteous, obey the law, respect everyone; but if someone puts his hand on you, send him to the cemetery.

(*Malcolm X Speaks,* 1965)

A segregated school system produces children who, when they graduate, graduate with crippled minds.

(Ibid.)

Sitting at the table doesn't make you a diner, unless you eat some of what's on that plate. Being here in America doesn't make you an American. Being born here in America doesn't make you an American.

(Ibid.)

Time is on the side of the oppressed today, it's against the oppressor. Truth is on the side of the oppressed today, it's against the oppressor. You don't need anything else.

(Ibid.)

Nobody can give you freedom. Nobody can give you equality or justice or anything. If you're a man, you take it.

(Ibid.)

If being a communist or being a capitalist or being a socialist is a crime, first you have to study which of those systems is the most criminal. And then you'll be slow to say which one should be in jail.

(Ibid.)

You show me a capitalist, I'll show you a bloodsucker.

(Ibid.)

You're not supposed to be so blind with patriotism that you can't face reality. Wrong is wrong, no matter who does it or who says it.

(Ibid.)

You can't separate peace from freedom because no one can be at peace unless he has his freedom.

(Ibid.)

Power never takes a back step—only in the face of more power.

(Ibid.)

It's easy to become a satellite today without even being aware of it. This country can seduce God. Yes, it has that seductive power—the power of dollarism.

(Ibid.)

Isoroku Yamamoto (1884–1943): *Japanese admiral*

I fear we have only awakened a sleeping giant, and his reaction will be terrible.

(Remark to officers after the attack on Pearl Harbor, 7 December 1941)

William L. Yancey (1814–1863): *Senator from Alabama*

If it is right to buy slaves in Virginia and carry them to New Orleans, why is it not right to buy them in Cuba, Brazil, or Africa and carry them here?

(Speech calling for the reopening of the foreign slave trade, Vicksburg Convention, 1858)

Jack Yellen (1892–   ): *Songwriter*

"Happy Days Are Here Again"

(Title of song, 1930, which became the slogan for Franklin D. Roosevelt's presidential campaign)

Ehud Yonay (?–?): *Israeli journalist*

One comes to the United States—always, no matter how often—to see the future. It's what life in one's own country will be like five, ten, twenty years from now.

(*New York Times*, 26 November 1972)

Andrew Young (1932–   ): *Ambassador to the United Nations*

What people want in the world is not ideology; they want goods and services.

> (Interview, *Newsweek*, 28 March 1977)

Nothing is illegal if one hundred businessmen decide to do it.

> (Remark to reporters, September 1980)

Art Young (1866–1943): *Radical cartoonist*

He built the Road—
With others of his class, he built the road,
Now o'er it, many a weary mile, he packs his load,
Chasing a job, spurred on by hunger's goad,
He walks and walks, and wonders why
In hell he built the road.

> (*Industrial Worker*, 23 April 1910)

Brigham Young (1801–1877): *Mormon leader*

This is the place.

> (Upon coming to the Great Salt Lake Basin where the Mormon Zion was constructed, 24 July 1847)

George W. Young (?–?): *Temperance advocate*

The lips that touch liquor must never touch mine.

> (Slogan, c. 1870)

Z

Joseph Zangara (1900–1935): *Attempted assassin of President-elect Franklin D. Roosevelt*

Too many people are starving to death.

> (While shooting a revolver at Franklin D. Roosevelt and killing Chicago mayor Anton Cermak, February 1933)

Israel Zangwill (1864–1926): *Russian-born writer*

A fig for your feuds and vendettas! Germans and Frenchmen, Irishmen and Englishmen, Jews and Russians—into the Crucible with you all! God is making the American.

(*The Melting Pot*, 1908)

America is God's Crucible, the great Melting-Pot where all the races of Europe are melting and re-forming!

(Ibid.)

The real American has not yet arrived. He is only in the Crucible, I tell you—he will be the fusion of all the races, the coming superman.

(Ibid.)

Arthur Zimmermann (1858–1940): *German foreign minister*

We intend to begin unrestricted submarine warfare on the first of February. We shall endeavor in spite of this to keep the United States neutral. In the event of this not succeeding, we make Mexico a proposal of alliance on the following basis: make war together, make peace together, generous financial support, and an understanding on our part that Mexico is to reconquer the lost territory in Texas, New Mexico, and Arizona.

(Coded telegram to the German ambassador to Mexico, 17 January 1917, intercepted by British intelligence and publicized in the United States)

Vladimir Kosma Zworykin (1889–   ): *Russian-born developer of television*

The technique is wonderful. I didn't even dream it would be so good. But I would never let my children to come close to the thing. It's awful what they are doing.

(Commentary on American television on the occasion of his ninety-second birthday, July 1981)

A Grab Bag of Slogans and Catch Phrases ===========

No taxation without representation.
(Colonial slogan, 1760s)

> We love our cup of tea full well,
> But love our freedom more.

(Ballad popular in wake of Boston Tea Party, 1774)

> Yankee Doodle went to town,
> Riding on a pony.
> Stuck a feather in his hat
> And called it macaroney.

(Marching song, Revolutionary War)

Jefferson and Liberty.
(Jeffersonian Republican campaign slogan, election of 1800)

Warhawks.
(Term given to prowar congressmen, 1812)

On to Canada!
(Rallying cry of the Warhawks, 1812)

> There stood John Bull in martial pomp,
> And here was Old Kentucky.

("Hunters of Kentucky," popular ballad after the Battle of New Orleans, 1815)

Era of Good Feelings.

(Terms given by a Boston newspaper to the administration of James Monroe, 1817–1825)

Corrupt Bargain!

(Jacksonian description of John Quincy Adams' appointment of Henry Clay as secretary of state after Clay helped elect Adams to the presidency, 1825)

Remember the Alamo!

(War cry, Texas War of Independence, 1835)

Tippecanoe and Tyler Too!

(Whig campaign slogan, election of 1840)

Who is Polk?

(Whig campaign slogan, election of 1844, referring to the relative obscurity of the Democratic candidate and eventual victor, James K. Polk)

Old Rough and Ready.

(Nickname given to Mexican War general and later president, Zachary Taylor, 1846)

Old Fuss and Feathers.

(Nickname given to Mexican War general and later presidential nominee, Winfield Scott, 1846)

I know nothing.

(Standard response of members of the Native American Party when asked about their semisecret organization, 1850s)

Free soil, free labor, Frémont.

(Republican campaign slogan, election of 1856)

On to Richmond.

(Union Army battle cry, 1861)

We'll hang Jeff Davis to a sour apple tree.

(Union soldiers marching song, Civil War)

Vote as you shoot.

>(Republican Party campaign slogan among Union soldiers, election of 1864)

The bloody shirt.

>(Describing the Republican Party's exploitation of bitterness toward the Confederate rebellion, late-nineteenth century)

Twisting the lion's tail.

>(In reference to the political practice of baiting Great Britain, late-nineteenth century)

Throw the rascals out.

>(Liberal Republican campaign slogan, election of 1872)

> Blaine, Blaine, James G. Blaine,
> The continental liar from the state of Maine.

(Democratic campaign jingle, election of 1884)

> Ma, ma, where's my Pa?
> Gone to the White House, Ha, Ha, Ha!

(Republican campaign jingle, election of 1884, referring to Grover Cleveland's admitted paternity of an illegitimate child)

> Hurrah for Maria.
> Hurrah for the kid.
> I voted for Grover
> And am damn glad I did.

(Democratic jingle after Cleveland was elected, 1884)

Free Silver.

>(Rallying cry of inflationist forces, late-nineteenth century)

N I N A

>(Common appendix to advertisements for help, "No Irish Need Apply," late-nineteenth century)

Yellow peril.

>(Catch phrase of anti-Chinese movement, late-nineteenth century)

Solid South.
> (Term describing the solidly Democratic vote of the southern states, late-nineteenth century)

As Maine goes, so goes the nation.
> (Political truism based on the fact that Maine voted earlier than the other states, *not* on any reality, late-nineteenth century)

Remember the Maine! To hell with Spain!
> (War cry, 1898)

Four more years of the full dinner pail.
> (Repubican campaign slogan, election of 1900)

Gunboat Diplomacy.
> (Referring to Theodore Roosevelt's interventionist policy in Latin America, early-twentieth century)

Dollar Diplomacy.
> (Referring to William Howard Taft's preference for asserting American policy through capital investment in Latin America, c. 1910)

The New Freedom.
> (Democratic campaign slogan, election of 1912)

The New Nationalism.
> (Progressive campaign slogan, election of 1912)

He kept us out of war.
> (Democratic campaign slogan, in reference to Woodrow Wilson, election of 1916)

You are working, not fighting.
> (Ibid.)

The Yanks are coming.
> (War cry, 1917)

Keep cool with Coolidge.
> (Republican campaign slogan, election of 1924)

Mellon pulled the whistle,
Hoover rang the bell,
Wall Street gave the signal
And the country went to hell.

(Song of the "Bonus Marchers," 1932)

No man is good three times.

(Republican campaign slogan, election of 1940, referring to Franklin D. Roosevelt's unprecedented candidacy for a third term)

Kilroy was here.

(Soldiers' graffito, World War II)

Had Enough?

(Republican campaign slogan, congressional election of 1946)

I like Ike.

(Republican campaign slogan, election of 1952)

Communism, Corruption, and Korea.

(Ibid.)

Madly for Adlai.

(Democratic campaign slogan, election of 1952)

Better dead than red.

(Catch phrase, 1950s)

Everything's booming but the guns.

(Republican campaign slogan, election of 1956)

The New Frontier.

(Democratic campaign slogan, election of 1960)

In your heart, you know he's right.

(Republican campaign slogan, election of 1964. "He" was candidate Barry Goldwater)

Freedom Now!

(Civil rights movement, early 1960s)

Black Power!
> (Black nationalist slogan, late 1960s)

Up Against the Wall, Motherfucker!
> (Black militant slogan, late 1960s)

Participatory Democracy.
> (New Left slogan, early 1960s)

Don't trust anyone over thirty.
> (Ibid.)

I am a student. Please do not fold, spindle, or mutilate me.
> (Student movement slogan, mid-1960s)

We are the people our parents warned us against.
> (Youth-movement slogan, 1960s)

Hey, hey, LBJ, how many kids did you kill today?
> (Antiwar movement chant, mid-1960s)

Our black brothers are our sisters.
> (Women's Liberation slogan, probably but not necessarily a parody, late 1960s)

Far out!
> (Catch phrase of the counterculture, late 1960s)

Oh Wow!
> (Ibid.)

INDEX OF PERSONS QUOTED

(See Index of Subjects for persons who are the subject of a quotation.)

INDEX OF SUBJECTS

(See Index of Persons Quoted for persons who are the source of a quotation.)